D0732667

Rhetorical Criticism

EMPOWERING THE EXPLORATION OF "TEXTS"

Theodore F. Sheckels

Randolph–Macon College

cognella® | ACADEMIC PUBLISHING

Bassim Hamadeh, CEO and Publisher

Todd R. Armstrong, Senior Specialist Acquisitions Editor

Tony Paese, Project Editor

Christian Berk, Associate Production Editor

Emely Villavicencio, Senior Graphic Designer

Danielle Gradisher, Licensing Associate

Natalie Piccotti, Director of Marketing

Kassie Graves, Vice President of Editorial

Jamie Giganti, Director of Academic Publishing

Copyright © 2019 by Theodore F. Sheckels. All rights reserved. No part of this publication may be reprinted, reproduced, transmitted, or utilized in any form or by any electronic, mechanical, or other means, now known or hereafter invented, including photocopying, microfilming, and recording, or in any information retrieval system without the written permission of Cognella, Inc. For inquiries regarding permissions, translations, foreign rights, audio rights, and any other forms of reproduction, please contact the Cognella Licensing Department at rights@cognella.com.

Trademark Notice: Product or corporate names may be trademarks or registered trademarks, and are used only for identification and explanation without intent to infringe.

Cover image copyright © 2016 iStockphoto LP/wellphoto.
copyright © 2017 iStockphoto LP/kanzefar.
copyright © 2015 iStockphoto LP/VickyRu.
copyright © 2016 iStockphoto LP/schalkm.

Printed in the United States of America.

BRIEF TABLE OF CONTENTS

TABLE OF CONTENTS

PREFACE

One writes a textbook such as this one because, in one's own experience as a teacher of rhetorical criticism, one has felt that students need an introduction to the subject that, first, is detailed without being overwhelming; second, offers enough examples to make critical practice something students might emulate with a degree of ease; and, third, is succinct. If a textbook can meet those three goals, it is likely to, first, be read, and, second, empower students. Students will go from staring at a text of whatever sort—speech, advertisement, memory site—to knowing a number of routes they might take in acquiring an understanding of both what it has to say and how it works in persuading or otherwise affecting an audience. So, there are four key goals informing this textbook: sufficient but not overwhelming detail; examples that help make critical praxis clear; a succinct treatment suitable for an undergraduate audience; and empowerment of those fledgling critics.

Chapter 1 develops this idea of empowerment further. It talks about how rhetorical theory offers a variety of lenses that bring into focus different aspects of a text. So, I'll let chapter 1 speak to why theory-based rhetorical criticism empowers. In this preface, I want to highlight the textbook's features, including material intended to facilitate the book's use in the classroom.

First, it is important to understand the textbook's target audience. One can come to the study of rhetorical criticism at a number of points in an academic career, ranging from fairly early in one's undergraduate study to graduate school. This text is targeted at the former group: Students who have had some basic courses in communication and are now embarking on a range of major courses. Quite often, at this point, students are sampling from the different areas of the communication discipline, taking a relational communication course, a mass communication course, and a rhetoric-oriented course. That students are sampling is important, for it means that only some of the students enrolled in the course I am imagining are going to become rhetorical critics, whereas for others, the course—and the textbook—represent an exposure to an endeavor that will end up in the background as they develop as media or interpersonal scholars. One hopes, of course, that the course—and this book—will attract many to the rhetorical enterprise. So, in addition to building an understanding of rhetorical criticism on a foundation of "the basics," the course—and the textbook—try to interest students in what we rhetorical critics do.

The audience, then, is neither graduate students nor my professional peers. This has implications on the audience. First, the style of the textbook is deliberately conversational. I want the students using the textbook to feel that they are being talked to. This does not mean talking down, but rather presenting some complicated matters as simply as possible without over-simplifying them. Second, the textbook does not quote the theorists heavily. Their words are not ignored, for it is useful to hear what the likes of Aristotle and Burke and Frye and Bakhtin had to say. But, as we all know, critical theorists tend to write dense prose. So, the textbook offers just a taste. Third, references are minimal. Yes, there would be far more if these chapters were journal articles, but they are not. The references serve three purposes: to point to sources when the ideas are not common fare among rhetorical critics, to point to the work of other critics whose insights are being noted, and to point students and instructors to some perhaps useful supplementary discussions.

We critics, of course, do not approach the task in the same way. Thus, there are many lenses used to illuminate texts. This textbook offers a wide range. It discusses traditional approaches such as classical and Burkean; it discusses newer practices rooted in Bakhtin, and it discusses a range of ideologies. The book also discusses a few approaches not especially common in rhetorical criticism books—the Chicago School, with its emphasis on final effect and pluralism; mythological criticism, with an emphasis on the theory of Northrop Frye and a glance at cultural and pop culture myths; and an approach rooted in constitutive rhetoric with a stress on identity formation. Whereas the third of these is well within the rhetorical tradition as those in the communication discipline might define it, the first and second are part of the broader rhetorical tradition shared by communication and literary scholars. There are some who may then reject them as too literary, but the position taken by this textbook is that all approaches, regardless of where in the academy they developed, are worth considering if they do indeed offer a lens that can illuminate a text. So, I hope users of the textbook will consider what these literary rhetorical critics have to offer.

There is a logic behind how the chapters are arranged—pretty much chronological—but one using the textbook need not follow this sequence. In fact, as a teacher of rhetorical criticism myself, I think it would be very difficult to cover all thirteen approaches in a semester. So, the chapters are designed to be free-standing. My guess is that instructors will choose many—maybe eight or nine—and my guess is that, if users were surveyed, we would see many different arrays.

Each chapter (after the introductory one), begins by explaining the theory the critical approach is based in. I assume here that following a critical approach without grasping the theory undergirding it is academically irresponsible, for critical approaches are not just tools like a particular statistic, but philosophically rich stances characterized by assumptions about human beings, their communication practices, and the worlds they inhabit. Sometimes the theory's history is important; almost always, its assumptions are. This discussion implies a critical praxis, but, then, the chapter makes the praxis explicit in two ways: first, by explaining what a critic of a certain sort does—not by offering step-by-step instructions but rather a discussion highlighting the critical process; second, by offering an extended example of the critical approach in use.

Each chapter offers one—in a few cases, two—extended examples, as well as many brief ones, as theory and praxis are explained. The examples are deliberately diverse. Some focus on the traditional subject of rhetorical criticism—famous speeches, ranging from Franklin Roosevelt in 1932 to Barry Goldwater in 1968, to Hillary Clinton in 1995, to Barack Obama in 2008, to Ellen Johnson Sirleaf in 2006, to Michelle Obama in 2016. Criticism, however, has extended far beyond speeches. It has extended to written texts, such as the Students for a Democratic Society's *Port Huron Declaration*; advertisements such as Chrysler's succession of Super Bowl ads featuring the unlikely trio of Eminem, Clint Eastwood, and Bob Dylan; popular Broadway shows such as *Grease* and *Hamilton*; popular films such as *Invictus*, *North Country*, and the *Adventures of Priscilla, Queen of the Desert*; popular television programs such as *West Wing*; and public memory sites such as a curious set designed to recall a POW camp for Confederate soldiers in southern Maryland.

Including both the traditional and the less traditional is deliberate, for undergraduates need to know that rhetorical criticism is more than "speech criticism," while not forgetting that it is still valuable to analyze speeches with both historical and contemporary relevance. The examples have also been chosen because they are interesting. Some students enjoy historical ones: We should not assume that rhetoric from previous times had no appeal. Most students, however, enjoy the more up to date. So, a large number of the examples in the text are fairly current. Will every example appeal to all? Of course not, but they all will appeal to some. The examples have also been chosen because they illustrate well how an approach works.

I earlier explained my assumption with regards to this textbook's audience. Similarly, I have an assumption about instructors. I posit that this course is rarely assigned to instructors unfamiliar with the subject. In fact, the opposite is probably more likely the case—instructors are very familiar with strong views on this approach and that approach. Such an audience probably needs a minimum of pedagogical aids. So, each chapter (after the first) offers a short list of essays that an instructor might refer students to if they wish to see the approach in practice. My experience is that many undergraduates find journal articles and book chapters daunting—after all, they are not the audience for these essays. However, there are some who will benefit. And, by looking at them, they will quickly discover that those who use a critical approach rarely proceed 1–2–3–4. Also, at the end of each chapter (except the first) is a short list of assignments that instructors might use. They are varied in their focus, with a deliberate distinction made between assignments focused on speeches and assignments focused on non-speech texts.

After discussing thirteen critical approaches, the textbooks offers two appendices. One is a glossary of rhetorical terms used in the discussions. The other is a brief discussion of how to write a critical essay. It does not offer a 1–2–3–4 approach. Rather, it begins by outlining how social science research reports are typically organized and offers a modification of this approach that is suitable to rhetorical criticism. Many of us place rhetoric and rhetorical criticism in the humanities, where writing an essay is an art, not the following of a pattern. But, communication as a discipline has become far more a social science enterprise than a humanities one. With that shift has come the expectation that criticism be written in a manner somewhat similar to social science research reports. The approach outlined in the first appendix is an easy-to-follow one that tries to bridge the gap between the humanities roots of rhetorical criticism and the growing social science orientation of the communication discipline.

Other textbooks may offer a 1–2–3–4 approach to writing an essay, but essays following such advice bear little resemblance to what real critics and real critical essays do. The model outlined in the last appendix, on the other hand, offers an approach viable beyond the immediate classroom if one were to pursue rhetorical criticism in professional contexts.

No book—especially a textbook—moves forward without the assistance of those who review its drafts and offer commentary. I have never seen commentary as varied as in this case: the same chapter was the best in the book and the worst in the book, etc. What the variability reveals is that we rhetorical critics have strong opinions on both what rhetoricians have to say and how to turn their ideas into critical praxis that undergraduates can practice. And that should surprise no one. All comments were helpful, some more than others. I'd like therefore to acknowledge the advice—whether I took it or not—of Teresa Bergman, University of the Pacific; Leila R. Brammer, Gustavus Adolphus College; Joni M. Butcher, Louisiana State University; Adrienne Christiansen, Macalester College; Kathleen Edelmayer, Madonna University; Jeffrey B. Kurtz, Denison University; Nancy J. Legge, Idaho State University; Raymie McKerrow, Ohio University; Joshua D. Phillips, Pennsylvania State University–Brandywine Valley; Jane S. Sutton, Pennsylvania State University–York; and Mary E. Triece, University of Akron.

Books such as these reflect classroom practice as well. What approaches appeal, what approaches are easily or not so easily grasped, and which examples "click" are matters one discovers only by teaching the course, looking at smiling or puzzled faces, and reading the essays undergraduates have written. So, I also am grateful to decades of students at Randolph-Macon College who have, through their reactions and writings in the undergraduate rhetorical criticism course, influenced many of the decisions I have made in writing this textbook.

Finally, thanks to the folks at Cognella: Acquisitions Editor Todd Armstrong, who has grasped, from the outset, what I was trying to accomplish in this textbook, and Project Editor Tony Paese, who has worked through the complex process of securing permissions and finding visuals to complement the text.

TFS

Michelle Obama addressing the 2016 Democratic National Convention.

CHAPTER 1

Introduction to Rhetorical Criticism

Many of you have heard of the interscholastic or intercollegiate activity called forensics. It features students competing in a variety of speaking activities. Quite a few years ago, one of the events was called rhetorical criticism. Many students shied away from it. Why? They weren't sure what it was and feared it might be a difficult and thing to do. (So, the name was changed to communication analysis, and interest increased a bit.)

The assumption that rhetorical criticism is difficult is one that this textbook will challenge. With guidance, rhetorical criticism is no more difficult than most academic tasks, and it leads to fascinating insights about how communication works. The fascinating insights are the pay-off. When you first read what scholars who are rhetorical critics do, you may wonder at the insights they offer and how they got there. Well, they knew what questions to ask, they knew what theories would assist them in answering the questions, and they knew how to apply those theories. This textbook is designed to help you proceed to fascinating insights of your own along this same path.

How exciting the process is really depends on two things: First, what you choose to analyze; second, what answers you come up with. If you analyze a very old speech and come up with conclusions that are rather obvious, the process will not be exciting. However, if you choose to analyze something interesting—be it a speech or an ad or a film or a website or a monument or a sports event—and come up with conclusions that might surprise a casual listener or viewer—the process can be quite exciting. This textbook is designed to help you do exciting things as a rhetorical critic.

But, before we get to those things, we need to go over some basics.

What Is Rhetoric?

Education in classical antiquity focused on the seven liberal arts—three, the trivium, being fundamental; four, the quadrivium, being areas that built on the fundamental three. One of the three fundamental areas of study was **rhetoric**, and, in a rhetoric course or curriculum, you would learn what choices to make to persuade an audience. Rhetoric, as an area of study, focused on the available means to persuade.

You might quickly think that persuasion is an activity that just those in government or politics do, but persuasion is broader than that. An ad persuades you to buy a product; a film or a novel persuades you to embrace a particular theme. Some rhetoricians will go so far as to argue that all or almost all "texts" (we'll talk about this term in a bit) persuade to one degree or another. Given the breadth of persuasion as a human activity, it is no wonder rhetoric was fundamental in a classical education.

What Is Criticism?

In that rhetoric course, you would be taught how to persuade. Criticism proceeds toward persuasion from the other direction: It looks at attempts to persuade and examines how they proceeded. Criticism may well assess whether a text succeeded or not, but criticism is really more interested in examining how a text persuades. Criticism is also alert to effects a text might have, besides the main one of persuading. Often, there are things going on that the audience—in some cases, even the speaker or writer or designer—might not be fully aware of.

What Is a "Text"?

Answering this question requires an excursion into academic history.

As the nineteenth century turned into the twentieth, American universities began to change. Following examples in Europe, especially in Germany, American universities became places featuring research, not just instruction. This transition was easy for science faculty to make—and fairly easy for social science faculty. Humanities faculty, such as those in English, had more difficulty. They had no laboratories to go to, no experiments to design.

Those who taught speech and rhetoric were, at that point in time, typically in English departments, so the story there is relevant. English faculty, needing a research agenda, typically did one of the following four tasks: (a) wrote well-researched biographies of noted authors; (b) wrote histories of literary periods such as the Renaissance or the Romantic Movement; (c) established the definitive version of literary works that existed in several versions, like many of Shakespeare's plays; and (d) compiled sources and analogues for a literary work, sources being previous versions of the plot the author likely looked at and analogues being the version of the plot that existed at the same time that the author may not have directly considered.

Speech and rhetoric faculty were often treated as second-class citizens in English departments. For this and other reasons, these faculty seceded from English in 1914. There was a professional gathering of college English teachers at a hotel in Chicago. Speech and rhetoric teachers walked out, went across the street to another hotel, and created a new professional group and a new academic discipline.

But these speech and rhetoric faculty needed a research agenda just as much as the English teachers. It was then becoming a university-wide expectation. So, what did they do? They wrote biographies of highly regarded orators and histories of important periods or public address. They established definitive versions of famous speeches when more than one version was out there, and they situated speeches within the context of other speeches on the same subject. In other words, they did the same kind of research as the English teachers, but, whereas the English teachers focused on literary texts, they focused on speeches as their texts.

Gradually, the rhetoric faculty will expand what they are looking at as texts. Prose documents such as the Declaration of Independence will be turned to as a text, as will, over the decades, ads, television programs, memory places such as monuments and museums, other places, and Internet sites. Rhetoric faculty will even consider films and literature, although doing so might seem to some to be crossing academic boundaries— as invading the turf of film studies programs or English departments. But, the questions posed and the methods used to answer them would be very much within the realm of rhetorical theory.

So, today, as this book reflects, the rhetorical critic's "text" can be any number of things, all of which use symbols, be they words or visuals entities, to produce meaning. Parallel to the expansion of texts has been an expansion in theory. So, critics are no longer just applying insights developed in classical antiquity, but are also applying insights that have emerged over centuries in many different countries. You will, in this text, become familiar with some of those insights and be able to speak knowledgeably about American Kenneth Burke, Russian Mikhail Bakhtin, Dutch Chaim Perelman, Canadian Northrop

Frye, and French Michel Foucault, among others. They have all offered theoretical insights that help rhetorical critics answer different kinds of questions.

Proceeding as a Critic

At the graduate level, many fledgling rhetorical critics act as if they must choose what kind of critic to be. Will they follow Kenneth Burke? Will they follow Michel Foucault? As this textbook will repeatedly insist, such choosing is not necessary. One can follow whoever offers the approach that best answers the critic's immediate question. However, there is a tendency for a critic to turn repeatedly to a given theorist—and to ignore others. This tendency exists because a given theorist's ideas resonate especially well with the critic. The ideas match how the critic feels communication or persuasion occurs. So, as you proceed through this textbook, ask yourself occasionally whether the approach feels right to you. But, do not become obsessed with finding your rhetorical critical identity too early. Your primary goal, as an undergraduate, should be to grasp what the different perspectives assume and how they proceed.

In fact, before even considering the matter of what approach you might be inclined to, you need to go through the steps outlined next. You need to go through them many, many times.

Choosing a Text

The first step is choosing a text. A critic does not just pick one; rather, he or she is drawn to a text that seems to pose a question worth asking and answering. Why did Donald Trump's 2017 inaugural seem so flat and unlike previous inaugural addresses? Why does the World War II Memorial on the Mall in Washington, DC, evoke dramatically divergent reactions from those who visit it? Why is the Super Bowl ad Apple ran in 1984 to announce the Macintosh (or Mac) computer considered so very effective? Who did Barack Obama quote, allude to, or echo over and over in his speeches?

The question should lead to a methodology, probably one of the twelve outlined in the following chapters. The question about Trump's inaugural address might evoke genre theory, and you would be asking how the address departs from what is ordinarily done when one assumes the presidency. The question about the World War II Memorial might evoke symbolic convergence—or fantasy theme—criticism and find you talking in terms of how the war has been socially constructed by World War II veterans as opposed to those, during and after the presidency of George W. Bush, who have socially constructed the monument's design and dedication in terms that highlight, first, what the memorial omits, and second, how the memorial seemed to serve immediate political purposes. The question about the 1984 Apple ad might evoke mythological criticism insofar as in the ad a heroic figure defeats an autocratic one who is reducing humanity to automatons. And the Obama speeches might evoke the work of Mikhail Bakhtin on the voices a speaker includes in the multi-voiced or polyphonic text he creates.

As you proceed through this textbook, you will understand more and more how the question you feel compelled to ask of a text will take you in a particular methodological direction. You may also feel that certain questions suit you more than others: you enjoy asking them and you think you are especially adept at answering them.

However, before you go too far down the path, you need to do two other things: You need to read the chosen text very closely, and you need to understand the chosen text's context.

Reading Closely

It should go without saying that you need to read the text you have chosen carefully. You need to attend to the words and the images. If the text is performed, you also need to attend to how it is performed. Closely and carefully does not just mean that you slow yourself down and read many times. Closely and carefully means that you read with certain elements in mind. The precise words and, if relevant, the precise visual images are always important, as is how the text is structured. Beyond these elements, what you attend to depends on the question you are trying to answer. If you are looking at Trump's inaugural, you know that this speech typically tries to unite the people after what might be a divisive election by defining who the people are. With this in mind, you would read the text, looking for how Trump defines the nation's people. Franklin D. Roosevelt in his 1933 inaugural described Americans as being without fear; John F. Kennedy in 1961 described Americans as a new generation of pioneers exploring a new frontier; Ronald Reagan in 1981 described Americans as heroes. What was Trump's definition? If you are considering the voices evoked in Obama's speeches, you highlight the voices as you encounter them, finding many different ones, but also finding a lot of Abraham Lincoln, John F. Kennedy, and Martin Luther King, Jr. Why, you might ask, does Obama echo these three?

Understanding the Context

The key here is understanding what brings the text into existence. Speeches do not just happen. Nor do memorials or ads or films. Rhetoricians refer to what brings the text into

Some types of exigencies
- define the situation
- Defend or attack a specific policy proposal
- Create an audience
- Get audience to take action
- Establish the advocate's ethos
- Explain failure
- Restore public confidence
- Create and/or remove distinctions

existence as its **exigence.** Exigence is not as simple as background. Rather, it entails the situation the text creator is in that necessitates that text.

When President Franklin Delano Roosevelt (FDR) spoke in 1933, the nation was panicky because of the Great Depression and the government's inability, during the late years of the Hoover administration, to do much about it. FDR needed to respond by assigning blame and pledging action. He also needed to convince the people not to be afraid. Those needs constituted his exigence. When Ronald Reagan spoke in 1981, the nation was, arguably, feeling depressed: Jimmy Carter, after all, had lectured the American people about their lack of confidence in the nation, suggesting that public officials lacked that confidence as well. Reagan's exigence was to restore confidence, and what better way than to evoke the nation's great heroes and then argue that the real heroes are the average Americans in his audience? Restoring confidence was the exigence underlying his 1981 address.

Sometimes, to understand the context, one has to dig a bit. The true exigence may not be immediately apparent. Martin Medhurst's analysis of President Dwight D. Eisenhower's 1961 farewell address is a very good example of this need to dig.[1] Farewell addresses are, as a genre, supposed to offer warnings: George Washington's did; therefore, all others must. So, many looking at Eisenhower's address immediately attended to the two warnings he offered—against the post–World War II "military industrial complex" that might well be producing military equipment or weaponry we did not need, and against the over-involvement of government in university scientific research. There is plenty of evidence in the comments from the speechwriters involved in preparing the address that these warnings were important to Eisenhower. Medhurst, however, looked beyond these warnings. He noted how often the word "balance" appeared in the speech and, using other archival evidence, argued that the true exigence of the speech was not what Eisenhower saw going on in industry or research but rather his fear that the very young Kennedy team coming in after January 1961 would act in a rash manner. The speech, in preaching balance, was designed to rein in potential Kennedy excesses. The exigence was the incoming Kennedy group—young and inexperienced—and what they might do in foreign and domestic affairs if not counseled to exhibit this requisite balance.

Back in time, after 1914, when scholars turned to speeches as the texts they would consider, they treated the context rather briefly. Many in literary criticism were ignoring context and insisting that a poem or a novel be read as a universal document not tied to a particular moment in time. A group of critics known as the Cambridge School were doing so in the United Kingdom; a group of critics, centered at Vanderbilt University in Nashville, Tennessee, and known as the New Critics, were doing so in the United States. Thus, it may be that speech critics were slighting the context of speeches because they wanted to be in academic vogue. Whatever the reason, they needed to be prompted to look more deeply into the context to discern what the exigence or exigencies might be. Good rhetorical criticism today investigates a text's context carefully and thoroughly.

Understanding the Rhetorical Situation

If you have pinpointed the exigence or exigencies for a text, you are well on the way to understanding what most rhetoricians refer to as "the rhetorical situation." Two other elements play a role in that situation, however.

The first is the person who is delivering the text. This will often be the speaker, but, if the text is a written one, such as the Declaration of Independence, it is a writer (or group of writers), and if the text is a public memorial, it is the designer, who was perhaps following design specifications as well as her or his creative impulses. The tricky thing about the speaker or writer or designer—referred to in rhetorical theory as "the rhetor"—is that this person usually presents the text using a **persona.**

The simplest way to understand the concept of a persona is to think about how we all choose to communicate differently with different audiences. A typical college student will communicate differently with a professor, a parent, a friend, and an intimate partner, right? What is true for a college students is true for anyone. Consider a president of the United States. This person is, besides any personal roles he or she might have, a chief executive, a party leader, a spokesperson for the nation to other nations, and a commander in chief. These are all different personae, and a president shifts among them just as a college student shifts between the persona he or she puts on when speaking to a professor and the persona he or she puts on when speaking to a very close friend.

Further complicating many of the texts rhetorical critics deal with is the fact that the rhetor sometimes must take on more than one persona. A president delivering a State of the Union address is speaking both as chief executive outlining what policies the nation needs and as party leader telling his or her partisan compatriots how to proceed. A rhetorical critic must identify the persona or personae the rhetor is using in order to understand fully the situation he or she is in.

The second is the audience being offered the text. If a critic can pinpoint a single or a primary audience, there are many questions the critic should ask about it. There are demographic characteristics such as age, gender, race, religious affiliation, sexual orientation, and the like. Perhaps more important are the attitudes that audience holds, especially the intensity with which the audience holds its attitudes and how personally important—or salient—these attitudes are to the audience.

The complication here is that rhetors are often addressing several audiences at the same time. The president delivering a State of the Union address is speaking to Congress, but also to a national television audience, as well as many abroad who will listen to the speech as it is delivered or shortly thereafter. A memorial designer—let's say Maya Lin, a university art student whose design for the Vietnam Veterans' Memorial won a national competition—must know that veterans will encounter her text, that political conservatives and political liberals will both encounter her text, and that young people not even born at the time of the Vietnam conflict will eventually encounter her text. This knowledge of multiple audiences will often affect how the rhetor chooses to communicate.

Choosing Your Rhetorical Perspective

A few pages ago, I suggested that the text you choose will probably evoke particular questions and that these questions will lead you to use a particular critical perspective, with the many that are surveyed in this text being the most common possibilities. Although that is generally true, two other phenomena might eventually ensue.

First, you may find yourself gravitating to a particular question—or a particular set of questions—more than others. A given text can be examined from a variety of perspectives, so you may find yourself, regardless of the text, almost always asking the same question(s). You might find yourself always inclined to ask about the story the rhetor is offering or how that story relates to larger cultural myths. You might find yourself always inclined to ask questions related to gender or to power. You might find yourself always inclined to ask how the rhetor creates a bond between the rhetor and his or her audience(s).

If there is such a gravitational pull, then you are becoming a particular kind of critic—a narrative critic, a mythological critic, a critical rhetorician, or a Burkean critic (i.e., one who is influenced by the writings of Kenneth Burke). That often happens, especially a bit farther along in one's education, but it is equally likely that you'll find that several questions intrigue you and, therefore, several perspectives fit you.

Second, you may find a particular critical theorist's understanding of persuasion—or criticism—especially compelling. Throughout the rest of this textbook, these views are presented, succinctly and objectively. Kenneth Burke, for example, believes humans are guilt-ridden and that persuasion is involved in the various ways they try to deal with this guilt. Walter Fisher, on the other hand, believes humans are storytellers and that all arguments can be thought of in narrative terms, with the compelling ones being those that connect to our values. Mikhail Bakhtin—for a third example—believes that humans exist in a sea of language full of words and phrases that have been voiced by many others. For Bakhtin, to be fully human, one must immerse one's speaking or writing in this sea. Some theorists may find you scratching your head in confusion; others may find you saying "Yes." If you say yes, you are, again, becoming a certain kind of critic. Certainly not required, but possible.

Even if you do not find *your* perspective, you will probably find that some of the perspectives offered in the chapters that follow will resonate with you and others will not. That's undoubtedly the case with all of us who have become rhetorical critics. But, as you work through these perspectives, one caution: Don't choose based just on how easy approaches are to understand or apply. Choosing how you work with texts is not the same as choosing how you perform a mechanical task such as replacing an electric light fixture. There, ease may be important. When it comes to criticism, ease is coincidental. An approach that rings true with you may well feel easy to use. Make sure that any ease in use is because you think the approach truly illuminates human persuasion (and communication), not because its steps are few or its terminology is immediately clear.

Rhetorical Theories as Critical Lenses

Whether you gravitate to one or a few approaches or you remain open to all, depending on the questions you have, theories function as lenses. This is a metaphor that will be used throughout this textbook, but it is not just a metaphor.

Lenses not only help you see; they can direct your sight. In a scientific laboratory, there are sophisticated microscopes that permit one to see in different ways, depending on the lens you choose. Lenses don't simply get you closer or farther away; it is not that simple. The same is true for camera lenses. Which lens you choose depends on what you want to see and record, and, having chosen a particular lens, you are better able to see and record what you are interested in.

Different theories focus on different elements in a text. I don't want to review the textbook just yet, chapter by chapter. So, let me just mention three examples.

Kenneth Burke's theory of terministic screens focuses on the words and phrases a rhetor uses. One using this theory would be trying to determine to what extent a text uses the terms that resonate with its audience and, thereby, create identification between rhetor and audience and, hence, persuasion. Using this theory as a lens, one is focusing on words and phrases that might well be overlooked if one were using a different theory as a lens.

For example, post-colonial theory, as a critical rhetorical theory, focuses on how those who hold power compel "others" to speak or write or design in a manner that conforms with the dominant group's norms. One using this theory to examine a text authored by "others"—those not in dominant group—would be trying to determine both how the text exhibits constraint and how it tries to break away from its bonds. A critic looking for a text's use of a terministic screen would probably not be considering these power dynamics.

Genre theory focuses on recurring forms of discourse. Used poorly, the theory becomes a checklist of usual characteristics that one marches a new text past; used well, the theory asks how a rhetor exhibits a particular trait and, if a trait is missing, why it is. One giving, for example, a presidential nomination acceptance speech at a political convention probably knows what typically characterizes that genre. For example, nominees usually try to sound "presidential," leaving the strongly partisan attacking for the vice presidential nominee. But what if a presidential nominee takes a different tactic and goes after his or her opponent vehemently? What's going on? Perhaps the nominee felt the genre was passe; perhaps the nominee was poorly advised; perhaps the precise political situation called for something stronger than the norm. Regardless of the answer, the question is worth asking. And one asking it would probably not be asking about other matters.

Michelle Obama at the 2016 Democratic National Convention

Nominees have accepted nominations for many decades—early on, back at their homes; after 1932, at the convention hall. But a speaking role was not given to first ladies (or potential first ladies) until 1992 when Barbara Bush chose to address the Republican National Convention. The rationale for such a speech has been two-fold: one, to allow one who knew the nominee intimately to address his or her character; two, to allow potential first ladies (or gentlemen) to audition for the role before the public. Post-Bush, we have heard from all the women—and the one man—who might hold the office. In 2016, Michelle Obama did something different: She spoke, not as one who might serve and has something to say about her partner, but as one who has served eight years and has something to say about who will serve as president in the future, as her partner's successor.

The speeches by first ladies past provide some context for understanding Michelle Obama's 2016 speech. More is provided by the particulars of the 2016 election year—that the Democrats were nominating a woman, that the Republicans had nominated a man who had both attacked Michelle Obama's husband, even questioning his citizenship and allegedly harassing women, and—perhaps—that prospective first lady Melania Trump had flagrantly plagiarized Michelle Obama in her RNC speech a few weeks earlier.

Michelle Obama was speaking as incumbent first lady, but also as a woman and as an African American. Her audiences included Democrats in and outside the convention hall, Americans from both parties and from no parties watching on television, and—especially—women and African Americans. In both these cases, Hillary Clinton's support was not as strong as her team had hoped. Michelle Obama's exigence was to help Hillary out with these two demographics.

All this is background information—important background but background nonetheless. What about "the text" itself? Here it is:

Thank you all. Thank you so much. You know, it's hard to believe that it has been eight years since I first came to this convention to talk with you about why I thought my husband should be president. Remember how I told you about his character and convictions, his decency and his grace, the traits that we've seen every day that he's served our country in the White House.

I also told you about our daughters, how they are the heart of our hearts, the center of our world. And during our time in the White House, we've had the joy of watching them grow from bubbly little girls into poised young women, a journey that started soon after we arrived in Washington.

When they set off for their first day at their new school, I will never forget that winter morning as I watched our girls, just 7 and 10 years old, pile into those black SUVs with all those big men with guns. And I saw their little faces pressed up against the window, and the only thing I could think was, what have we done? See, because at that moment, I realized that our time in the White House would form the foundation for who they would become and how well we managed this experience could truly make or break them. That is what Barack and I think about every day as we try to guide and protect our girls through the challenges of this unusual life in the spotlight, how we urge them to ignore those who question their father's citizenship or faith. How we insist that the hateful language they hear from public figures on TV does not represent the true spirit of this country. How we explain that when someone is cruel or acts like a bully, you don't stoop to their level. No, our motto is, when they go low, we go high.

With every word we utter, with every action we take, we know our kids are watching us. We as parents are their most important role models. And let me tell you, Barack and I take that same approach to our jobs as president and first lady because we know that our words and actions matter, not just to our girls, but the children across this country, kids who tell us I saw you on TV, I wrote a report on you. Kids like the little black boy who looked up at my husband, his eyes wide with hope and he wondered, is my hair like yours?

And make no mistake about it, this November when we go to the polls that is what we're deciding, not Democrat or Republican, not left or right. No, in this election and every election [it] is about who will have the power to shape our children for the next four or eight years of their lives. And I am here tonight because in this election there is only one person who I trust with that responsibility, only one person who I believe is truly qualified to be president of the United States, and that is our friend Hillary Clinton.

That's right. See, I trust Hillary to lead this country because I've seen her lifelong dedication to our nation's children, not just her own daughter, who she has raised to perfection[,] but every child who needs a champion, kids who take the long way to school to avoid the gangs, kids who wonder how they'll ever afford college, kids whose parents don't speak a word of English, but dream of a better life, kids who look to us to determine who and what they can be.

You see, Hillary has spent decades doing the relentless, thankless work to actually make a difference in their lives[,] advocating for kids with disabilities as a young lawyer, fighting for children's health care as first lady, and for quality child care in the Senate.

Call for unity

Michelle Obama, Selections from Speech at 2016 Democratic National Convention, 2016.

And when she didn't win the nomination eight years ago, she didn't get angry or disillusioned. Hillary did not pack up and go home, because as a true public servant Hillary knows that this is so much bigger than her own desires and disappointments. So she proudly stepped up to serve our country once again as secretary of state, traveling the globe to keep our kids safe. And look, there were plenty of moments when Hillary could have decided that this work was too hard, that the price of public service was too high, that she was tired of being picked apart for how she looks or how she talks or even how she laughs. But here's the thing. What I admire most about Hillary is that she never buckles under pressure. She never takes the easy way out. And Hillary Clinton has never quit on anything in her life.

And when I think about the kind of president that I want for my girls and all of our children, that's what I want. I want someone with the proven strength to persevere, someone who knows this job and takes it seriously, someone who understands that the issues a president faces are not black and white and cannot be boiled down to 140 characters. Because when you have the nuclear codes at your fingertips and the military in your command, you can't make snap decisions. You can't have a thin skin or a tendency to lash out. You need to be steady and measured and well-informed.

[handwritten margin note: "fear of this happening"]

I want a president with a record of public service, some whose life's work shows our children that we don't chase [fame] and fortune for ourselves, we fight to give everyone a chance to succeed. And we give back even when we're struggling ourselves because we know that there is always someone worse off. And there but for the grace of God go I.

I want a president who will teach our children that everyone in this country matters, a president who truly believes in the vision that our Founders put forth all those years ago that we are all created equal, each a beloved part of the great American story. And when crisis hits, we don't turn against each other. No, we listen to each other, we lean on each other, because we are always stronger together. And I am here tonight because I know that that is the kind of president that Hillary Clinton will be. And that's why in this election I'm with her.

You see, Hillary understands that the president is about one thing and one thing only, it's about leaving something better for our kids. That's how we've always moved this country forward, by all of us coming together on behalf of our children, folks who volunteer to coach that team, to teach that Sunday school class, because they know it takes a village.

[handwritten margin note: "Community, unity"]

Heroes of every color and creed who wear the uniform and risk their lives to keep passing down those blessings of liberty, police officers and the protesters in Dallas who all desperately want to keep our children safe. People who lined up in Orlando to donate blood because it could have been their son, their daughter in that club. Leaders like Tim Kaine[,] who show our kids what decency and devotion look like. Leaders like Hillary Clinton who ha[ve] the guts and the grace to keep coming back and putting those cracks in that highest and hardest glass ceiling until she finally breaks through, lifting all of us along with her.

That is the story of this country, the story that has brought me to this stage tonight, the story of generations of people who felt the lash of bondage, the shame of servitude, the sting of segregation, but who kept on striving and hoping and doing what needed to be done so that today I wake up every morning in a house that was built by slaves. And watch my daughters, two beautiful, intelligent, black young women playing with their dogs on the White House lawn.

And because of Hillary Clinton, my daughters and all our sons and daughters now take for granted that a woman can be president of the United States.

> So look, so don't let anyone ever tell you that this country isn't great, that some-
> how we need to make it great again. Because this right now is the greatest country
> on earth!
>
> And as my daughters prepare to set out into the world, I want a leader who is wor-
> thy of that truth, a leader who is worthy of my girls' promise and all our kids' promise, a
> leader who will be guided every day by the love and hope and impossibly big dreams
> that we all have for our children.
>
> So in this election, we cannot sit back and hope that everything works out for the
> best. We cannot afford to be tired or frustrated or cynical. No, hear me. Between now
> and November, we need to do what we did eight years ago and four years ago. We
> need to knock on every door, we need to get out every vote, we need to pour every
> last ounce of our passion and our strength and or love for this country into electing
> Hillary Clinton as president of the United States of America! So let's get to work. Thank
> you all and God bless.[2]

Much might be said about this speech, but what I want to illustrate, here, is how one's questions determine one's rhetorical perspective or lens.

Chapter 2 in this textbook discusses classical criticism. As you will see, this approach is thorough: It discusses everything from the arguments in a text to how well a rhetor handled both his or her body and his or her notes. The approach is usually chosen for a basic heuristic reason: The critic does not yet know what a single focus might be and wants to explore the possibilities as he or she engages in analysis. The critic assumes that certain aspects will jump out, others recede, giving the approach a less mechanical feel than it might seem to have as it marches the text through the five divisions or canons of rhetoric.

What might such an approach highlight about Michelle Obama's speech? Classical rhetoric sometimes seems to compel critics to treat *logos* (the arguments a text makes) and *pathos* (the emotional appeals a text makes) as two separate matters. Obama's major argument for electing Hillary Clinton is that she has and will continue to serve the needs of our children. That logical argument is, however, encased by Obama within the very emotional story of raising her two daughters from youngsters to young women during eight years in the White House. Obama merges *logos* and *pathos* to offer a compelling argument for why voters should elect Hillary Clinton.

Chapter 3 in this textbook discusses the Chicago School, which is often blurred with classical criticism. The blurring, however, obscures the fact that although both approaches are rooted in Aristotle, they are rooted in different Aristotelian works. The Chicago School, strongly influenced by the *Poetics*, asks what effect the text has and, then, what brought about that effect. Many, at the end of Michelle Obama's speech, felt both triumphant but not yet triumphant. They felt triumphant because Obama told of the nation's victory over racial prejudice in its election of her husband. That she, a black woman, wakes up every morning in "a house that was built by slaves" is evidence of this triumph. However, in her next sentence, Obama alludes to the triumph that has not yet occurred but, she presumes will, when the nation overcomes gender prejudice in its election of Clinton. Obama evokes the election triumphs of 2008 and 2012, and she evokes Clinton's lengthy record of public service (framed as for the benefit of children) to promote this triumphant but not yet fully triumphant feeling.

Chapter 4 and chapter 5 deal with two aspects that are drawn from the multiple volumes of rhetorical theorizing, authored by American Kenneth Burke. Chapter 4 deals with the words and phrases a text uses and how they help create identification between rhetor and audience(s). Using this approach, a critic would note how Michelle Obama uses phrases associated with Clinton in praising her: "stronger together," "with her," "it takes a village." These terms are ones that should bind together Michelle Obama, Hillary Clinton, and those listening to Obama's praise of Clinton.

Chapter 5 deals with the drama that a persuasive text presents and, very importantly, what elements are dominant in the drama and how their dominance affects persuasion. So, what is the drama Michelle Obama sketches? It is the twinned one of her quest to raise her daughters well during the White House years and Hillary Clinton's quest to serve all daughters—all children—well throughout her long career. Dominant in the drama offered is the element of purpose. Other elements of drama are present—the actors and actions, for example—but purpose dominates. And Obama wants us to focus on that noble, humane purpose in choosing Clinton as the next president.

Chapter 6 deals with how groups—rhetorical communities—create stories or themes that they strongly believe in. They are termed "fantasy themes," but they are very real to those who socially construct these stories or themes. The critic's task is to ascertain the extent to which the theme in a text matches that held by its audience and, thus, sways that audience.

What was Michelle Obama's theme? It had to do with the children whose lives are foregrounded in the speech, but indirectly. The theme was that this nation is already great because of the opportunities it has provided those once neglected and, worse, discriminated against. The nation, in Michelle Obama's "fantasy," has overcome its problems with race, will soon overcome its problems with gender, and—with Clinton as president—"will be guided every day by the love and hope and impossibly big dreams that we all have for our children." This is the American Dream, of course, but with the obstacles of race and gender playing a prominent role.

Chapter 7 is similar to chapters 5 and 6 insofar as it focuses on what we might term "the story" a text presents, but, whereas chapter 5 deals with elements of drama and chapter 6 deals with socially constructed "fantasies," chapter 7 deals directly with narrative. All arguments, Walter Fisher argues, are narratives. They are persuasive if they are coherent and possess fidelity. Fidelity is the key: events, characters, and values must "ring true." So, a critic using this theory would not only identify Obama's story but consider its coherence and fidelity. The story is, once again, twinned: that of the Obama girls mixed with that of Hillary Clinton's political career. Because factually true and well-enough known, they are coherent. They exhibit fidelity because they fit what Obama trusts her audience will assume about both her character as a mother and Hillary's character as a political player. They also exhibit fidelity because they match the high value we, in this culture, place on creating a better future for our children.

Chapter 8 deals with genre. This speech fits into a group—speeches by prospective or incumbent first ladies at a major party political convention; however, it departs from the group because it is delivered by an outgoing first lady. This difference allowed Michelle Obama to depart repeatedly from the generic norm. Michelle did not need to speak about her husband: he was leaving office. So, she instead speaks about those who would succeed him. She speaks overtly about Hillary Clinton, but she also speaks somewhat covertly about Donald Trump. Obama says she wants a president "who understands that the issues a president faces are not black and white and cannot be boiled down to 140 characters," who doesn't "have a thin skin or a tendency to lash out," who doesn't "chase fame and fortune for" himself, and "who truly believes in the vision that our Founders put forth all those years ago that we are all created equal … [a]nd, when crisis hits, we don't turn against each other."

Michelle Obama is, thus, being more political than first ladies usually are at conventions. She has earned this right, but she may also be engaging in what rhetorician John Schilb called a "rhetorical refusal" and, as such, calling attention to the constraints that first ladies are typically under.[3] She is, in a way, suggesting that the first lady's rhetoric ought to have the political power her 2016 speech does, that the first lady need not exhibit the rhetorical constraints and, perhaps, the other constraints that have limited what first ladies can say or do in public life.

Chapter 9 discusses mythological criticism. This may seem to be an approach quite remote from a convention speech, but mythological critics are interested in the patterns that texts follow. So, what is Michelle Obama's pattern? There is a sense of cycles in her speech: She and Barack have triumphed over racism, Hillary Clinton will triumph over sexism, and all who sustain their focus on the children and commit to working together as equals will triumph over whatever evil may lurk. However, there is also a recognition that these triumphant cycles do not just occur, as she concludes the speech by rejecting tiredness, frustration, or cynicism and calling for her auditors to "pour every last ounce of our passion and our strength and our love for this country into electing Hillary Clinton as president of the United States."

Chapter 10 presents Mikhail Bakhtin's contributions to rhetorical theory. One of his concepts is that of polyphony, which suggests that most texts participate in a larger discourse in which many other voices are heard in various ways. The rhetor has some control over the process: He or she can choose which voices to bring in for strategic reasons. So, who does Michelle Obama voice? Early she voices—but does not quote—those who attacked her husband. She also alludes to words he had said as well as words she had said as they struggled to overcome attacks. But then she shifts to the voice of Hillary Clinton. To an extent, Clinton is allowed to speak through Michelle Obama in the latter part of this convention address.

Chapter 11 deals with questions of power—who has it? How is it used? How is it resisted? Neither a Marxist perspective or a post-colonial perspective, which are reviewed in chapter 11, seem directly applicable to Michelle Obama's speech, but the larger issue of power is. Consider her remark on waking up every morning in a house that slaves built. In this remark, she alludes to both the power she—and others like her—have gained, but also the power that may still, in some haunting manner, enclose her. That power may well be in the past, but her awareness of it means that it is still, to some degree, present.

Chapter 12 deals with feminist criticism, a specific approach to raising questions of power that warrants separate consideration because of both the numbers attracted to it and the insights about texts that it has offered. This mode of criticism is equally interested in critiquing how those gendered female are constrained by sexist assumptions and practices and in revealing and saluting how those gendered female are breaking rhetorical glass ceilings through both parody and their own gendered style. I've already mentioned how Michelle Obama may be somewhat constrained by a genre thus far restricted to women. But what in her convention address has her speaking as female? Without apology, she, now a powerful political entity, speaks primarily as a mother. In so doing, she is embracing a female role often treated as politically unimportant and re-inscribing it as politically crucial—for her, for her husband, and for Hillary Clinton.

Finally, chapter 13 deals with constitutive rhetoric. As you will discover, this approach represents a turn away from thinking about rhetoric as persuasive of an audience to thinking about rhetoric as creating an identity for the rhetor and his or her audience. From this perspective, a critic would be interested in how Michelle Obama may be participating in creating a new identity for women and, probably more interestingly, for African-American women. Much is made of the strength evident in Michelle Obama's arms and shoulders. Perhaps this physical strength stands for a broader strength that is part of the identity she is trying to constitute for herself and other African-American women. The address is, without a doubt, a strong one. She is not speaking in the unassuming manner Barbara Bush did back in 1992; she is also not echoing anyone else's words and sentiments. She is speaking as herself, from her heart, in terms that poignantly present her eight years in the White House and powerfully endorse Clinton to be that house's next occupant.

Twelve approaches; a dozen different sets of questions. Yes, there are overlaps, but, at least at the beginning of your exploration of rhetorical criticism, it is useful to keep the approaches separate. In your practice as a rhetorical critic, they may well merge: There is no rule against blending perspectives in a single critical essay. Just as a biological scientist may examine an organism using two or three different lenses designed to reveal different things, a rhetorical critic may proceed from a couple of theoretical bases. When one looks to the assumptions behind the theories, one may find some problems of compatibility. So, there is a need to be cautious as you proceed; however, the richness of what rhetorical criticism can reveal is best pursued by—to the extent possible—asking the many questions a given text poses.

Notes

1. Medhurst, Martin J. "Reconceptualizing Rhetorical History: Eisenhower's Farewell Address." *Quarterly Journal of Speech*, 80 no. 2 (1994): 195–218.

2. Obama, Michelle, "Democratic National Convention Speech," 2016.

3. Schlib, John. *Rhetorical Refusals: Defying Audiences' Expectations.* Carbondale, IL: Southern Illinois University Press, 2007.

Figure credit

Fig. 1: Source: https://commons.wikimedia.org/wiki/File:Michelle_Obama_DNC_July_2016_(cropped).jpg.

Hillary Clinton delivering one of the many
speeches during her political career.

CHAPTER 2

Classical Criticism

When communication scholars began examining texts such as famous speeches, they needed a framework to guide them. It was readily available in a body of work we term classical. We term it such because it originates in classical antiquity, in ancient Greece and Rome. However, as you will shortly learn, it has endured well into the twentieth century. Along the way, new insights have been offered and merged in with the framework established long ago by the Greek Aristotle, the Roman Cicero, and others.

The Origins of Classical Criticism

Rhetoric was a fundamental area of instruction in antiquity. The liberal arts were the seven areas of study thought to be appropriate for the "free man" ("liber" in Latin). Three, the trivium, were fundamental; four, the quadrivium, were supplementary but nonetheless important. Rhetoric was part of the trivium.

Back then, there were no textbooks, so what we have in print is based on students' notes as learned men lectured about the art. Aristotle was one such man, and his teachings are compiled in *The Rhetoric*. And the Romans Cicero and Quintillian reproduced much of what Aristotle had said as he taught the art. They undoubtedly made some changes, elaborating on some concepts, stressing matters that Aristotle had not. We, however, assume that what we get in the Roman writers is based on a foundation Aristotle laid. Given how the critical approach discussed in this chapter is derived from the works of several (those mentioned and others), referring to the theory as classical is more accurate than referring to it as Aristotelian.

Classical Criticism through the Centuries

The supposed dark ages followed classical antiquity. During this time, much classical thought was either lost or pushed aside. Then, there were a number of revivals of that thought. The Renaissance represents one, as does the eighteenth century's embrace of reason. During these revivals and during smaller ones, classical rhetoric reasserted itself.[1]

In the Renaissance, in England, theorists George Puttenham and Henry Peacham elaborated on what the classical theorists had said about style. Later, in Scotland, George Campbell and Hugh Blair added to our understanding of how effective arguments are constructed, building into a discussion of what options one might have as a rhetor, several insights which were derived from the very beginnings of the psychology discipline. From the nineteenth century onward, many Americans (among them, President John Quincy Adams) have refined classical concepts. And, although some might not put them in the classical category, Chaim Perelman and Lucie Olbrechts-Tyteca in *The New Rhetoric* have offered a valuable update on what the classical theorists said about the kinds of arguments a rhetor could make.

Some rhetorical theorists have suggested that classical criticism is now passe. It is not the approach that is most in vogue. However, some critics use this theoretical basis to this day to produce very valuable essays. And, used explicitly or not, it is the framework that more avant-garde rhetoricians knowingly depart from.

The Five Canons

Classical rhetorical theorists, in offering their instruction, divided the subject into five parts, or divisions or canons. Using the Latin terms, they are *inventio, dispositio, elocutio, pronuntiatio,* and *memoria*. I will treat each, but it will become quickly apparent that, as we proceed down the list, theorists have offered us progressively less to go on.

Inventio

This canon deals with how a rhetor finds the materials necessary to persuade an audience. Right off the bat, theorists note that the materials fall into three categories. Some are what we think of as the substantive arguments. They may cite comparisons; they may point to consequences; they may quote authorities. These are termed **logos**.

In our day and age (after Descartes, some would say), we value logos over all else, but, back in classical antiquity, two other categories were equally important. The emotional appeals one might make—evoking fear, pride, and the like—are termed **pathos**. Aristotle, in what we have of *The Rhetoric*, devotes many, many pages to pathos. It was not something either unimportant or fallacious to him!

Then, there is **ethos**. If one of the three is most important, according to Aristotle, ethos is it. But what is ethos? The similarity between the Greek word and the English term "ethics" has misled many into discussing ethos as if it were a code of conduct for rhetors. Rather, it is a set of qualities a rhetor has in the eyes of his or her audience(s). Aristotle's words on ethos are worth noting:

> The character [ethos] of the speaker is a cause of persuasion when the speech is so uttered as to make him worthy of belief; for as a rule we trust men of probity more, and more quickly, about things in general, while on points outside the realm of exact knowledge, where opinion is divided, we trust them absolutely. This trust, however, should be created by the speech itself, and not left to depend upon an antecedent impression that the speaker is this or that kind of man. It is not true, as some writers on the art maintain, that the probity of the speaker contributes nothing to his persuasiveness; on the contrary, we might almost affirm that his character [ethos] is the most potent of all the means to persuasion.[2]

Classical theorists divide ethos into three dimensions: competence, character, and good will. Some contemporary rhetoricians, seeing good will as part of character, have replaced it with dynamism. So, before a rhetor even begins, his or her audience has a sense of how competent he or she is, whether he or she is of good character, and whether he or she is thought to be dynamic as a presenter.

The rhetor can—Aristotle said must—do things during a speech to affect ethos. For example, a strong organization can increase one's ethos on the competence dimension, and citing arguments that opponents might make can increase one's ethos on the character dimension. So, ethos is not outside the rhetor's control. However, there are instances in which a rhetor would find it very difficult to alter how his or her audience views him or her. During the early 1970s, student anti-war activists were fiercely opposed to President Richard Nixon. His ethos, in the minds of this audience, was low on the character dimension, and he probably had no possibility of altering it. But ethos can work the other way, too. After his 1963 address at the Lincoln Memorial in Washington, DC, Martin Luther King, Jr.'s ethos soared for many audiences. For a while afterward, his words were golden (i.e., highly likely to be received well because of his high ethos). More recently, President Donald Trump has had a negative ethos in the minds of many, as had California Congresswoman Nancy Pelosi in other minds.

So, logos-pathos-ethos is one construct one studying classical invention or *inventio* must be aware of. Another is the rhetorical triangle of argument, audience, and rhetor. Classical theorists were aware of how these three variables might affect an attempt at persuasion, but they did not stress it. Why? Probably because of the homogeneity that characterized the context they were in. The liberal arts, as noted before, were for free men (i.e., the elite in these societies). So, the audience did not exhibit much by way of diversity, and the rhetor trying to persuade the audience was much the same as the audience members. There was also likely to be quick agreement between rhetor and audience on what the context, an element outside the triangle, but often referred to, was.

Since classical antiquity, the terms in the triangle have become more complex. A rhetor is likely now to not only have a diverse audience, but face multiple audiences. A rhetor is also much more aware now of the different roles or personae he or she might adopt in trying to persuade this complex audience. We are now, as classical critics, more likely to explore the audience and the rhetor and ask how arguments—the third point in the triangle—will be affected by the audience's demographics and attitudes and the rhetor's chosen persona.

The diverse audience also means that more attention than in classical times needs to be paid to context, for there may not be the quick agreement on it as there was in ancient Athens or Rome. In fact, one change from ancient times to present times may well be the need the rhetor now has to establish a context in his or her text in such a manner that the majority in the audience nods yes to it.

Context is not part of the rhetorical triangle, although some revise the concept—and diagram—and insert context into the triangle's center. Purpose is not part of the triangle either, but it needs to be attended to as well. Back in classical times, a rhetor's purpose was clear—to persuade that homogenous audience to say yes. As time passed, the whole notion of persuasion became more complex. Those who revived classical rhetoric in the eighteenth century, at a time when the academic discipline of psychology was emerging, tried to bring some of its insights into rhetoric. They recognized that the means that one might use to persuade were broader than classical theorists had suggested. They also recognized that persuasion was not as simple as yes or no.

Perhaps because new types of text emerged—most significantly, advertising—the discussion of persuasion began to stress rhetorical goals short of gaining a yes and strategies that were more peripheral or less direct. Given how complex persuasion may well be, focusing on a list of argumentation strategies may seem simplistic. But, offering such lists has informed the classical discussion of *inventio* from the start. The classical rhetoricians—as well as logicians—make a distinction between inductive and deductive reasoning. If practicing induction, one assembles arguments and evidence and draws a conclusion from them; if practicing deduction, one begins with statements already granted to be true, such as "All men are mortal." This induction-deduction distinction, although useful in some realms, may not be as useful to rhetors as the concept of ***topoi*** or ***topica***, expanded a bit to include the ways deduction typically shows up in everyday discourse.

Where does one go to find the arguments and evidence he or she will assemble? Classical rhetoricians offer lists of the places one might go. They did not mean places literally (e.g., go to the library's reference room); rather, they meant place to be a metaphor for the common types of support one might choose to offer. Aristotle termed these *topoi*, the Greek word for "places"; Cicero termed them *topica*, the Latin word for "places." Classical rhetoricians offered lists, and rhetoricians through time have offered revised lists. Aristotle's common or universal *topoi* offer a starting point. As reformulated by Edward P. J. Corbett in the several editions of *Classical Rhetoric for the Modern Student*, they are seventeen in number, divisible into five broad categories. Let's use the controversial issue of gun control for our examples. (Some will be pro; others, con.)

Common Topoi *of Classical Rhetoric*

Definition
  Genus
  Division

Comparison
  Similarity
  Difference
  Degree

Relationship
  Cause and effect
  Antecedent and consequence
  Contraries
  Contradictories

Circumstances
  Possible and impossible
  Past fact and future fact

Testimony
  Authority
  Testimonial
  Statistics
  Maxims
  Law
  Precedents

Under definition, there are two types—a definition based on genus (e.g., an AR 15 rifle is a military weapon) and a definition based on division (e.g., firearms fall into a number of separate categories). Under comparison, there are three *topoi*—similarity (e.g., a rifle is like a knife), difference (e.g., an AR 15 rifle is different than the typical hunting rifle), and degree (e.g., an AR 15 rifle is a more advanced weapon for self-protection than a simple handgun). Under relationship, there are four *topoi*: cause and effect (e.g., firearms in the home result in tragic accidents); antecedent and consequence (e.g., playing violent video games often precedes—and leads to—gun violence by young people); contraries (e.g., protecting one's home and restricting firearms don't coincide); and contradictions (e.g., since we restrict the First Amendment, why can't we restrict the Second?).

Under circumstance, there are two *topoi*—possible and impossible (e.g., gun control will not get firearms out of the hands of "bad guys") and past fact and future act (e.g., gun control efforts in past decades have failed to reduce gun violence significantly). Finally, under testimony, there are six *topoi*—authority (e.g., quoting/citing an expert on crime); testimonial (e.g., quoting/citing someone well-known but not an expert); statistics (e.g., citing number of accidental gun-related deaths in the home); maxims (e.g., "the best defense is a good offense"); law (e.g., the text of the Second Amendment); precedents (e.g., quoting/citing the Supreme Court decision in *Heller v. District of Columbia*); and examples (e.g., noting positive gun control efforts in Canada or Australia).

Rhetoricians in the centuries since have offered different, perhaps more manageable lists. In the twentieth century, a very good one has been offered by rhetoricians Chaim Perelman and Lucie Olbrechts-Tyteca in *The New Rhetoric*. In offering their list, these rhetoricians collapse deduction and induction together because, in their view, in every-day arguments (which is what rhetoric deals with), true deduction does not exist. Rather, we have arguments that resemble deductive ones, which Perelman and Olbrechts-Tyteca term "quasi-logical." Their conceptualization has been made even more accessible in the work of Barbara Warnick and Susan Kline.[3]

Warnick and Kline explain what Perelam and Olbrechts-Tyteca are attempting to do—and their rigorous research procedure—in an article in the journal *Argumentation & Advocacy*:

> The conventions for conducting arguments also grow out of practices and norms mutually accepted by interlocutors who participate together in a common culture. Likewise, the inferential schemes that move the audience to accept the arguer's claims are generated through commonplaces and structures recognized and accepted by Western society. Over two-thirds of *The New Rhetoric* was devoted to describing these agreed-upon liaisons that make inferences possible, for Perelman and Olbrechts-Tyteca believed that in practical reasoning, inferential moves are made possible rhetorically.

Prior to *The New Rhetoric*, our vocabulary for describing inference patterns was limited to formal logical patterns (e.g., categorical, disjunctive, and conditional syllogisms) and the standard classifications of inductive reasoning (analogy, generalization, cause, and sign). Perelman and Olbrechts-Tyteca generated their schemes through a careful empirical process in which they collected discursive arguments for over ten years, typed them, and added new categories (dissociations, symbolic liaisons, and double hierarchy arguments, among others), thus providing a richer vocabulary for describing reasoning structures. In addition, Perelman and Olbrechts-Tyteca explicitly incorporated a rhetorical theory of argument by shaping audience-accepted commonplaces into the inference structure of schemes.[4]

Let's start with deduction, as it is traditionally defined. The key here is the syllogism, of which there are three types: categorical, hypothetical, and disjunctive. Here is an example of each:

CATEGORICAL
All men are mortal.
Socrates is a man.
Therefore, Socrates is mortal.

HYPOTHETICAL
If the University of Alabama wins the game, they will be the national champion.
Alabama has won the game.
Therefore, Alabama is the national champion.

DISJUNCTIVE
I will travel to New York City by either airplane or train.
I will not travel by airplane.
Therefore, I will travel by train.

If you were in a logic class, you would not only deal with more sophisticated examples than these, but also learn the many rules for carefully constructing such syllogisms. But, you're not in a logic class, and rhetors rarely lay out syllogisms in a 1–2–3 manner. Instead, they offer pieces of such syllogisms in ordinary language. These are termed *enthymemes*. What a rhetor expects of his or her audience is that they will supply missing pieces and assemble the syllogism. Kathleen Hall Jamieson in *Dirty Politics* even argues that this supplying and assembling will enhance persuasion because the audience becomes a co-creator of the argument with the rhetor.[5] For example, let's say a rhetor argues, "Global warming threatens our planet: We must stop it!" That statement is an enthymeme. Given a different structure and with pieces added, it becomes a categorical syllogism:

Phenomena that threaten the planet must be stopped.
Global warming is a phenomenon that that threatens the planet.
Therefore, global warming must be stopped.

In everyday discourse, one would probably not voice the initial premise, but the audience, in completing the *enythmeme*, would provide it without uttering it.

Topoi *Offered by Perelman and Olbrechts-Tyteca*

Quasi-logical
  Transitivity (categorical)
  Incompatibility (disjunctive)
  Reciprocity (hypothetical)

Analogy
  Literal
  Figurative

Generalization
Cause
Coexistence
  Sign
  Act to character
  Character to act

Dissociation

Perelman and Olbrects-Tyteca (and Warnick and Kline) refer to syllogism-like enthymemes as quasi-logical arguments (because they do not believe the deduction logicians talk about really exists in everyday argumentation). The one that resembles the categorical syllogism is an argument based on transitivity; the one that resembles the disjunctive syllogism is an argument based on incompatibility; and the one that resembles the hypothetical syllogism is an argument based on reciprocity. These are the first three places or *topoi/topica* a rhetor might turn to for his or her arguments.

There are four more.

The fourth is analogy, which has two types: literal and figurative. If one were to argue that the United States should have a single-payer national healthcare system, one might argue that the system would be analogous or similar to Medicare. That's a literal analogy.

One might argue that the system would be analogous to the care a parent provides a child. That's a figurative analogy. Figurative analogies are more decorative than literal ones, and they therefore lack persuasive force, but they are not without some power to persuade.

The fifth is generalization from examples. Here, the rhetor would cite the many other nations that have a single-payer system. The rhetor would hope that the examples were found by the audience to be both sufficiently like what was being suggested for the United States and sufficiently numerous.

The sixth is cause. A rhetor would argue, for example, that our present healthcare system causes many harms. Causes are difficult to prove—because there are so many variables that might affect an outcome. So, a variation on the cause *topos* would be arguing based on a strong correlation between our present healthcare delivery system and some dire consequence.

The seventh is coexistence. One variation on it is a sign argument, where the rhetor suggests that something observable is a sign of either a problem or its opposite. Long waits in the emergency room may be a sign of a healthcare system that is not working; a decline in cancer deaths may be a sign of a healthcare system that is working. Two other variations are noteworthy. In one case, a rhetor would argue that an act's positive or negative qualities are a sign of a person's character. So, one might argue that a billionaire's significant donations to charity indicate his or her beneficence. The flip of that would be to argue that a person's character or credentials are a sign of the validity of what he or she says. For example, to argue that either an admired figure's endorsement of universal healthcare suggests that it is a great idea or a noted authority's endorsement suggests that it is such. This flip—what others might term "arguing from authority"—is a very popular way of arguing in academic circles as well as in our culture at large.

The eighth is dissociation. Here, a rhetor argues that what is proposed is better than an alternative—universal health care is better than what we have under the Affordable Care Act. When one argues "better," one is usually explicitly or implicitly playing off a given culture's value hierarchy. Some culture's value efficiency quite highly; others do not. A culture that did would prefer—find "better"—a policy option argued to be efficient.

If you were in a class teaching rhetoric, you would learn how to use these *topoi* to create arguments. But, you're presumably in a criticism class. So, your goal is to identify the arguments a rhetor offers. Although lists perhaps do simplify what goes on in human persuasion, they nonetheless offer you a useful vocabulary for talking about the stuff in a text. Notice, however, how both this list and the one derived from Aristotle's work focus on logos. As I suggested earlier, we, post-Descartes, here in the West, tend to privilege logos over pathos and ethos. But, in assessing how a text persuades, don't neglect the emotional appeals a text makes and don't neglect how the audience's sense of the rhetor's competence, character, and dynamism (the rhetor's ethos) affects persuasion. California

Senator Kamala Harris's initial speech in the United States Senate powerfully criticized the Trump administration's emerging immigration policies. She heavily used patho*s*. At about the same time, Arizona Senator John McCain declined to vote for a Republican attempt to repeal portions of the Affordable Care Act (Obamacare). He said little; his argument (basically that regular procedures featuring amending and debating had not been followed) relied greatly on his accumulated ethos as a long-serving senator, noted for both integrity and frankness. Pathos and ethos cannot be neglected when assessing how a text works!

Dispositio

Classical theorists say far more about how to discover one's arguments than they do about how to organize them. In classical times, there emerged what seemed to be an assumption that all persuasive discourse proceeded according to a pattern best outlined by Cicero. Following this pattern, one would announce one's position, divide it into parts, provide proof for each part, perhaps refute arguments that might be advanced against the position, and then grandly conclude in what classical rhetoricians term the "**peroration**." Since Cicero, many have offered variations on this pattern. Early in the twentieth century, for example, communication professor Alan Monroe offered what has come to be known as "Monroe's motivated sequence." (It is discussed in just about any public speaking textbook one might pick up.) This sequence is much like Cicero's but adds a step Monroe terms "visualization," where the rhetor invites the audience to picture whatever is being proposed in existence and see how beneficial it will be.

As psychology emerged, some notions derived very loosely from the new discipline began adding nuances to this structure of the oration. The notion of recency (coming last) and primacy (coming first) as being more compelling positions in a list alerted rhetors to a sound strategy for arranging arguments within the oration's proof section. Notions from psychology are what led communication scholar Alan Monroe to tweak the oration into Monroe's motivated sequence, adding the visualization step. Notions from psychology are also what leads just about every speech teacher to stress the need to begin and end strongly. The roadmap that instructors talk about is a way to not only preview one's arguments but also to make one's audience co-creators of the text (and its arguments) as it is executed. The ending (peroration) is not just a time to review, but an important opportunity to rally one's audience into action. When critically considering speeches, you will find yourself often gravitating toward how the speaker began and how the speaker concluded because of what we know about how audiences respond.

Public speaking textbooks also advise rhetors to use organizational strategies that are easy for the audience to follow. This advice is not just based on courtesy. If an audience can very easily follow a text's organization, then that audience has more space in its limited short-term memory to focus on arguments. Also, if the organization is easy to follow, then the audience is more likely to feel like a co-creator of the message and, thereby, be more easily swayed to accept its argument.

What, then, is easy to follow? Narrative theorists will, of course, say story-like structure. This guess is probably correct: It seems intuitively true. Research in linguistics on what are termed "rhetorical predicates" offers more than guesses.[6] Rhetorical predicates are larger—perhaps one paragraph in length—units of discourse than the sentence, and they often take four forms: list-like, narrative, cause-effect, and contrastive. Research has been undertaken on how these forms seem to affect one's ability to remember what the paragraph says. Based on this research, the most effective predicates seem to be cause-effect and narrative.

Again, if you were learning rhetoric, you would now know how you might want to structure your speech or essay. As a critic, you know what you might use to assess how effective a rhetor is in organizing his or her text. The presidential speechwriting process is often quite messy: Different writers contribute, and then staffers (i.e., those responsible for policy areas) insist on insertions and deletions. Presidents too frequently direct "the speech shop" to meld it all together. One consequence is poor organization, since no single scheme is being followed. So, often, a rhetorical critic will find problems with a text's persuasiveness by flagging down a structure that just does not work.

Elocutio

This is the trickiest Latin term. We association elocution with speaking clearly and perhaps dramatically, but the classical theorists use it to refer to what we might term "style."

Back in classical antiquity, not much seems to have been said about style. Tropes and schemes—more on those in a bit—were mentioned, but the most useful concept seems to be the distinction among high, middle, and low style. Now, this might seem a rather simple notion, but it is really more insightful than it seems, since there is an insistence on finding the appropriate style for both one's audience and one's situation. Discourse on important public occasions require high style; arguing about most legislative matters and offering instruction require middle. The use of low style is rare. One can update this advice by noting how two well-known presidential genres are stylistically different. The inaugural should be and typically is in high style; the State of the Union address, middle. Presidents have sometimes erred by making the inaugural too low or the State of the Union too high.

How does a rhetor move up the scale from low to middle to high? Two common ways are by using **tropes** and **schemes**. The more they are used, the higher the style.

Tropes are figurative uses of language; schemes are creative ways of arranging words and phrases to create aural, rhythmic patterns. Mentioned in classical treatises on rhetoric, tropes and schemes are developed to a length that some think absurd, in the English Renaissance by George Putnam in his *The Arte of English Poesie* (1589) and Henry Peacham in his *The Garden of Eloquence* (1577). They list hundreds of these stylistic techniques.

I have neither the space nor the inclination to list hundreds, but let me, for both tropes and schemes, outline some common and effective ones. Having used healthcare as my topic thus far, let me use gun control and infrastructure as my topics, here.

Tropes are figurative uses of language. The very familiar simile and metaphor are examples, as are the less familiar **synecdoche** and **metonymy**. In the former, a part stands for the whole:

America should not let its miles of iron rail rust.

In the latter, an attribute stands for an entity:

America should not allow its quick movement from city to city to become a thing of the past.

In the first, "miles of iron rail" represents the entirety of the nation's railroading system and, by extension, all the nation's transportation infrastructure; in the second, the quick movement (a trait) stands for what our highway permits. (And, yes, they are quite similar tropes.)

If one were to use the trope of **hyperbole**, one would exaggerate for effect:

Thousands of miles of concrete roadway are crumbling every year.

If one were to use the trope of **litotes**, one would understate for effect:

Travelers were hardly inconvenienced: They only had to wait three hours to get through the toll gate.

Schemes are artful ways of arranging words, phrases, or clauses. Parallelism is the most basic; more artful are **anaphora, epistrophe, antithesis, antimetabole, asyndeton,** and **polysyndeton**. Here's an example of each.

Anaphora: The nation's roads are crumbling, the nation's bridges are collapsing, the nation's pipes are rusting, and the nation's electrical grid is about ready to short-out.

(Here, "The nation's" is repeated at the beginning of successive clauses.)

Epistrophe: The bridges are collapsing, the tunnels are collapsing, the huge water conduits are collapsing, and, along with them, the economy is collapsing.

(Here, "collapsing" is repeated at the end of successive clauses. Insofar as the last item is arguably bigger than the others, the sentence exhibits the scheme of **climax**.)

Antithesis: We need high-speed railways, not always-late trains; we need safe water mains, not pipes that leach lead; we need bridges that span rivers, not ones that seem ready to fall in.

(Here, in three instances, two items are contrasted with the use of "not." "But," "yet," and other words can strike the antithetical relationship as well.)

Antimetabole: Better highways get goods to warehouses on-time, Goods arriving on time get to retail outlets soon, goods on the retail shelves get purchased quickly, and quick purchases speed up the entire economy.

(Here, something like a chain is created, with what is at the end of a clause reappearing at the beginning of the next.)

Asyndeton: This nation's infrastructure is breaking, bursting, collapsing, crumbling, rusting, failing.

(Here, a list is offered without a conjunction between the last two items. The scheme suggests that the list goes on even farther.)

Polysyndeton: The nation must deal soon with its dangerously deteriorating highways and bridges and tunnels and rail lines and water pipes and sewers.

(Here, the overuse of the conjunction creates a "piling-on" effect.)

If you were in a rhetoric class, you'd be urged to use these and many other flourishes when appropriate. But, as a budding rhetorical critic, your task is to pinpoint tropes and schemes and assess their effect and their effectiveness.

Pronuncitatio

This canon focuses on delivery. Evidently, back in classical antiquity, everyone could speak well, for not much on delivery is to be found in classical treatises. Perhaps, social class has something to do with the absence both in classical times up through the eighteenth century. Right or wrong, it was presumed that the elite, who received the rhetorical education, were competent as speakers.

In the eighteenth and nineteenth centuries, attention shifts to educating those other than the elites. Evidence of that attention is the Elocutionary Movement. This movement offered training in public speaking based on—at best—guesses as to what effect techniques of delivery might have. It is very easy to mock this movement. It, for example, catalogued various gestures the speaker might make, arguing what effect the gesture would have. Sometimes, the advice seems common sense; at other times, it seems rather silly. Hands extended; palms up. That gesture evokes pity. One asks, "Really? Based on what?" The advice also, one might add, assumes that gesture is the same from culture to culture, even from gender to gender—an assumption that is not valid.

The Elocutionary Movement perhaps slowed down sound school instruction in public speaking, but such instruction did emerge. Although the research underpinning advice on how to use one's voice or how to use one's body is still limited, those teaching public speaking are cautious in making claims. What they say usually passes the test of common sense. This advice, primarily from twentieth- and twenty-first-century textbooks, adds to the body of classical rhetorical theory.

As far as the voice is concerned, we think we know how volume (high and low), pace (fast and slow), and pitch (high and low) affect communication. We know enough to critique speeches that are consistently at the extremes as likely ineffective. We know enough to critique speeches that exhibit variety—for strategic reasons—as effective. We also know that other variables, such as gender, alter how a vocal quality is received. A high-pitched male is seen as effeminate and, therefore, weak; a high-pitched female is seen as shrill and, therefore, potentially irrational. There are, of course, stereotypes galore functioning in that statement, but, no matter how we feel about stereotypes, they do enter how audiences respond to rhetors.

We also seem to know—based on common sense—that some movement is preferable to standing rigidly or pacing endlessly. Standing rigid suggests lack of confidence; pacing suggests nervousness. We also seem to know—with higher confidence—that eye contact with audience enhances persuasion both by gaining and sustaining the audience's attention and by suggesting a personal connection—perhaps one of caring—between the rhetor and the audience. Gestures are a trickier matter. We know that not gesturing is foregoing a persuasive resource, but that over-gesturing calls attention to the gesturing itself and away from what is being said. A tricky dimension of gesturing largely deals with gender. For deeply rooted social reasons, those gendered female tend to use close-to-the-body gesturing, whereas those gendered male use broader ones. An implication is that, should a female use gesturing associated with males, she may be seen as overly assertive, and, should a male use gesturing associated with females, he may be seen as weak. We also know that ethnicity may affect one's gesturing: Certain ethnicities do gesture more than others; preferred gestures also seem to vary from ethnicity to ethnicity.

When one is in the public forum, the best advice is to avoid extremes. A rhetorical critic might then find him- or herself critiquing negatively any under- or over-use. At least in the short term, the critic might also find him- or herself critiquing negatively any delivery behavior significantly out of line with the rhetor's gender. I say "in the short term" because there are suggestions that gender differences may be vanishing in the public forum, suggestions that an androgynous style may be emerging, at least in arenas such as commerce and government.

One other nonverbal behavior is worth noting. Many rhetors over-use what are termed "vocal interrupters." These are sounds or words, such as "umm," that a rhetor inserts while trying to assemble the next words he or she will utter. Vocal interrupters are quite common: It is almost impossible to eliminate them entirely. They become a problem when they are so noticeable that audience members begin counting how many umm's are used. At that point, the interrupters are a problem because they distract from the substance of the text and they suggest that the rhetor is unsure of what he or she is saying. A speech with too many such interrupters can lose its effectiveness because of these interrupters alone.

This commentary on *pronuncitatio* ought to alert those who will analyze speeches to an important part of that analysis: actually hearing or, better, seeing and hearing the speech. Although we cannot do this for speeches far back in time, the internet, with all its resources, has made listening and/or watching more possible than it once was. Beyond a certain point in the twentieth century, performances of most major public addresses can be accessed online. Sometimes, the critic is stuck with radio; sometimes, grainy newsreel footage. But gradually the sound and images get better, and, at a magical point in the 1960s, living color appears!

Memoria

This last canon is the one that is most neglected, back in classical antiquity and today. In Ancient Greece and Rome, orations were typically delivered from memory. Thus, treatises offered some advice for committing a speech to memory. Today, this advice is largely irrelevant, for speeches are rarely memorized. In a classroom setting, or even in a business setting, they are usually delivered extemporaneously. So, in a public speaking class, an instructor might critique how well a student prepares and uses notecards. But in most public situations that critics examine, speeches are typically read—from a large-print script or from a teleprompter. Often, a rhetor will extemporize (i.e., depart from the prepared text to offer additional comments). A rhetorical critic, then, can examine both how well a rhetor works with a script or a teleprompter. Some presidents, for example, have had a difficult time with the technology. A rhetorical critic can also examine any extemporaneous moments to discern both how well they fit into the flow of the speech and whether the addition in any way distracts from the main thrust of the message. President Bill Clinton, for example, could depart from his script without anyone noticing: He would flow into and then out of unplanned remarks, rarely sending any signals that they were unplanned. Rarely did the detours cause problems: Clinton was indeed "slick." President Lyndon Johnson, on the other hand, could move smoothly in and out of a script, but his additions often shifted the audience's attention to him—what he'd done or wanted to do—and thereby distracted from a text's primary message.

You may note that, in talking about the five canons classical rhetoric explored, the texts referred to are almost always speeches. Although the canons could easily be applied to written texts, a fair amount of adaptation would be necessary to apply the approach to visual texts such as advertisements, films, or public memory sites. A few classical concepts might fit, but, for the most part, the classical approach is tied to speeches, which are the most traditional kind of text rhetorical criticism deals with. But that seems appropriate: the most traditional approach being tied to the most traditional kind of text.

In keeping with this emphasis on speeches, two quick case studies will exhibit how classical criticism might be used to illuminate a famous 1933 speech, President Franklin D. Roosevelt's first inaugural, and a famous 1995 speech, First Lady Hillary Clinton's address to an international conference on women's rights held in Beijing, China. An experienced classical critic would rather quickly settle on certain aspects of each to discuss, but let me slow the process down and outline the method he or she would use.

Method

There is a great deal to classical rhetorical theory—much to consider—because the approach was designed to be comprehensive. It covers all aspects of a text, usually a speech. Thus, a critic using the approach ranges through all aspects. Initially, the critic's procedure is heuristic. It is a way to discover what a critical essay might focus on. Heuristics work best if they are structured, and the five canons provides a perfect structure.

Under *inventio*, ask, first, if there are aspects of the rhetor's person, the audience, and the context that are important. Make sure you understand the exigence behind the text/ speech.

Then, proceed through logos, pathos, and ethos. Identify the arguments that the text/speech makes. Either the classical common *topoi* or their reformulation by Perelman and Olbrechts-Tyteca should help you identify and name what the logical bases in the text/speech are. Identify the emotional appeals as well. Then, consider how the rhetor, based on who he or she is, persuades. Note the rhetor's presumed competence, character, and dynamism going in, and note what the rhetor does to enhance these variables of ethos.

Under disposition, discern the text's structure, noting the overall pattern as well as how the rhetor handles the text's beginning and its ending. Ask if organizational resources are being used effectively.

Under *elocutio*, ask about the level of style the rhetor uses and if that level is appropriate. Then, look for tropes and schemes, not just noting them, but asking if they are used to good effect.

It is important, if the text before you is a speech, that you see and/or hear the speech. Not always possible, this viewing and/or hearing allows you to ask questions under the canon of *pronuncitatio*. What you are looking for are elements of delivery that enhance a speech and elements of delivery that detract from a speech.

Finally, under *memoria*, you should ask how, if your text is a speech, the speaker works with the manuscript or the notes. In some cases, that manuscript may be scrolling by on a teleprompter. Quite a few speeches have been weakened by rhetors who handled their materials in a manner that called undue attention to their existence and use.

Having proceeded through the canons as a heuristic, the critic—you—are ready to choose among the insights you have gained. Some are unimportant; some are curious; and some are very important in making the text/speech effective. The aspects in the latter category are the ones you should develop in a piece of criticism. A good essay using classical criticism could deal with just one aspect, but, more likely, it will focus on a handful that work together, providing the essay with an overall theme. Back in time, you will find, in print, pieces of classical criticism that do proceed, sometimes mechanically, through all five canons. This proceeding as a classical critic is rare today, but classical critics still proceed that way as they think through what they will eventually write.

The examples that follow illustrate how the classical critic zeroes in on certain aspects of a text after using the canons as a heuristic.

Application: Franklin D. Roosevelt in 1933

Newly elected President Franklin D. Roosevelt spoke to the nation on March 4, 1933. The nation had fallen into the Great Depression four years earlier, and years of Hoover policies had not altered the economic plight significantly. So, Roosevelt's exigence was to lift the people—at least emotionally—out of the depression they were in.

President Hoover, Mr. Chief Justice, my friends: This is a day of national consecration, and I am certain that on this day my fellow Americans expect that on my induction into the presidency I will address them with a candor and a decision which the present situation of our people impels. This is preeminently the time to speak the truth, the whole truth, frankly and boldly. Nor need we shrink from honestly facing conditions in our country today. This great nation will endure as it has endured, will revive and will prosper.

So first of all, let me assert my firm belief that the only thing we have to fear is fear itself—nameless, unreasoning, unjustified terror which paralyzes needed efforts to convert retreat into advance. In every dark hour of our national life a leadership of frankness and of vigor has met with that understanding and support of the people themselves which is essential to victory. And I am convinced that you will again give that support to leadership in these critical days.

*****

And yet our distress comes from no failure of substance. We are stricken by no plague of locusts. Compared with the perils which our forefathers conquered because they believed and were not afraid, we have still much to be thankful for. Nature still offers her bounty and human efforts have multiplied it. Plenty is at our doorstep, but a generous use of it languishes in the very sights of the supply.

Primarily, this is because the rulers of the exchange of mankind's goods have failed through their own stubbornness and their own incompetence, have admitted their failure, and have abdicated. Practices of the unscrupulous moneychangers stand indicted in the court of public opinion, rejected by the hearts and minds of men.

True, they have tried. But their efforts have been cast in the pattern of an outworn tradition. Faced by failure of credit, they have proposed only the lending of more money. Stripped of the lure of profit by which to induce our people to follow their false leadership, they have resorted to exhortations, pleading tearfully for restored confidence. They only know the rules of a generation of self-seekers. They have no vision, and when there is no vision, the people perish.

Yes, the moneychangers have fled from their high seats in the temple of our civilization. We may now restore that temple to the ancient truths. The measure of that restoration lies in the extent to which we apply social values more noble than mere monetary profit. Happiness lies not in the mere possession of money; it lies in the joy of achievement, in the thrill of creative effort. The joy, the moral stimulation of work, no longer must be forgotten in the mad chase of evanescent profits. These dark days, my friends, will be worth all they cost us if they teach us that our true destiny is not to be ministered unto but to minister to ourselves, to our fellow men.

Recognition of that falsity of material wealth as the standard of success goes hand in hand with the abandonment of the false belief that public office and high political position are to be valued only by the standards of pride of place and personal profit; and there must be an end to a conduct in banking and in business which too often has given to a sacred trust the likeness of callous and selfish wrongdoing. Small wonder that confidence languishes, for it thrives only on honesty, on honor, on the sacredness of obligations, on faithful protection, and on unselfish performance. Without them, it cannot live.

Franklin D. Roosevelt, Selection from Inaugural Address, 1933.

Restoration calls, however, not for changes in ethics alone. This nation is asking for action, and action now.

*****

If I read the temper of our people correctly, we now realize as we have never realized before our interdependence on each other: that we cannot merely take but we must give as well; that if we are to go forward, we must move as a trained and loyal army willing to sacrifice for the good of a common discipline because without such discipline, no progress can be made, no leadership becomes effective. We are, I know, ready and willing to submit our lives and our property to such discipline because it makes possible a leadership which aims at the larger good. This I propose to offer, pledging that the larger purposes will bind upon us, bind upon us all as a sacred obligation with a unity of duty hitherto evoked only in times of armed strife.

With this pledge taken, I assume unhesitatingly the leadership of this great army of our people dedicated to a disciplined attack upon our common problems. Action in this image, action to this end is feasible under the form of government which we have inherited from our ancestors.

*****

And it is to be hoped that the normal balance of executive and legislative authority may be wholly equal, wholly adequate to meet the unprecedented task before us. But it may be that an unprecedented demand and need for undelayed action may call for temporary departure from that normal balance of public procedure. I am prepared under my constitutional duty to recommend the measures that a stricken nation in the midst of a stricken world may require. These measures, or such other measures as the Congress may build out of its experience and wisdom, I shall seek, within my constitutional authority, to bring to speedy adoption.

But in the event that the Congress shall fail to take one of these two courses, in the event that the national emergency is still critical, I shall not evade the clear course of duty that will then confront me. I shall ask Congress for the one remaining instrument to meet the crisis—broad executive power to wage a war against the emergency, as great as the power that would be given to me if we were in fact invaded by a foreign foe.[7]

A critic could march the speech through the five canons, seeing what there is to see. Let me shorten the process by suggesting that such an examination would point to several key elements in the speech: (a) FDR's reliance on his ethos; (b) FDR's use of pathos; (c) an organization that led gradually to an unprecedented assertion of power on his part; (d) his effective use of two tropes; and (e) his powerful delivery despite his largely unknown physical disability. Let's consider each one.

A great deal of optimism accompanied Roosevelt's election. He was viewed as a successful governor who, despite his patrician roots, had a great deal of sympathy for those who were suffering the most because of the Depression. He was also thought to be a highly effective orator. So, on all three ethos dimensions of competence, character, and dynamism, FDR scored highly with his audience. The task facing FDR in 1933 was immense. Contrary to myth, Herbert Hoover did not just sit around and let people suffer: He worked to both overcome the suffering and address the fundamental economic problems. So, FDR had to develop strategies more radical than anything Hoover had thought of. He needed to bank on a high ethos to initiate his plans, and he does so in the 1933 inaugural.

FDR was also facing a nation living in fear. He had to not only negate that fear but replace it with a determination most in his audience thought they lacked. He told the audience that their fears were misplaced, that they had "nothing to fear but fear itself." He also evoked both American pride and American determination by talking about how America had overcome challenge after challenge in its past. He replaced the emotion of fear with an opposite one.

FDR's inaugural is not especially long. He tells the American audience what it must do; then, he tells the American audience what he must do. Having rallied the audience, he can count on them to cheer his pledged actions. But that pledge expands as the speech progresses. He begins by talking about what he will do in concert with the Congress; he ends by threatening, because the nation is at war against the Depression and the forces that caused it, to assume war-time powers if Congress fails to act. FDR effectively carries the audience along with him so that he gains assent to an unprecedented assertion of executive power. Structured in a different manner, the inaugural address might not have gained this assent.

Many tropes characterize FDR's address. Two are especially noteworthy. Early in the speech, he compares those responsible for the Great Depression to the moneychangers Jesus Christ threw out of the temple in Matthew 20 and Mark 10. The Biblical metaphor associates corporate interest with irreligious greed. It also associates him and his incoming administration with Jesus. Throughout the speech, he uses another metaphor, comparing the effort he will lead to making war. Not only is this metaphor powerful, but it sets up the assertion of presidential power he concludes the address with.

FDR voices these tropes—and the entirety of the speech—powerfully. His voice is, perhaps, more of a radio one than the television one we have become accustomed to, but, as he moves slowly through the speech, in tones both serious and uplifting, he inspires confidence on the part of auditors. His performance is even more powerful if one is aware of how disabled he already was. Afflicted with polio at a younger age, Roosevelt could not easily support himself as he stood before the U.S. Congress. Looking at his performance very closely, one sees how he uses one hand to support himself while gesturing and turning the pages of his script with the other. His need for support will increase during the years of his presidency, but it is already apparent. He knew he needed to counter any suggestion or appearance of physical weakness, for that would lead the people to believe he was weak in other ways. In this 1933 speech, he "powers through," much as he wants the nation to "power through" in response to the Great Depression.

Application: Hillary Clinton in 1995

Hillary Clinton's stint as first lady was far from smooth. Attacked before she even entered the White House as spouse by Republican firebrand Patrick Buchanan, she faltered when assigned the major responsibility for getting a comprehensive healthcare bill through Congress. After that, she only gradually took on causes. One of them was women's rights. As an advocate, she attended an international meeting in 1995 in Beijing and addressed the assembled delegates.

The speech she gave was still being finalized as the Clinton party flew across the Pacific. The controversial matter was what she might say about women's rights in China. Strong statements might not only be perceived as ungracious, but do damage to U.S.-Chinese relations.

As with the FDR 1933 inaugural, a classical critic would—at least in his or her mind—consider all the five canons. Let me focus again on four points that an essay using classical criticism as a lens might emphasize: (a) The breadth of Clinton's arguments; (b) the restrained pathos of her comments; (c) how she moves toward the climactic equivalence she strikes between women's rights and human rights; and (d) her effective delivery exhibiting a restrained passion.

> By gathering in Beijing, we are focusing world attention on issues that matter most in our lives, the lives of women and their families—access to education, health care, jobs, and credit; the chance to enjoy basic legal and human rights and to participate fully in the political life of our countries.
>
> There are some who question the reason for this conference. Let them listen to the voices of women in their homes, neighborhoods, and workplaces. There are some who wonder whether the lives of women and girls matter to economic and political progress around the globe. Let them look at the women gathered here and at Huairou—the homemakers and nurses, the teachers and lawyers, the policy makers and women who run their own businesses. It is conferences like this that compel governments and peoples everywhere to listen, look, and face the world's most pressing problems. Wasn't it, after all, after the women's conference in Nairobi ten years ago that the world focused for the first time on the crisis of domestic violence?
>
> *****
>
> The great challenge of this conference is to give voice to women everywhere whose experiences go unnoticed, whose words go unheard.

Hillary Clinton, Selection from Address to International Women's Conference in Beijing, 1995.

Women comprise more than half the world's population, 70 percent of the world's poor, and two-thirds of those who are not taught to read or write. We are the primary caretakers for the world's children and elderly. Yet much of the work we do is not valued—not by economists, not by historians, not by popular culture, not by government leaders.

At this very moment, as we sit here, women around the world are giving birth, raising children, cooking meals, washing clothes, cleaning houses, planting crops, working on assembly lines, running companies, and running countries. Women also are dying from diseases that should have been prevented or treated. They are watching their children succumb to malnutrition caused by poverty and economic deprivation. They are being denied the right to go to school by their own fathers and brothers. They are being forced into prostitution, and they are being barred from the bank lending offices and banned from the ballot box.

Those of us who have the opportunity to be here have the responsibility to speak for those who could not. As an American, I want to speak for women in my own country—women who are raising children on the minimum wage, women who can't afford health care or child care, women whose lives are threatened by violence in their own homes. I want to speak up for mothers who are fighting for good schools, safe neighborhoods, clean air, and clean airwaves; for older women, some of them widows, who find that after raising their families, their skills and life experiences are not valued in the marketplace; for women who are working all night as nurses, hotel clerks, or fast-food chefs so that they can be at home during the day with their children; and for women everywhere who simply don't have the time to do everything they are called upon to do each and every day.

*****

But we must recognize that women will never gain full dignity until their human rights are respected and protected. Our goals for this conference—to strengthen families and societies by empowering women to take greater control over their own destinies—cannot be fully achieved unless all governments, here and around the world, accept their responsibility to protect and promote internationally recognized human rights.

*****

Tragically, women are most often the ones whose human rights are violated. Even now, in the late twentieth century, the rape of women continues to be used as an instrument of armed conflict. Women and children make up a large majority of the world's refugees, and when women are excluded from the political process, they become even more vulnerable to abuse.

I believe that now, on the eve of a new millennium, it is time to break the silence. It is time for us to say, here in Beijing and for the world to hear, that it is no longer acceptable to discuss women's rights as separate from human rights. These abuses have continued because, for too long, the history of women has been a history of silence. Even today there are those who are trying to silence our words. But the voices of this conference and of the women at Huairou must be heard loudly and clearly.

It is a violation of human rights when babies are denied food or drowned or suffocated or their spines broken simply because they are born girls.

It is a violation of human rights when women and girls are sold into the slavery of prostitution for human greed, and the kinds of reasons that are used to justify this practice should no longer be tolerated.

It is a violation of human rights when women are doused with gasoline, set on fire, and burned to death because their marriage dowries are deemed too small.

It is a violation of human rights when individual women are raped in their own communities and when thousands of women are subjected to rape as a tactic or prize of war.

It is a violation of human rights when a leading cause of death worldwide among women ages fourteen to forty-four is the violence they are subjected to in their own homes by their own relatives.

It is a violation of human rights when young girls are brutalized by the painful and degrading practice of genital mutilation.

It is a violation of human rights when women are denied the right to plan their own families—and that includes being forced to have abortions or being sterilized against their will.

If there is one message that echoes forth from this conference, let it be that human rights are women's rights and women's rights are human rights once and for all.[8]

You may have heard of Second Wave Feminism. This social movement sparked many advances for women, but its impact was largely felt in the developed world. In fact, many within the broader women's movement had critiqued the second wave negatively for ignoring issues faced by women of color, especially women of color in less-developed nations. Clinton, in her speech, surveys the problems facing women. She—we assume deliberately—deals with problems facing women worldwide. She refers to issues dominant in developed nations such as the United States: low salaries, inadequate healthcare and childcare, domestic abuse. She also refers to issues dominant in less-developed nations: rape as a tool of war, genital mutilation, forced abortions. The breadth she achieves plays a role in transforming the women's movement from one characterized by a privileged position to one that is truly global.

Many of her examples, especially those involving the less-developed nations, are shocking. In recounting them, Clinton could have stressed the shocking and evoked the strong emotions we might summarize under the term "horror." Instead, Clinton exercised a degree of restraint. She states the facts and keeps her and the audience's emotional reactions from going to an extreme. Why?

Feeling horror may be cathartic for those assembled—and those watching. Catharsis, however, tends to be a purging—as if the problem has been removed. She was trying to achieve a different emotional response—a strong condemnation (rooted in both her logos and her pathos) that might lead governments (and other groups) to address the abuses.

Many who would need to act were male. That audience might respond defensively if accused. Clinton's approach, mixing logos and restrained pathos, might be argued to be carefully orchestrated to avoid that defensive response. Whereas an extremely emotional approach might have evoked the defensiveness, she holds back a bit on emotion and makes sure there is a dose of cool reason every time that there is a dose of warm passion.

That male audience beyond the auditorium is made up of international political players. In the arena they play, human rights has been an issue—a mantra for some—since the 1970s. It was an issue one wanted to be behind, even if one's nation's record was far from perfect on the score. Human rights could not be labeled a safe issue, but is far more of part of the political mainstream than some of the women's issues, such as genital mutilation, raised by Clinton. Clinton, therefore, constructs her speech so that, at its climactic moment, it merges the women's issues she raises, which some (male) might want to dismiss, with the human rights issues that were not only more acceptable political fare, but matters given considerable *gravitas* in international political circles. Linking women's rights and human rights made it very, very difficult for Clinton's larger audience—not the women in the room—to dismiss her comments.

We think of Hillary Clinton as a seasoned political player, but, at the time she delivered this speech, she was a lawyer who had become first lady who was, arguably, far more comfortable behind the scenes working on policy matters than speaking to a large international audience. She had, of course, delivered speeches during her political career thus far, but speaking was husband Bill's gig. In Beijing, she was faced with a very difficult speech to deliver. She was going to be saying many controversial things. Some of those things might be considered an affront to her Chinese hosts. The tone had to be right. If too strident, the speech would backfire, but, if too restrained, it would be quickly forgotten. She had to get the tone just right, and she did. A rhetorical critic has a difficult time talking about tone: The critic cannot play an audio- or videotape at this point in his or her essay. One can only invite those reading to Google the speech, listen to it, and assess what the tone is and how Clinton hits the mark between strident and restrained to achieve maximum effect.

Strengths and Limitations

Some rhetorical critics claim that the classical approach is passé, even dead. Those who still practice the approach chuckle at this comment. What's dead, perhaps, is bad rhetorical criticism, where the critic proceeds mechanically, canon by canon. Good critics use the canons as a heuristic and then zero in on the elements that seem to be most likely to produce an understanding of how a text did its persuasive work. But, a limitation of the classical approach is that it might be used too mechanically.

Another limitation is that the approach focuses heavily on the text. M. H. Abrams in *The Mirror and the Lamp* (1953) offers an overview of literary criticism that is useful at this point.[9] He uses a triangle (much like the one used by rhetoricians) to suggest that critics might be focused on artist, audience, reality, or the text. The first three are the triangle's points; the text is central. Criticism that focuses on the artist he terms "expressive"; criticism that focuses on the audience he terms "affective"; criticism that focuses on reality he terms "mimetic"; and criticism that focuses on the text he terms "objective." In Abrams's terms, classical rhetorical criticism might be too objective. The text is in the center of Abrams' triangle, so objective criticism necessarily touches on the other three. However, objective criticism can just touch, and that seems to be what classical rhetorical criticism can be faulted for.

It can also be especially faulted for not addressing some dimensions of reality that have become increasingly important as the decades have passed. Matters of power and matters of gender, which mix in matters of power, can be ignored if the reality apex of Abrams' triangle is just touched.

Despite the limitations of the Classical approach, it does have the advantage of being comprehensive in its examination of the text. As a heuristic, it does lead the critic to ask about the arguments, the organization, the style, and the delivery of a speech. It even leads the critic to ask modern-day variations on the memory questions of old. But this very description of the approach's comprehensiveness reveals one more limitation: The approach does seem tied to speeches. Yes, the approach can be adapted, but, in its core form, classical criticism would seem to be tied to just one type of text.

Exemplars

Black, Edwin A. "Gettysburg and Silence." *Quarterly Journal of Speech* 80, no. 1 (1994): 21–36.

Murphy, John M. "'Our Mission and Our Moment': George W. Bush and September 11th." *Rhetoric & Public Affairs* 6, no. 4 (2003): 607–32.

Reid, Ronald F. "Edward Everett: Rhetorician of Nationalism, 1824–1855." *Quarterly Journal of Speech* 55 (October 1956): 273–82.

Zarefsky, David A. "Philosophy and Rhetoric in Lincoln's 1st Inaugural." *Philosophy and Rhetoric* 45, no. 2 (2012): 165–88.

Suggested Applications

Speech Applications

- Dr. Martin Luther King, Jr.'s famous "I Have a Dream" speech delivered in Washington, DC, in August 1963

- President Barack Obama's second inaugural address delivered in January 2013

Non-Speech Applications

- At certain hours, when many over fifty-five are watching, network television offers many advertisements by pharmaceutical companies, often for treatments for ailments that those in that fifty-five-plus group are more susceptible to. Watch a few. Pick one and analyze it using classical criticism as your lens.

- The Martin Luther King, Jr. Memorial in Washington, DC stresses certain elements of King's message while minimizing others. It also presents the King story in a certain order and, arguably, in relation to other monuments and memorials nearby. It has the style that is neither the grand one of the Lincoln Memorial nor the narrative one of the FDR Memorial. Analyze it using classical criticism and assess the many choices the designers made in remembering Dr. King.

Notes

1. A good review of rhetoric's history is Corbett, Edward P. J., and Robert J. Connors. *Classical Rhetoric for the Modern Student*. 4th ed. New York, NY: Oxford University Press, 1999.

2. Corbett, Edward P. J., and Robert J. Connors. *Classical Rhetoric for the Modern Student*. 4th ed. New York, NY: Oxford University Press, 1999. 110

3. Warnick, Barbara, and Susan L. Kline. "The New Rhetoric's Argument Schemes: A Rhetorical View of Practical Reasoning." *Argumentation & Advocacy* 29, no. 1 (1992): 1–15.

4. Warnick and Kline, 1–2.

5. Jamieson, Kathleen Hall. *Dirty Politics: Deception, Distraction, and Democracy*. New York, NY: Oxford University Press, 1992.

6. The concept of rhetorical predicates is explored in several articles by Bonnie J. Meyer, perhaps most fully in Meyer, Bonnie J., and Roy O. Freedle. "The Effects of Different Discourse Types on Recall." *American Educational Research Journal* 21, no. 1 (1984): 121–43.

7. Roosevelt, Franklin D. "First Inaugural Address." Speech. https://www.archives.gov/education/lessons/fdr-inaugural.

8. Clinton, Hillary. "Beijing Address." Speech, United Nations. http://www.un.org/esa/gopher-data/conf/ fwcw/conf/gov/950905175653.txt.

9. Abrams, M. H. *The Mirror and the Lamp: Romantic Theory and Critical Tradition.* New York, NY: Oxford University Press, 1971.

Figure credit

Fig. 2: Source: http://www.miaminewtimes.com/news/hillary-clinton-leads-donald-trump-by-51-points-among-florida-hispanics-8409537.

Nelson Mandela, South Africa's first democratically elected president.

CHAPTER 3

The Chicago School

A critical movement is termed a "school" if it has a very strong association with the faculty (and graduates) of a particular academic institution. Thus, at various points in this textbook, we will be referring to the Cambridge School or the Frankfurt School. Well, this chapter deals with an approach to criticism that emerged from the work of a group of scholars at the University of Chicago. Foremost among them was Ronald Salmon (or R. S.) Crane. These faculty were concerned with both how literary criticism was traditionally undertaken **and** the responses advanced in England by the Cambridge School and in the United States by a group primarily at Vanderbilt University, termed "the new critics," not the Vanderbilt School, although the latter term might well have fit.

Because the Chicago School's approach focused on literary, not speech texts, it is often misunderstood by those in communication. They treat it as either classical criticism or as a variation on classical criticism. This association makes some sense because both approaches are rooted in the work of Aristotle; however, it also does not make sense because the two approaches root their work in very different studies by the famous Greek.

Literary Studies in the Early Twentieth Century

In 1910, a university professor teaching Shakespeare would be primarily interested in inspiring his or her (probably his) students to appreciate "the Bard." Then, thanks to the influence of the German university, professors in the United States were compelled to do research, research that, although not scientific, had to have a scientific feel to be thought worthy. Professors would engage in such tasks as assembling the definitive text of a literary work (when there were multiple versions) and assembling the sources an author might have consulted or analogues to the story he or she (probably he) had offered. They would also write biographies of authors or histories of literary periods.

Some of this quasi-scientific work has proven quite valuable; some was amateurish biography or amateurish history, for, after all, literary critics were not trained to be either biographers or historians. But this work, good or bad, failed to do one crucial thing— look at the literary text itself. To some extent, this ignoring of the text was because the professors presumed that readers could, on their own or with a bit of nudging, "get it." This ignoring, however, bothered literary scholars as the century progressed.

In England, specifically at Cambridge University, those bothered were led by I. A. Richards. He believed that the literary text was primary and that it ought to be studied apart from either biographical or historical concerns. Also driven by the pressure to be scientific, he conducted experiments in which he would present a text, devoid of any background information, to subjects to see what meaning they would make of it. He wondered to what extent readers would interpret texts the same way, as well as whether they would focus on the same textual clues in constructing their meaning. Richards presents his work in a 1929 book entitled *Practical Criticism*.

Meanwhile, in the United States, primarily at Vanderbilt University, those bothered, led by the likes of Cleanth Brooks, Robert Penn Warren, and William Wimsatt, announced a "new criticism," also tied to approaching a text devoid of biographical or historical context. They went a step further: They argued that literature—and by literature they primarily meant poetry—was written in a special language. This language, rife with imagery, was heightened in such a way that it gave the poet and his or her (Emily Dickinson was sometimes considered) work a universal moral meaning. The founders of this group had religious rootings in Southern Protestant Christianity. This rooting very much colored their insistence on the strong moral purpose of literature.

The View from Chicago

Faculty at the University of Chicago undoubtedly also felt the pressure to do research. The highly regarded great-books approach, taken in the undergraduate curriculum there, perhaps took some of the pressure off, for the men (yes, men) had a quite rigorous, interdisciplinary teaching job to do (leading undergraduates in the discussion of books such as Euclid's *Elements*, even though their PhD might be in literature or history), but, still, they felt the pressure to do something akin to scientific research and, like the Cambridge and Vanderbilt groups, do something with the literary texts themselves.

In other words, they agreed with these two groups that biographical and historical critics had gone too far. They, however, did not reject their work as completely as did the Cambridge and Vanderbilt groups. Biographical work might be useful; historical work might be useful. The problem, as the Chicago group saw it, was that all their predecessors were going to extremes. And this feeling extended to the Cambridge and Vanderbilt groups: They were going too far in focusing exclusively on the text, with the latter also occasionally going too far in its insistence on all literature having a strong moral purpose.

The great-books curriculum tended to focus those teaching and those studying on classical texts (Euclid, Homer, Herodotus); thus, it is not altogether surprising that the Chicago School critics looked to Aristotle for a foundation for their critical enterprise, but, as scholars of literature, they turned to his *Poetics*, not his *Rhetoric*. The *Poetics* was, we think, an unfinished product. We think Aristotle planned to go through all the literary types known at his time and explain, much as a scientist would, how they worked. We know he wrote about tragedy and comedy. The latter discussion has been lost. We think the plan was to continue on and consider other literary genres, such as the ode and the elegy.

How Aristotle proceeded is explained by other works he wrote, specifically *Physics*, *Metaphysics*, and *Posterior Analytics*. As their titles might suggest, these works have little to do with literature. They seem philosophical or scientific. But, in them, Aristotle outlines a view of effects. According to Aristotle, all that might be analyzed has both a final effect (i.e., the ultimate goal) and ancillary effects (i.e., those phenomena that lead to the ultimate goal). When applied to tragedy in the *Poetics*, Aristotle points to the purging of pity and fear as the final effect and characteristics, such as noble characters and elevated language as ancillary effects that help bring about the final one. (We might well use the term "effect" just for the final one, calling the others "causes," but the Aristotelian vocabulary used "effect" for both.)

Critical Praxis

R. S. Crane and the Chicago School borrow this approach. Although genre is important to the Chicago School critics, they proceeded work by work as often as genre by genre. So, for a given literary work, they would ask what its final effect was and what techniques helped bring about that effect on the audience. Both parts of this analysis require further explanation.

All we have of the *Poetics,* Aristotle's discussion of tragedy, might suggest that he was primarily interested in an emotional effect. He, after all, speaks of pity and fear. The Chicago School critics saw the final effect more broadly as mixing ideas and emotions. A literary work, then, would make its audience think about something *and* feel something. Shakespeare's *Hamlet* then might be argued to evoke both anxiety and horror, but it would also make an audience think about the costs of hesitation, the problems that might arise if one waited and waited for evidence that might not ever become available. A first step that a Chicago School critic would take would be positing a final effect for a work.

Then, these critics would engage in a recursive process of identifying elements of the work that help bring the final effect about. But, if elements are found that do not fit the theory, then the critics go back to the posited final effect—the critics recurse—and rethink it.

To what elements might the critic turn? The answer, quite simply, is any. Crane's student Wayne C. Booth's answer is more precise:

> What marks the mode is the search for particular causes that operated in the poet's art, in some sense within his control. Whether such causes are any more literal than all the other forces that move into and out of poems, as revealed by other modes, the fact remains that Crane's search for maximum precision in pointing to what he called "reasons of art" yielded a kind of knowledge about poems that is inaccessible to other modes.
>
> Crane would, of course, strike first and last for some kind of satisfactory picture of the whole, so that all references to parts could be functional—referred not to abstract qualities desirable in all or some poems, but to the precise demands of this poem. How have (a) the object represented (character in thought and action) and (b) the verbal devices, the imagery, the ironies, the meter and the rhyme, and the technical control of (c) point of view, all been made into a coherent unity that produces (d) an effect that can be talked about because it is not just one reader's accidental response but is somehow demonstrably in the poem? *This* monism is thus unusually comprehensive for it covers author's intentions, readers' responses, the world reflected in the poem, and the potentialities of the medium. It finds all of these *in* the poem, the life of each part implicit in its relations to an achieved whole.[1]

The language of the work would, of course, be on the list: The Chicago School critics shared with the Cambridge School and the New Critics at Vanderbilt a strong interest in literary language. Structure, genre, and media would also be on the list. Others elements might be characterization and point of view if the work were fiction, or rhythm if the work were poetry. The Chicago School critics would not turn their back on biographical and historical work. If readers of Milton's *Paradise Lost* knew of the poet's blindness and that knowledge affected how they read lines, then that bit of biography would be connected to the epic poem's final effect. If readers of Swift's *Gulliver's Travels* knew how the relationship between horses and humans was played with in the logic textbooks school-boys in the 1720s would all know and, thus, how eighteenth-century readers would read voyage four, then that bit of history would be connected to the satire's final effect. (This example might seem odd to those using this textbook, but those logic textbooks were an important element in R. S. Crane's rather famous essay on Swift's satire).[2] In other words, the Chicago School critics were open to any and all elements as having a bearing on a work's final effect. They were nowhere near as narrow as the Cambridge School or the Vanderbilt group they reacted against. R. S. Crane and his colleagues were interested in language, yes, but also in elements that contribute to the effect of a text that extend far beyond language. In Booth's terms, the approach was "comprehensive."

Wayne C. Booth

Critical approaches continue only if those who initiate an effect manage to influence their students to continue. R. S. Crane taught many graduate students at the University of Chicago. Foremost among them was Wayne C. Booth, who we've already quoted. During his long career in literary studies, Booth had many achievements relevant to the advancement of criticism. Here are three of them.

First, he made it clear that the Chicago School was just as interested in genre as in individual works. The analysis of Swift's *Gulliver's Travels* glanced at previously was based on a journal article authored by R. S. Crane. To a scholarly work such as that, add Booth's landmark *Rhetoric of Fiction* (1961) and *Rhetoric of Irony* (1974). In these two studies, Booth extended Aristotle's work in the *Poetics* by systematically examining how two interesting genres worked. He explored what the genre's final effect typically was and what techniques were usually used to achieve it.

Second, Booth, by the range of texts he chose to consider, narrowed the gap between rhetorical studies in literature departments (such as English) and rhetorical studies in communication departments. Irony (i.e., saying the opposite of what you mean while giving signals as to your true meaning), after all, is a characteristics of both great works of literature and a fair amount of political discourse. Many in the 1970s saw the two—the literary and the practical—as not only separate but hostile. Booth saw that the two had much common ground. Thus, Booth's work and his name are known to students in both literary and communication fields.

Third, Booth expanded on the case Crane had made for critical pluralism. In his *The Language of Criticism and the Structure of Poetry* (1953), Crane made it clear that the understanding of poetry, broadly defined, required a critic to be open to a variety of critical approaches. He was writing in response to the New Critics of Vanderbilt who had promoted a number of intense but limited approaches that were rooted in the use of figurative language. Crane's response was that these critics were correct for some literary texts but not for others. A good critic, according to Crane, needed the ability to shift his or her focus from literary dimension to literary dimension depending on the work before him or her. In other words, reading *Paradise Lost* would require a very different set of critical probes than examining a sonnet by Emily Dickinson or an ode by John Keats. Crane and the other Chicago School critics were attacked for this approach. They were termed "poachers" or "cannibals" because they would freely steal from or ingest approaches that supposedly belonged to other groups of critics. Crane's position, which tried to put the ideal critic above the warfare among groups here and groups there, unfortunately had the effect of drawing fire from all these warring groups.

Booth wrote frequently on what Crane had termed "pluralism," most notably in *Critical Understanding: The Power and Limits of Pluralism* (1979). Those who had attacked Crane suggested that his approach was "easy," for the Chicago School critic was simply borrowing the hard work of others. Booth makes it very clear that critical pluralism is far from easy. First, the pluralist must understand the other critical approaches he or she turns to; second, the pluralist must know when to turn where.

Examples make Booth's points clearer. Some texts may come, without influence, out of the minds of creative authors; however, others may be connected to narrative patterns that have appeared often before, so much so that they are considered part of a culture's mythology. A pluralist needs to discern if the evocation of something mythological is accidental and not relevant to the work's final effect or important to readers' experience and quite relevant. Making that determination is not easy. Having determined that the mythological is relevant, then the critical pluralist has to be able to talk about mythological matters just as does the critic who chooses to just focus on that narrower element.

Let's talk about context. A writer who is part of the literary establishment (let's say male, white, highly educated, living in London or New York) may not feel, as he writes, how that establishment's norms are affecting his writing. He has internalized the norms so much so that they are there but not of special critical interest. But what if the writer is outside the establishment? Then, the norms may be either pressures acceded to or pressures rebelled against. What the writer does vis-à-vis these norms now becomes of critical interest. The critical pluralist needs to discern when the writer's response to norms becomes an important category in a work's effect on its reader. Then, should that response be important, the critical pluralist needs to understand a large body of what we term "post-colonial" critical theory to be able to speak with authority about how, for instance, a work might be trying to write "against the metropolitan center" by using its norms but parodying them.

Focusing on the final effect and the means, whatever they might be, is one hallmark of the Chicago School. Critical pluralism (i.e., thoroughly and intelligently discussing the means, whatever they might be) is another. Together, they create an intellectually rigorous criticism that requires a great deal of sophistication on the part of its practitioners. The goal of criticism in Booth's view is understanding. The work of Chicago School critics is characterized by a degree of fluidity, for they went wherever a text took them in accounting for its final effect. Before applying the approach to a text that is neither a work of literature nor a speech, let's discuss, with a little less fluidity or openness, the Chicago School's approach.

Method

The starting point is theorizing what a text's final effect on an audience is. The critic tries to escape his or her reaction and to discern how the intended audience reacted. That reaction, very importantly, is both intellectual and emotional.

Once a final effect has been theorized, then the critic considers all the resources the author (the rhetor) had available. The goal is to pin down the ones that lead to the final effect. Here, the critic uses instincts and develops habits. The critic can often guess, based on his or her reading of the text, what the crucial elements might be. It might be the language; it might be the way the text twists a genre; it might be how the text spins the historical situation. The critic, after a while, will also develop habits—always considering mythological dimensions or always considering point of view. These guesses and habits should not be resisted, but the critic must go beyond them and consider other aspects of the text.

The goal is to show how each aspect helps bring about the final effect. The critic may well be able to show the connection, but there are two other possibilities. Should the critic judge that a particular aspect has no discernible effect, then it is an aspect of art (be it literary or oratorical or something else) that is not of importance in the case under consideration. But, should the critic judge that a particular aspect has an effect other than the theorized final effect, then the critic must recurse (i.e., go back to the beginning and revise the theorized final effect).

The goal is to end up with a final effect and a sizeable number of artistic choices that can be argued to produce that final effect. I like to conceive of the finished criticism visually as a circle. At the center is the final effect; around the circumference are various artistic choices, with arrows pointing to the center. If the arrows can be boldly drawn, then the criticism has considerable explanatory power. The artistic choices arrayed around the circle will vary from text to text. Even when considering a poem (what Crane did) or a speech, the choices focused on will vary. But, the most striking variance occurs when the critic moves from type of text to type of text. In other words, one will not look for the same techniques when analyzing a speech and analyzing an advertisement. The example that follows illustrates how the chosen techniques will differ from type of text to type of text by considering a feature film.

Application: The Film *Invictus*

Back when Crane wrote, poetry was the number one genre, joined by drama that was written in poetry, such as many Shakespearean plays. By the time Booth wrote, prose fiction had become ascendant. Today, there are many types of writing and speaking and designing to which a Chicago School critic might attend. To demonstrate both the reach of the critical approach and some of the difficulties applying it, we will consider the 2009 film *Invictus*.

Directed by Clint Eastwood, the film tells the story of the early years of Nelson Mandela's presidency in South Africa. The film, in both its initial shots and in scattered early comments, attempts to offer the viewer enough background to grasp the film's premise. The audience needs to know what apartheid was, that Mandela was, for twenty-five-plus years, an imprisoned anti-apartheid activist, that in the early 1990s the different political groups in the nation decided to avoid bloody civil war by staging a truly democratic election that all knew would put the African National Congress (ANC) and Mandela in the presidency, and that the nation was—as Mandela began the presidency—still badly divided along racial lines. To understand how the film achieves its final effect, one would not have to know minute political particulars but would have to know how badly divided South Africa was in 1994. Today, most think of Mandela in heroic terms, but, in 1994, some in South Africa saw him as a noble, long-suffering crusader while others saw him as a dangerous (probably Communist) revolutionary intent on confiscating white-owned property and destroying the nation the white colonists had, over centuries, built.

The film leaves its audience cheering. The audience feels joy; the audience also thinks that a spirit of perseverance and forgiveness and unity is necessary to bring about the "miracle" that Mandela performs in the film. This posited final effect—one should note—is both emotional and intellectual. One feels the movie: It brings many to tears, but one can nonetheless point to the governing characteristics Mandela exhibits in the course of his early years as president.

The film does deal with governing, but it much more explicitly deals with sport. The South African rugby team, the Springboks, was a revered institution in apartheid South Africa. The team was also deeply resented by the majority of Africans who were the victims of injustice under apartheid. In the film, Mandela decides to use Springbok rugby to unite the nation.

About twenty minutes into the film, Mandela addresses a sports council meeting that has just acted against Springbok rugby:

> **MANDELA:** Brothers, sisters, comrades, I am here because I feel strongly that you made a decision today without sufficient information or foresight. I am aware of your earlier vote. I am aware that it was unanimous. Nonetheless, I propose that we restore the Springboks. Restore their name, their emblem, and their colors, immediately. Let me tell you why.
>
> On Robben Island, in Pollsmoor Prison, my jailers were all Afrikaners. For twenty-seven years, I studied them. I learned their language, I read their history, I read their poetry. I had to know my enemy, in order to prevail against him.
>
> And we prevailed, did we not? All of us here … we prevailed.
>
> Our enemy is no longer the Afrikaners. They are our fellow South Africans, our partners in democracy.
>
> And they treasure Springbok rugby. If we take that away, we lose them. We prove that we are what they feared we would be. We have to be better than that. We have to surprise them with compassion, with restraint, and generosity.
>
> Yes, I know. All the things they denied us.
>
> But this is not the time to enjoy a moment's pretty revenge. This is the time to build our nation using every single brick available to us—even if that brick comes clothed in green and gold.
>
> You elected me. You elected me to be your leader. Let me lead you now.
>
> Who is with me on this?
>
> Who is with me?

At the end of the film:

> **MANDELA:** Francois, I want to thank you most sincerely for what you have done for your country.
>
> **FRANCOIS:** Mr. President, I want to thank you for what you have done.[3]

Mandela decides to use sport—specifically the South African rugby team, the Springboks—to effect change. So, he decides to recruit the team's captain, Francois Pienaar, to help him. Initially, the captain focuses on Mandela's desire that the team win the World Cup, but, gradually, he begins advocating Mandela's core principles, such as perseverance and unity, as well as pushing the team to perform well beyond expectations in the tournament, which was being hosted by South Africa.

The actions Mandela takes (plot elements) promote the film's final effect; so do Pienaar's actions and words. So, the film's main plot plays a major role in its rhetoric. But films use far more than plot to achieve their effects.

There are a number of subplots in the film. They are largely developed through scenes that contrast with each other as the film progresses. Early, Mandela expands his security detail by adding to his ANC bodyguards (all black) several members of the apartheid-era security forces (all white). Initial scenes depict the tension between the two contingents; gradually, we see them working together, even playing rugby (a white sport) together.

Clint Eastwood, Selection from *Invictus*. Copyright © 2009 by Warner Bros. Entertainment Inc.

When the South African team wins, we almost see the leaders of the two contingents hug. Early we see the tension between the police and black youth, long the victims of aggressive police behavior. At the end, we see a black boy and white police officers cheering together for the Springboks while enjoying refreshments. Early we see how hated the Springboks are among the nation's black majority. At the end, we see groups representing all racial groups cheering on the winning team. Early, we hear Mandela booed at a rugby game while the majority attending wave the old South African flag and reject the nation's new anthem. At the end, Mandela is cheered, the new flag is prominent, and the new anthem is sung enthusiastically.

Cinematography is used to enhance these contrasts. Early scenes show fences and other barriers separating racial groups; they reinforce early scenes that depict the two very different worlds that existed in the nation, the wealthy one occupied by whites and the poor ones occupied by blacks. Gradually, fences and other barriers vanish. The suggestion that there are different worlds persists, but many scenes show white and black side by side, at least suggesting that the different worlds are beginning to merge.

Cinematography and editing are used to make sure the audience sees and feels the changes that have miraculously occurred in South Africa. Later scenes are longer, feature quickly-paced editing suggestive of positive action, and use slow motion during the rugby games' most dramatic moments. Perhaps these scenes are overdone and, thus, overly melodramatic, but they do stress both the joy-producing victory—on the rugby field and off—and the qualities that led there.

Not surprisingly, music reinforces both the drama and the joy. Film critics distinguish between ambient and non-ambient music, non-ambient being background music the characters cannot hear and ambient being music that is part of the scene. Initially, there is little of either in the film. As the film progresses, ambient music appears—usually at scenes of celebration. Then, we get a mix of non-ambient music: solemn non-ambient music when the Springboks visit Robben Island, where Mandela had been held as a prisoner; tense and triumphant non-ambient music during the rugby games. Near the film's end, at the stadium, we get music that is ambient (i.e., it is being performed on stage) but seems grander and non-ambient. Nothing is especially unusual in the film's orchestration, although the way it moves from tense and quiet to joyous and boisterous is worth noting, for the transition is clearly a means to enhance the final effect. Music also sometimes operates without the audience being fully aware of its effect, so it is well worth calling attention to how the music here is what the Chicago School would point to as an ancillary effect that helps to bring about the film's final effect.

Thus far, we've considered elements tied to *Invictus* being a film as ways the text brings about its final effect—feeling the joy and recognizing the qualities of governing necessary to effect change and joy. To talk about these film elements (and others that might be raised) requires that the critic knows how a film works. One perhaps does not need to know about the differences among film stocks and camera lenses, but one does need to know certain fundamentals about camera angles, camera shots, continuity and non-continuity editing, and ambient and non-ambient music to offer a critical analysis of a film. But not all the relevant matters a Chicago School critic might bring to a full discussion of *Invictus* are tied to its being a film.

Consider the fidelity of the narrative: Are the events and characters believable, and are the values inherent in the narrative faithful to the values of those viewing? This particular narrative might have mythological resonance. It might be connected to the many stories of victorious underdogs found in the literature—and the mythology—of western nations. This particular narrative might be connected to other positive civil rights stories found in the literature, film, and history of the United States. If so, the narrative may be tied to a socially constructed fantasy theme (a term and approach discussed in another chapter) shared by political progressives in this nation. (And, although the film is about South Africa, it is an American film, so the U.S. audience's response may be the one to focus on.)

That the previous paragraph has to refer to chapters in this textbook that you may not have read yet illustrates how the Chicago School's pluralistic approach can embrace ideas one might associate more with other critical approaches. Crane and Booth both argued that it was silly to think that a group of scholars or critics "own" an approach. In their view, these many groups have succeeded in illuminating different questions a critic might ask about how a text achieves its final effect. They feel free to ask these questions, for, in their view, the critic's goal is understanding how a text works, and a wide variety of questions might be necessary to grasp how the rhetoric works. Importantly, the specific questions will not be the same from work to work. The good critic, as Crane and Booth would define him or her, ranges from question to question—aspect to aspect—based on what seems to be contributing to the given work's final effect.

Strengths and Limitations

The discussion of *Invictus* should point to the Chicago School's major strength: It covers many, many aspects of a text. It is not limited to language or limited to narrative. The critic goes wherever he or she thinks appropriate to understand why the text works as it does.

The approach's two most striking weaknesses are inherent in its very approach. One is that the critic, to go wherever is necessary to illuminate how a text works, inevitably will step outside of his or her area of expertise. One can try to grasp the many different critical approaches that exist, but being a true critical pluralist is a daunting task. Try as the Chicago School critic might, he or she runs the risk of amateurism when a work requires that one very, very comfortable using certain approaches go far afield to another approach where the critic has familiarity but not expertise. What the Chicago School aspires to, as Booth describes it in *Critical Understanding: The Power and Limits of Pluralism*, is noble, but may be difficult, if not impossible.

Another limitation is found in the Chicago School's emphasis on effect on an audience. There is a risk in this approach that audience will be defined in a limiting way—that the diversity of the audience will be lost as the critic creates, for critical purposes, the idealized audience; that the broader social impact of a text will be lost as the critic thinks of audience in the more limited way as those who are directly addressed by a text. The solution, of course, is to broaden the audience. But, there is a problem inherent in doing so—that some contributing effects might be relevant to some audiences but not to others. For example, mythological resonance might be something a highly educated audience would experience but not others. For example, the social construction behind a shared fantasy theme might involve some but not all the members of the broader audience. So, as the audience broadens, the analysis can get messier and messier. There may be a temptation to streamline the analysis by unwittingly using what rhetorical theorists Chaim Perelman and Lucie Olbrechts-Tyteca referred to in *The New Rhetoric* (1958) as the universal audience. They talk about how the rhetor tries to construct this audience because this audience is without the prejudices that real audiences might have. The Chicago School critic would create this audience, not to promote a higher level of decision making on the part of the public, but simply as a critical convenience. Care must be taken to avoid pushing aside the complexities rooted in the diversity of the audience in order to create a very systematic analysis that consists of a single final effect and a finite number of contributing traits.

The Chicago School does, however, have a major strength in both its attention to numerous traits or ancillary effects in its analyses. More is better, not just because it is more, but because texts are complex and the more ancillary effects one explores, the more likely one is to reveal the rhetorical complexity. Related is the strength the Chicago School has because of its critical pluralism. The good pluralist is willing to go wherever the text takes him or her. The only limitation is that the place must seem to have a connection to the effect that the text under consideration is posited to have on its audience. One, then, does not go to a critical approach because it is in vogue; rather, one goes to an approach because it illuminates how a text brings about its emotional, intellectual effect.

A last strength is that the Chicago School is attentive to both the emotional and intellectual effects a text might have. French philosopher Rene Descartes influenced western thought (and mathematics) in many positive ways, but one negative way was splitting the emotional and intellectual aspects of our being apart and privileging the intellectual. A result, for example, is that some popular logic textbooks treat appealing to emotions as fallacious as opposed to what Aristotle recognized when he lists pathos along with logos and ethos as persuasive resources. In the latter pages of *Rhetoric*, many, many pages discuss the emotional appeals a rhetor might make. Was Aristotle counseling fallacious reasoning? No, he was recognizing that humans are rational *and* emotional and that persuasion is affected by both rational and emotional means. The Chicago School, in defining final effect as it does, is in line with this bit of Aristotelian wisdom and, arguably, more in touch with how texts work. Consider *Invictus* one last time. It is a moving film. Yes, it makes a rational statement one might extract, but it would not be the moving film it is without the strong emotional appeals it makes.

The Chicago School is considered by many in communication studies as offering an approach to literary criticism, not rhetorical criticism. That its major proponents were literary scholars makes this association logical. But, the association is unfortunate, for the Chicago School's approach can be used to illuminate much of what goes on in the kinds of texts the rhetorical critic typically studies. That the Chicago School approach has been applied more often to novels than to speeches does not mean that this critical praxis cannot offer valuable, thoroughgoing analyses of speeches, films, advertising, or memory sites.

Exemplars

Antczak, Frederick J. "Learning to Read Martin Luther King's 'Pilgrimage to Non-Violence': Wayne Booth, Character, and the Ethical Criticism of Public Address." In *Rhetorical Pluralism: The Legacies of Wayne C. Booth*, 153–63. Columbus, OH: Ohio State University Press, 1995.

Daughton, Suzanne M. "Metaphorical Transcendence: Images of the Holy War in Franklin Roosevelt's First Inaugural." *Quarterly Journal of Speech* 79, no. 1 (November 1993): 427–46.

Rood, Craig. "'Understanding' Again: Listening with Kenneth Burke and Wayne Booth." *Rhetoric Society Quarterly* 44, no. 5 (2014): 449–69.

Weiler, Michael. "Arguing in Fiction." In *Argumentation Theory and the Rhetoric of Assent*, 103–16. Tuscaloosa, AL: University of Alabama Press, 1990.

Suggested Applications

Speech Applications

- At the 1992 Republican and Democratic National Conventions, featured speakers addressed in rather moving ways the AIDS crisis affecting America. What were the speeches' effects, and how did the two speakers bring about these effects?

- In 1995, after the bombing of the Oklahoma City Federal Building, President Bill Clinton gave a very effective eulogy. It did what a eulogy should do, but it also helped bolster the faltering Clinton presidency. What was the final effect of Clinton's speech and how did he achieve it?

Non-Speech Applications

- The Astronauts Memorial in Cape Canaveral is, according to Carole Blair and Neil Michel, a well-designed memory site that fails.[4] What effect(s) does it evoke? Why?

- Katie Perry's song "Roar" was used throughout the 2016 Hillary Clinton campaign. What was its effect on the audience and why?

Notes

1. Booth, Wayne C. *Critical Understanding: The Powers and Limits of Pluralism.* Chicago, IL: University of Chicago Press, 1982. 58–60.

2. Crane, Ronald S. "The Houyhnhnms, the Yahoos, and the History of Ideas." In *Reason and Imagination: Studies in the History of Ideas, 1600–1800,* 231–53. New York, NY: Columbia University Press, 1962.

3. *Invictus.* Directed by Clint Eastwood. Performed by Morgan Freeman and Matt Damon. United States: Warner Bros. Pictures, 2009. Film. http//www.imsdb.com/scripts/Invictus.html.

4. Blair, Carole, and Neil Michel. "Commemorating in the Theme Park Zone: Reading the Astronauts' Memorial." In *At the Intersection: Cultural Studies and Rhetorical Studies,* 29–93. New York, NY: Guilford Press, 1998.

Figure Credit

Fig. 3: Copyright © South Africa The Good News (CC by 2.0) at https://commons.wikimedia.org/wiki/File:Nelson_Mandela-2008_(edit).jpg.

Barry Goldwater, the Republican's very conservative 1964 presidential candidate, with his strong supporter Ronald Reagan.

CHAPTER 4

Kenneth Burke and Terministic Screens

Kenneth Burke is, without a doubt, the most influential American rhetorical theorist of the twentieth century. To understand his work, one needs to understand how he came to do the work he did.

Burke was highly educated, but not in the traditional manner. Much of what he learned, he learned in the classroom, but much of what he learned, he learned by reading on his own, not paying all that much attention to the categories that academic institutions have set up and now defend as if they were fortresses. It is therefore not surprising that Burke's work is read in a number of these academic disciplines, and it is also not surprising that these different disciplines tend to read different books by Burke and point to different Burkean ideas as *the* central Burkean ideas. Later in this textbook, I will note that there are "many Bakhtins," depending on what book by the Russian theorist one chooses to emphasize. The same is true for Burke: There are many Kenneth Burkes.

This textbook tries to focus on the Burke most relevant to the practice of rhetorical criticism. Even with that narrower focus, there are many ideas to choose from. Based on the utility of the concepts—as well as the difference between them, this textbook deals with terministic screens in this chapter and dramatism in the next. But these are most certainly not the only contributions Burke has made to rhetorical criticism. (Your instructor, if he or she is a Burkean, may want to add others.)

Another characteristic of Burke's work that arises from his reading in a wide variety of fields is that he can be difficult to read because he presumes that his audience knows philosophy, theology, a variety of literatures, and rhetoric as he does. Burke's many works—books and collected essays—are well worth reading, but the student should not expect reading Burke to be easy-going. His catholicity of reading and knowledge (i.e., its universal reach) poses problems for even a person educated well but more narrowly in just one of the many academic fields that Burke moves around in with ease. For example, a highly trained rhetorician may not immediately get all of Burke's literary references.

So, this discussion will try to get to the core of Burke's work. It may oversimplify, but, if you or your instructor feels that is the case, the solution is to read Burke with all the difficulties inherent in doing so.

Division, Guilt, Consubstantiality

The core Burke sounds like both social commentator and theologian. He finds the human race to be horribly divided, and he finds the human race to be horribly guilty because of this division and, perhaps, other human foibles. This is not an optimistic view Burke offers. It is perhaps colored by the environment he lived in—a Western world seeing the rise in fascism and the reality of global war featuring weapons and casualties never before seen. It might be easy to link Burke to this context and then dismiss the relevance today of his observations. However, although the historical causes may now be different, we are still horribly divided, both internationally and within the nation. So, Burke is not irrelevant.

The fortunate part of Burke's core observation is that he notes both division and guilt—fortunate because the guilt might evoke positive action. Burke, in fact, assumes that we do not want to be divided. Furthermore, he thinks of rhetoric as the means of persuasion that will get us from division—and its related guilt—to what he terms **identification** or **consubstantiality**. One can pick the term one wants, but the latter seems a tad richer, for it suggests a degree of unity more profound than identification. Identification means we can see ourselves in others, that there is a mirroring. Consubstantiality means we share substance, that there is some kind of merging at the bodily level. (I prefer the metaphor under-girding consubstantiality, so I will use that term.)

Routes to Consubstantiality

So, how does Burke posit that we get from division and guilt to consubstantiality? He suggests several. Before discussing how he suggests we get there through the language choices we make, I want to note two other responses to division and guilt that Burke speaks about.

The first is the passage Burke traces through mortification to purification and redemption. There exists a large body of work in the communication discipline on how to deal with things that have gone wrong or things one has done wrong. Those who study political communication have noted how the various strategies have been used well or not so well by political figures. Richard Nixon explained a "secret fund" in 1952 and tried to explain Watergate in the 1970s; Edward Kennedy explained a wrong turn he made on a dark road on a dark island in 1969; Ronald Reagan explained the illegal supplying of arms to anti-communists fighters in Nicaragua in 1985–87; and Bill Clinton tried to explain his sexual relationship with a White House intern in 1998. Those who study organizational communication have noted how the strategies have been used by a large number of companies, some guilty and some not, to explain what happened and restore the corporate image. Those who study sports communication have done the same, looking at a range of sports stars who have been touched by something scandalous and have needed to explain.[1]

B. L. Ware and Wil A. Linkugel provided these critics with a list of strategies to look for; William Benoit has offered a revised one that many have chosen to use.[2] These lists assume that sometimes you are guilty and need to either confess or escape blame, and sometimes you are not guilty and need to explain matters so that all understand the situation. Burke is interested in the former. Although the terms of analysis these critics use could be cross-applied to Burke-inspired work, they rarely are, for Burke is not interested in how the rhetor chooses a strategy. He is also less interested in the specific organizational or political problems than these communication scholars are. Rather, Burke is interested in how the guilty, presumed to be humankind, enacts the specific strategy (or set of strategies) termed mortification. The goal of that mortification is purification. Once purified, one, now redeemed, can then rejoin the body he or she has divided himself or herself from through whatever the transgression was. Burke sees this as a comic enlightening process, not because it is funny, but because it has a positive outcome.

But not all who are divided, whether through a transgression they can specify or through circumstances they cannot precisely define, want to take the mortification and purification and redemption route. Burke sees another, often negative, route often exemplified in literature. These others might want to shift the blame to others (another strategy on the lists). This is scapegoating, examples of which are found in classical literature such as famed Greek-Roman tragedies. It is also found in the politics that surrounded Burke. For example, in Nazi Germany, Adolph Hitler was using this strategy to get Germans who were suffering economically after World War I to blame Jews, gypsies, homosexuals, and others for their plight. They need not feel guilty, for the fault for all the ills of Germany could be placed on these groups. Hitler's rhetoric, as described by

Burke in his famous essay "The Rhetoric of Hitler's 'Battle,'" created consubstantiality, but his uniting of bodies was at the expense of other bodies.[3]

The rhetorical strategy of scapegoating has not gone in the aftermath of World War II. Consider the 2016 American presidential election. How did Donald Trump's early rhetoric create consubstantiality among his supporters? By scapegoating immigrants, depicting them negatively and then urging their exclusion from America. How did Bernie Sander's rhetoric in the same election create consubstantiality among supporters? By scapegoating the richest one percent or scapegoating Wall Street, depicting them negatively and then urging legislation to combat their alleged greed.

Mortification and purification and scapegoating are two routes to consubstantiality that Burke speaks of. They are frequently found in both the literature he refers to and in reality. Also common is a route that is less dramatic than saying *mea culpa* or pointing the finger at some evil other. It is, however, a rhetorically powerful route used by many. Ironically, it is often used to promote division at the same time it overcomes division.

Terministic Screens

Burke is using analogies here:

> When I speak of "terministic screens," I have particularly in mind some photographs I once saw. They were *different* photographs of the *same* objects, the difference being that they were made with different color filters. Here something so "factual" as photographs revealed notable distinctions in texture, and even in form, depending upon which color filter was used for the documentary description of the event being recorded.
>
> Similarly, a man has a dream. He reports his dream to a Freudian analyst, or a Jungian, or an Adlerian, or to a practitioner of some other school. In each case, we might say, the "same" dream will be subjected to a different color filter, with corresponding differences in the nature of the event as perceived, recorded, and interpreted.[4]

Let me follow Burke's use of analogies with another that deals a bit more with how terministic screens function in persuasion, as opposed to the creation of one's view of the world. A screen, like the one in a window or a door, lets air in but keeps larger entities like pieces of dirt and bugs out. The screen connects the outside and the inside, but not completely. If we imagine the rhetor on the outside and the audience with whom he or she wants to be consubstantial on the inside, what should the rhetor do to get through the screen and what should the rhetor not do?

The dirt and bugs in this analogy are the terms—words and phrases—that the audience is not receptive to. The air that gets through the screen are the terms that the audience is receptive to, the ones the audience has constructed its perspective on the world using.

Undergirding this analogy are fundamental assumptions about language: that it is not neutral and that different prospective audiences are not receptive to the same language choices. After Burke, linguists Lakoff and Johnson have studied at length how political conservatives and political liberals tend to use different vocabularies. Burke senses this, suggesting to rhetors who wanted to be consubstantial with specific audiences that they use the terms that the desired audience use and revere. Rhetors would then pass through the terministic screens that divide rhetor from audience and can block consubstantiality.

Lakoff and Johnson have offered their insights in both scholarly (*Moral Politics* [1996, 2001]) and popular (*Don't Think of an Elephant* [2004]) works. (Lakoff with Elsabeth Wehling, has added *The Little Blue Book* [2012]). Much of what they say seems commonsensical—conservatives preferring the term "liberty" to the term "justice," preferring government as stern father saying no more often than government as benevolent mother offering bounty and saying yes. What Burke's analysis points to, however, is broader than just conservatives and liberals. Any audience, Burke says, will have its preferred terms. So, consider the following questions: What are the preferred terms of business executives? Of teachers? Of members of Greek-letter fraternal or sororal organizations? Of members of a particular church? Burke's point is that, if you wish to become consubstantial with an audience, you need to use its terms in order to get through the screen that has been erected to keep the dirt and bugs (the terms not in favor) out.

Other Approaches to Language

What Burke says about language is connected to what other rhetorical theorists have said about language. Richard Weaver has noted how, in our language, there are what we might term "god terms" and "devil terms."[5] Weaver and others have noted that these terms are, of course, culture specific. What might be a devil term in our culture—"communism" in years past; "terrorism" now—may be neutral or even positive in another. The rather obvious rhetorical advice these theorists offer is to use god terms and devil terms strategically. They discuss the terms in conjunction with persuasion but not in conjunction with the Burkean notion of creating consubstantiality and persuading.

Another approach was developed by Michael Calvin McGee. He noted that certain terms in our culture are so rich with meaning that they function as what he termed ideographs.[6] With his seminal article in 1980, he began a minor mode of criticism that focuses on the use of **ideographs**—conventionally enclosed in square brackets—in a text. The bracketing is designed to suggest that these terms are rife with meaning, that, if and when unpacked, evoke a range of attitudes as well as historical people and events. They are, then, different from the terms Burke points to. Burke is talking about the words and phrases a prospective audience prefers; McGee is talking about culturally loaded constructs that are less keys to gain access and more bomb-like entities that can explode within a text with a power that far exceeds a single term. In Burke's thinking, "freedom" is a term that gets through to an audience with a particular political inclination. It facilitates consubstantiality. In McGee's, [freedom] is a construct that, when unpacked, evokes texts, episodes, people important within a culture. This difference notwithstanding, both Burke and McGee are pointing to the power word choice can have in a text. McGee is more interested in how ideographs present, in a compressed form, dominant ideologies; Burke is more interested in how the very language we choose to use represents "a *reflection* of reality" that is both "a *selection* of reality" and "a *deflection* of reality" and, thus, how we choose to see the world and not see the world.[7] Both, however, point to the power language has in persuasion.

Method

A critic using Burke's concept of terministic screens must be a close reader of a text. If the text is a speech or manifesto, take "reader" quite literally, but the same attentiveness is necessary if one is to see what, by way of written and visual symbols, might be found in an advertisement or a television program. The close reading looks for recurring words and phrases; then, it assembles them in clusters. Thus, this approach is sometimes termed "cluster criticism."

One should not just assemble four clusters and say "I'm done." A next step is discerning how the clusters might be connected. One might be able to assemble them into something akin to a narrative. If not a narrative, then perhaps a logical structure with causes, effects, and the like. Assembling this structure gets one closer to how those who have chosen certain language have thereby chosen to structure their world view.

Another step is also important, if one is to push this approach to its logical endpoint, and that is to see how another text and audience connect or do not connect. The basic question here is does the second text in question use the words and phrases that get through the screen that accepts certain terms but rejects others. If the text successfully passes through, then identification occurs between the rhetor and his or her text and the audience. Some texts can be judged to be tremendous successes; others, failures. The case that follows, although focused on a speech from more than fifty years ago, is one that quite dramatically shows how a text can powerfully connect with a target audience through its use of words and phrases. Presidential candidate Barry Goldwater—or his speechwriters—seem to know, in penning their text, what terministic screen the intended audience has created (one that might be discerned by analyzing the text or texts that the audience has developed).

Application: Barry Goldwater in 1964

Very aware of the terms that would get through to some Republicans in 1964 was their presidential nominee, Arizona Senator Barry Goldwater. The key word in that sentence was "some." To understand it and how Goldwater's nomination acceptance speech worked, one needs some background on Republican politics way back then.

There had long been a split in the Republican Party between what might be termed conservative and progressive wings. In 1964, the split was wide. The conservative wing's candidate was Barry Goldwater, and, going into the San Francisco convention, he was the presumed nominee. The progressive wing had tried to stop him. First, there was New York Governor Nelson Rockefeller. He failed to garner sufficient support. His divorce and remarriage bothered voters, as did his more moderate East Coast Republicanism. Second, there was a last-minute candidate, Pennsylvania Governor William Scranton. He also failed to derail the Goldwater train. Their efforts won them no love from the majority Goldwater delegates assembled at the convention—so much so that Rockefeller, given his opportunity to address the gathering on a platform matter, was booed off the stage. On Goldwater's night to speak, the Rockefeller-Scranton delegates took their revenge: They walked out rather than listen to Goldwater's words.

Goldwater was, of course, addressing a television audience, but he seemed much more attentive to the one directly in front of him. It is clear from his script that he planned to address his fellow conservatives there. It was, then, just as well the progressives had walked out: They would not have responded as positively to Goldwater's terms as the conservative audience did.

> I accept your nomination with a deep sense of humility. I accept, too, the responsibility that goes with it, and I seek your continued help and your continued guidance. My fellow Republicans, our cause is too great for any man to feel worthy of it. Our task would to be too great for any man did he not have with him the hearts and the hands of this great Republican Party. And I promise you tonight that every fiber of my being is consecrated to our cause—that nothing shall be lacking from the struggle that can be brought to it by enthusiasm, by devotion, and plain hard work. In this world no person, no party can guarantee anything, but what we can do and what we shall do is to deserve victory, and victory will be ours.
>
> This good lord raised this mighty republic to be a home for the brave and to flourish as the land of the free—not to stagnate in the swampland of collectivism, not to cringe before the bullying of communism. Now, my fellow Americans, the tide has been running against freedom. Our people have followed false prophets. We must, and we shall, return to proven ways—not because they are old, but because they are true. We must, and we shall, set the tides running again in the cause of freedom. And this party, with its every action, every word, every breath, and every heartbeat, has but a single resolve, and that is freedom—freedom made orderly for the nation by its constitutional government, freedom under a government limited by the laws of nature and of nature's God, freedom balanced so that order lacking liberty will not

Barry Goldwater, Selection from Address to 1964 Republican National Convention, 1964.

become the slavery of the prison cell, balanced so that liberty lacking order will not become the license of the mob and of the jungle.

Now, we Americans understand freedom. We have earned it, we have lived for it, and we have died for it. This nation and its people are freedom's model in a searching world. We can be freedom's missionaries in a doubting world. But, ladies and gentlemen, first we must renew freedom's mission in our own hearts and in our own homes.

During four futile years, the administration which we shall replace has, has distorted and lost that vision. It has talked and talked and talked and talked the words of freedom, but it has failed and failed and failed in the works of freedom. Now failures cement the wall of shame in Berlin. Failures blot the sands of shame at the Bay of Pigs. Failures mark the slow death of freedom in Laos. Failures infest the jungles of Vietnam. And failures haunt the houses of our once-great alliances and undermine the greatest bulwark ever erected by free nations—the NATO community. Failures proclaim lost leadership, obscure purpose, weakening will, and risk of inciting our sworn enemies to new aggressions and to new excesses.

*****

It was Republican leadership under Dwight Eisenhower that kept the peace and passed along to this administration the mightiest arsenal for defense the world has ever known. And I needn't remind you that it was the strength and the believable will of the Eisenhower years that kept the peace by using our strength, by using it in the Formosa Straits and in Lebanon and by showing it courageously at all times. It was during those Republican years that the thrust of Communist imperialism was blunted. It was during those years of Republican leadership that this world moved closer not to war, but closer to peace, than at any other time in the last three decades.

And I needn't remind you, but I will, that it's been during Democratic years that our strength to deter war has stood still and even gone into a planned decline. It has been during Democratic years that we have weakly stumbled into conflict, timidly refusing to draw our own lines against aggression, deceitfully refusing to tell even our own people of our full participation, and tragically letting our finest men die on battlefields unmarked by purpose, unmarked by pride or the prospect of victory. Yesterday it was Korea. Tonight it is Vietnam. Make no bones of this. Don't try to sweep this under the rug. We are at war in Vietnam. And yet the President, who is the commander and chief of our forces, refuses to say—refuses to say, mind you—whether or not the objective over there is victory. And his Secretary of Defense continues to mislead and misinform the American people, and enough of it's gone by.

And I needn't remind you, but I will, it has been during Democratic years that a billion persons were cast into Communist captivity and their fate cynically sealed. Today, today in our beloved country we have an administration which seems eager to deal with communism in every coin known—from gold to wheat, from consulates to confidences, and even human freedom itself.

Now, the Republican cause demands that we brand communism as the principal disturber of peace in the world today. Indeed, we should brand it as the only significant disturber of peace. And we must make clear that until its goals of conquest are absolutely renounced and its relations with all nations tempered, communism and the governments it now controls are enemies of every man on earth who is or wants to be free.

Now, we here in America can keep the peace only if we remain vigilant and only if we remain strong. Only if we keep our eyes open and keep our guard up can we prevent war. And I want to make this abundantly clear: I don't intend to let peace or freedom be torn from our grasp because of lack of strength or lack of will—and that I promise you, Americans.

I believe that we must look beyond the defense of freedom today to its extension tomorrow. I believe that the communism which boasts it will bury us will instead give way to the forces of freedom. And I can see in the distant and yet recognizable future the outlines of a world worthy of our dedication, our every risk, our every effort, our every sacrifice along the way. Yes, a world that will redeem the suffering of those who will be liberated from tyranny. I can see, and I suggest that all thoughtful men must contemplate, the flowering of an Atlantic civilization, the whole of Europe reunified and freed, trading openly across the world.

Now, this is a goal far, far more meaningful than a moon shot. It's a, it's a truly inspiring goal for all free men to set for themselves during the latter half of the twentieth century. I can see, and all free men must thrill to, the events of this Atlantic civilization joined by its great ocean highway to the United States. What a destiny, what a destiny can be ours to stand as a great central pillar linking Europe, the Americas, and the venerable and vital peoples and cultures of the Pacific. I can see a day when all the Americas, North and South, will be linked in a mighty system, a system in which the errors and misunderstandings of the past will be submerged one by one in a rising tide of prosperity and interdependence.

*****

Now, I know that freedom is not the fruit of every soil. I know that our own freedom was achieved through centuries, by unremitting efforts of brave and wise men. And I know that the road to freedom is a long and a challenging road; and I know also that some men may walk away from it, that some men resist challenge, accepting the false security of governmental paternalism. And I, and I pledge that the America I envision in the years ahead will extend its hand in health, in teaching, and in cultivation so that all new nations will be at least encouraged, encouraged to go our way, so that they will not wander down the dark alleys of tyranny or the dead-end streets of collectivism. My fellow Republicans, we do no man a service by hiding freedom's light under a bushel of mistaken humility.

*****

We Republicans see in our constitutional form of government the great framework which assures the orderly but dynamic fulfillment of the whole man, and we see the whole man as the great reason for instituting orderly government in the first place. We see, we see in private property and an economy based upon and fostering private property, the one way to make government a durable ally of the whole man, rather than his determined enemy. We see in the sanctity of private property the only durable foundation for constitutional government in a free society.

And, and beyond that we see and cherish diversity of ways, diversity of thoughts, of motives, and accomplishments. We don't seek to live anyone's life for him. We only seek, only seek to secure his rights, guarantee him opportunity, guarantee him opportunity to strive, with government performing only those needed and constitutionally sanctioned tasks which cannot otherwise be performed.

We Republicans seek a government that attends to its inherent responsibilities of maintaining a stable monetary and fiscal climate, encouraging a free and a competitive economy, and enforcing law and order. Thus do we seek inventiveness, diversity, and creative difference within a stable order. For we Republicans define government's role where needed at many, many levels, preferably, though, the one closest to the people involved—our towns and our cities, then our counties, then our states, then our regional compacts, and only then the national government. That, let me remind you, is the ladder of liberty built by decentralized power. On it also we must have balance between the branches of government at every level.

Balance, diversity, creative difference—these are the elements of the Republican equation. Republicans agree, Republicans agree heartily to disagree on many, many of their applications, but we have never disagreed on the basic fundamental issues of why you and I are Republicans. This is a party for free men, not for blind followers and not for conformists.

*****

Today, as then [1858], but more urgently and more broadly than then, the task of preserving and enlarging freedom at home and of safeguarding it from the forces of tyranny abroad is great enough to challenge all our resources and to require all our strength. Anyone who joins us in all sincerity, we welcome. Those, those who do not care for our cause, we don't expect to enter our ranks in any case. And let our Republicanism, so focused and so dedicated, not be made fuzzy and futile by unthinking and stupid labels. I would remind you that extremism in the defense of liberty is no vice. Thank you. Thank you. Thank you. Thank you. Thank you. And let me remind you also that moderation in the pursuit of justice is no virtue.

*****

Our Republican cause is not to level out the world or make its people conform in computer-regimented sameness. Our Republican cause is to free our people and light the way for liberty throughout the world. Ours is a very human cause for very humane goals. This party, its good people, and its unquenchable devotion to freedom will not fulfill the purposes of this campaign we launch here and now until our cause has won the day, inspired the world, and shown the way to a tomorrow worthy of all our yesteryears.[8]

What was clear from his script were the words and phrases he used. They were carefully selected to connect with the conservatives in the room. The word that repeats throughout the speech was "freedom," a term with special resonance for political conservatives. It signaled both freedom from federal government control and, in a global context, freedom as opposed to captivity within an evil, totalitarian communist system. In keeping with this dual resonance, the term "freedom" in Goldwater's speech often segues into phrases in which he expresses his awareness of the threat posed by communism.

The first excerpt offered in this chapter shows the heavy use of the word "freedom." The excerpt is from early in the speech, but Goldwater does not stop using the word after its initial minutes. The third excerpt points to Goldwater's references to communism as a major threat facing the nation, especially in his eyes and those of his supporters. The second excerpt is heavy with another word—"failure." Here, Goldwater perhaps uses a term that would have worked with all Republicans, for they would join him in indicting the Kennedy-Johnson administration. Democrats, however, listening at home to the address would find the term "failure" abrasive.

The crowd—that is, those remaining—cheered Goldwater's address loudly. The line that the media zeroed-in on is Goldwater's declaring that "extremism in the defense of liberty is no vice." A rhetorically effective line, yes, but not why the speech worked so well with the audience. The speech worked so well because he made it through the terministic screen between himself and his audience, and Goldwater thereby became strongly consubstantial with them.

The speech was covered heavily by the media, but they emphasized how he threw down the gauntlet to those not conservative, in and out of his party. What the media missed (but scholars have noted) is how his speech appealed powerfully to a particular audience because of the words and phrases—the terms—he used in it. In other words, yes, the speech did highlight a conflict between groups, and the media loves conflict. However, the speech was probably more noteworthy rhetorically for how it united those on the conservative side of the political spectrum. In 1964, they would be united in defeat, but, in many ways, Goldwater's candidacy laid the rhetorical foundation for the ascendancy of another conservative, Ronald Reagan, sixteen years later.

Strengths and Limitations

All speeches are composed of words and phrases, so one would expect this Burkean approach to have wide applicability. It does, but not all speeches as dramatically use a particular audience's key terms as does Goldwater's in 1964. In other words, this use of language to create consubstantiality is only occasionally *the* crucial dimension in a text. So, the approach's applicability is limited to only some speeches.

The approach is also limited to texts heavy in terms—probably spoken texts and written texts. Advertisements use terms more lightly, relying heavily on the visual. Memory sites—and places in general—also are just as visual as verbal, if not more so. This limitation does not mean that one should not try to extend Burke's approach to these less verbal media. For example, an ad might heavily use the word "new" and heavily offer images one associates with technology. Or a memory site, in its few words, might use ones we associate with patriotism and might use visual icons—flags, eagles, men and women in uniform—that we also associate with patriotism.

Also, in texts that are heavily verbal, there are dimensions other than the words and phrases used. The arguments made might be important, the emotional appeals made might be important, and how the speech proceeds through a structure might be important. This approach pushes those matters aside and just focuses on the terms used and if they get through to the audience. In Goldwater's speech, he does more than salute freedom, evoke fear of communism, and indict Kennedy-Johnson policies. That "more" should not be lost.

Quite a few critical approaches share this limitation of focusing narrowly on one aspect. With all of them, the key is using the approach when it is useful. In other cases, the critic would have to use another lens.

The strength is the obverse of this limitation. The approach does highlight a dimension of a text that might well be crucial. Critics generally do pay attention to the words in a text, but this Burkean approach takes the critic beyond just attention. It has the critic asking if the words have a special power, a power that gets the message through to its intended audience in a manner that creates that special connection Burke terms consubstantiality. When Lakoff and Johnson published *Moral Politics*, many readers were surprised at how the words and the metaphors used separated political conservatives from political liberals. They, linguists, argued that liberals were not succeeding politically because they did not know how to talk to conservatives. In 1996, when they published their book, that was perhaps true, but the larger point is that no matter who you are trying to connect with (i.e., become consubstantial with), you need to know what in the terms you use will get you through the screens that can divide one group from another. Burke's concept of terministic screens is very useful in understanding how language itself can be a powerful tool in overcoming division and guilt.

Exemplars

Aden, Roger C. "Entrapment and Escape: Inventional Metaphors in Ronald Reagan's Economic Rhetoric." *Southern Communication Journal* 54, no. 4 (1989): 384–400.

Cooks, Leda, and David Descutner. "Different Paths from Powerlessness to Empowerment: A Dramatistic Analysis of Two Eating Disorder Therapies." *Western Journal of Communication*, 57 no. 4 (1993): 494–514.

Corcoran, Farrel. "The Bear in the Back Yard: Myth, Ideology, and Victimage Ritual in Soviet Funerals." *Communication Monographs*, 50 no. 4 (December 1983): 305–20.

Perry, Stephen. "Rhetorical Functions of the Infestation Metaphor in Hitler's Rhetoric." *Central States Speech Journal*, 34 no. 4 (1985): 229–35.

Suggested Applications

Speech Applications

- At the Conservative Political Action Committee's annual gathering, many speeches are delivered by political figures who want—then or in the future—the support of the gathered group. Look at one or more. How did they play to the terministic screens of the ardently conservative audience?

- Bill Clinton was called on at the 2012 Democratic National Convention to discuss President Barack Obama's economic program, which was, at that point, only very slowly achieving results. How does Clinton use language to sway this partisan gathering?

Non-Speech Applications

- Television, especially before Christmas, is flooded with advertisements for luxury automobiles. How do these ads speak to those who might want such cars and be able to afford them?

- Boston has a designated "Freedom Trail" of sites important during the Revolutionary War period. In what terms are the sites—and the trail as a whole—presented and why? (Information on the trail is readily available online: you don't need to visit Boston.)

Notes

1. Blaney, Joseph R., Lance R. Rippert, and J. Scott Smith, eds. *Repairing the Athlete's Image: Studies in Sports Image Restoration.* Lanham, MD: Lexington Books, 2012.

2. Ware, B. L., and Wil A. Linkugel. "They Spoke in Defense of Themselves: On the Generic Criticism of Apologia." *Quarterly Journal of Speech* 59, no. 3 (1973): 273–83. and Benoit, William. *Accounts, Excuses, and Apologies: A Theory of Image Restoration.* Albany, NY: State University of New York Press, 1995.

3. Burke, Kenneth. "The Rhetoric of Hitler's Battle." *Southern Review* 5 (1959): 1–21.

4. Burke, Kenneth. *Language as Symbolic Action*. Berkeley, CA: University of California Press, 1966. 45–46.

5. Weaver, Richard M. *The Ethics of Rhetoric*. Davis, CA: Hermagoras Press, 1985.

6. McGee, Michael C. "The 'Ideograph': A Link between Rhetoric and Ideology." *Quarterly Journal of Speech* 66, no. 1 (1980): 1–16.

7. Burke, *Language as Symbolic Action*, 45.

8. Goldwater, Barry. "Nomination Speech." Speech, Republican National Convention. https://www.washingtonpost.com/wp/srv/politics/daily/may98/goldwaterspeech.htm

Figure credit

Fig. 4: Source: https://commons.wikimedia.org/wiki/File:Goldwater-Reagan_in_1964.jpg.

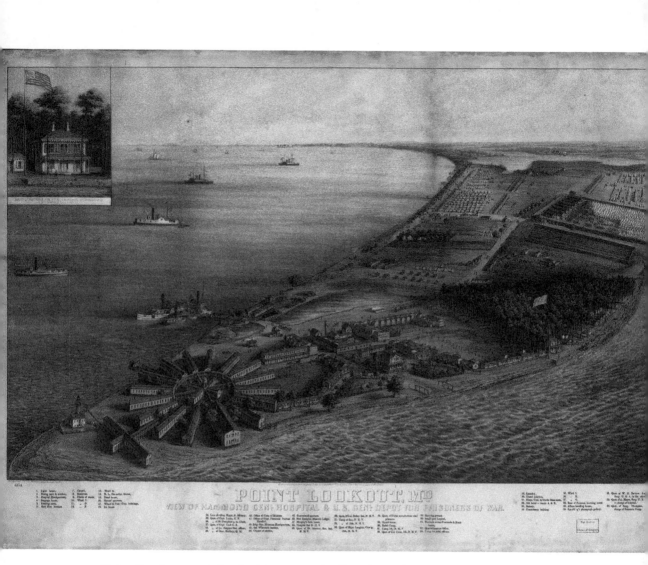

Point Lookout as it looked in ca. 1863. Fort Lincoln is in upper right corner.

CHAPTER 5

Kenneth Burke
and Dramatism

Kenneth Burke is a major twentieth-century American theorist. Calling him just a rhetorical theorist is selling his large body of thoughtful prose short, but most of what he says has a bearing on both rhetorical practice and rhetorical criticism. There are many ideas that one might extract from Burke's work. One, the idea of terministic screens and their role in achieving identification with an audience is discussed in the previous chapter. Another very popular idea is what has come to be known as dramatism. This chapter discusses this central Burkean idea.

For Burke, persuasion was far more than just getting an audience to embrace a message. Burke believed that humans were suffering from guilt because of their divisions. So separated from others, communal life was bleak. Persuasion, insofar as it created connection, was a tool to overcome this bleak state. And Burke sought not just mere connection; rather, he sought a condition far more meaningful and profound that he termed identification or consubstantiality. Burke explored the various means a rhetor had to produce this state.

As noted in an earlier chapter, Burke read widely and without the bounds sometimes imposed by academe. He would read theology and philosophy and literature. In the course of these readings, Burke noted the communal power possessed by drama in classical antiquity. Back in ancient Greece, comedies, and especially tragedies, were not just entertainment; rather, they were part of highly ritualized festivals intended to promote community and identity. They brought auditors together, creating a consubstantiality back then that Burke wanted to see in this troubled twentieth-century world.

Drama today rarely has the powerful communal effect it evidently did back in classical antiquity, but Burke hypothesized that it still had power. The power was apparent less on the stage *per se* than in discourse that was implicitly dramatic. As Burke saw things, we are continually presenting drama to each other, even though we may not be thinking of what we are doing in dramatic terms. When a legislator talks about the crumbling infrastructure in her district, she is implicitly offering a drama; when a president attempts to explain something that has gone very wrong in his administration, he is implicitly offering a drama. These dramas have actors and have actions, and they occur in scenes that those speaking may or may not paint in some detail.

Like the comedies and tragedies of old, these dramas can have not only a persuasive effect, but a larger unifying one. That legislator and that president are not just talking about a particular matter but how, in broader and grander terms, the nation operates and what the culture has come to assume about how the nation operates. These dramas, then, are important insofar as they have effects both small and large. Burke, as rhetorician, was interested in not only studying the effects, but in parsing how these implicit dramas worked to achieve these effects. Burke's structured approach, dramatism, is an attempt to explain how these dramas worked.

The Pentad

Burke divided a drama into five parts: act, actor, agency, scene, purpose. Here is Burke's explanation of the parts:

> We shall use five terms as generating principles of our investigation. They are as follows: act, scene, agent, agency, purpose. In a rounded statement about motives, you must have some word that names the *act* (names what took place, in thought or deed), and another that names the *scene* (the background of the act, the situation in which it occurred); also, you must indicate what person or kind of person (*agent*) performed the act, what means or instruments he or she used (*agency*), and the *purpose*. Men may violently agree about the purposes behind a given act, or about the character of the person who did it, or how he did it, or in what kind of situation he acted; or, they may even insist on totally different words to name the act itself. But be that as it may, any complete statement about motives will offer *some kind of* answer to these five questions: What was done (*act*), when or where it was done (*scene*), who did it (*agent*), how he did it (*agency*), and why (*purpose*)?[1]

Let's further define each term by considering two real, well-known examples. The first is President Franklin Delano Roosevelt's speech to the Congress in 1941, in which he asks that body to recognize that a state of war exists between the United States and the Empire of Japan. The second is President George W. Bush's address to the nation on the evening of September 11, 2001, in which he tells the nation to stand strong.

Act

The drama that FDR creates is what happened that ill-fated Sunday morning in Pearl Harbor, Hawaii. The crucial act is, of course, the aerial attack. The drama Bush creates is similar. It is the set of attacks launched by terrorists that September morning against iconic American structures, the twin World Trade Center towers in lower Manhattan in New York City, the Pentagon, and whatever a fourth hijacked commercial jet was heading for before its passengers brought the plane down in a field in southwestern Pennsylvania. In both cases, the acts are described vividly, dramatically.

Actor

FDR knows who launched the attack on Pearl Harbor—and on other sites in the Pacific. It was the Japanese, and he describes them as cunning, deceitful, and vicious. Bush does not know definitively who is behind the 9/11 attacks, so his description lacks specificity, but he makes it very clear to the American people that those responsible epitomize evil.

Agency

The question here is how (i.e., by what means) the actor(s) performed the act. In the case of Pearl Harbor, the immediate means were aircraft, but FDR also talks about misleading messages and actions that preceded the attack as means the Japanese used to make us think that an attack was not immediately forthcoming. In the case of 9/11, the means was four commercial jet airliners. Bush mentions them but does not dwell on this mechanism the terrorists used to murder thousands. Bush, perhaps, did not want to scare people from flying anymore than they already were. Bush instead focuses on how the terrorists are trying to evoke fear as a means—an agency—to weaken the United States.

Scene

FDR talks about the peaceful sunny Sunday morning that Hawaii was experiencing before the Japanese aircraft attacked. He also talks more broadly about what will later be referred to as "the Pacific theatre." FDR thereby puts the scene at Pearl Harbor into a much larger scene throughout which aggressive Japanese actions were taking place. Bush talks about the peaceful sunny Tuesday morning before the terrorists struck, but he also talks about the scene they created and how first responders heroically did what they could at the chaotic, fiery sites. Both FDR and Bush broaden the scene from the immediate point of attack, but in different directions with different goals. Roosevelt wants his audience to see what Japan had been doing throughout the Pacific so that the audience would conclude that the attack on Pearl Harbor was an isolated incident but part of a pattern. Bush wants his audience to see how the American people heroically responded to the 9/11 attack because his goal is to inspire strength.

Purpose

Both FDR and Bush could not know definitively why enemies launched these two attacks, but, in their speeches, they offered conjecture. In FDR's case, the purpose was imperialistic—to spread the Japanese empire's reach throughout the Pacific. Knocking out the American capability to resist this expansion by destroying much of the Pacific fleet was a necessary prerequisite to this expansion. In Bush's case, the purpose was vaguer. Yes, the terrorists intended to do material damage, and, given their targets, they intended to cripple American commerce and American government. However, Bush presents their purpose less in strategic terms and more in philosophical ones. The terrorists, according to Bush, attacked us to affront our cherished values and to weaken our long-noble spirit.

These two parallel cases are not difficult to analyze in terms of act-actor-agency-scene-purpose. Other cases may be more complex because there may well be more than one drama implicit in the discourse that is being examined. For example, in President Lyndon B. Johnson's famous March 1965 address to Congress demanding the passage of voting rights legislation, Johnson had two dramas in view. The first was the one that had occurred days earlier in Selma, Alabama, where authorities violently drove back a peaceful march back across the Edmund Pettus Bridge; the second was the one that would occur as Congress, pushed by LBJ, enacted a new law guaranteeing voting rights for all.

When the implicit drama is double (or multiple), a Burkean analysis would consider each. That consideration begins with describing the elements in the drama as presented. But the analysis does not stop there.

The Ratios

In such dramas, rarely are all five terms stressed equally. Usually, one—maybe two—are stressed. It is important to ascertain what term or terms are dominant if one is to understand how the drama works rhetorically. A critic could just ask himself or herself which one is stressed, but Burke offers a procedure to help one along. It is referred to as "the ratios."

If the five terms of the pentad are mapped onto themselves and duplicate pairs eliminated, there are ten possible ratios:

Act: Actor
Act: Agency
Act: Scene
Act: Purpose
Actor: Agency
Actor: Scene
Actor: Purpose
Agency: Scene
Agency: Purpose
Scene: Purpose

For each, a critic can ask which of the two elements is more prominent in the drama. Let's do so with just the FDR 1941 speech in mind:

Act: Actor – Act
Act: Agency – Act
Act: Scene – Act
Act: Purpose – Act
Actor: Agency – Actor
Actor: Scene – Equally stressed
Actor: Purpose – Equally stressed
Agency: Scene – Scene
Agency: Purpose – Scene
Scene: Purpose – Equally stressed

What looking at these ratios tells the critic is that the drama implicit in FDR's address to Congress stressed the horrible act. The drama also may have secondarily stressed the scene on which the aggressive act was performed. That act and scene are stressed suggests that FDR wanted his audience to visualize what had happened at Pearl Harbor and elsewhere in the Pacific and react with anger to it. The specific evil actor mattered less; that actor's weaponry (agency) and purpose (imperialism) mattered even less.

How the Dominant Term Affects Discourse

Burke discusses how discourse with different stresses reflects different philosophies of life. Agency-focused discourse is pragmatic, and scene-focused discourse is materialist, while act-oriented is realistic, actor-oriented is idealistic, and purpose-oriented is mystic. Few Burkean critics, based on what they have written, find this extension of dramatism into philosophy as useful or intriguing as Burke (who had a strong interest in competing philosophies) did, but they do find identifying the dominant term within a text's drama useful, for—put simply—actor-focused discourse is far different than scene-focused discourse. Consider each term.

Act

The stress is on what happened. Who did it is not as important, nor are the specifics of where and when. A president asking for relief efforts in the wake of a hurricane might stress the act (the devastation the storm brought). Which hurricane is not important. No one is trying to assign blame. And it little matters if the affected area is in Texas or Florida or Puerto Rico.

Actor

The stress is on who did it. Much prosecutorial courtroom oratory will have this focus because it is the function of court proceedings to assign guilt or innocence to an actor. Oratory used by the defense might keep the focus on the actor (by, for example, stressing his or her exemplary character), but defense oratory might also try to shift the focus to the scene (to external circumstances the defendant could not overcome). The accused did not perpetrate fraud; rather, he or she was caught up in the complex operations of a company and could not readily judge whether actions were fraudulent or not.

Agency

In Congress, those arguing for tax reform may focus on the specific means they are advocating to reduce the tax burden and stimulate the economy. Lowering corporate tax rates, eliminating the estate tax, and ditching the so-called "alternative minimum tax" are all means to the desired end. Those in Congress would not be focusing on who is doing the reform or even the status of the U.S. economy (the scene) as much as the means to be used. (An important U.S. House of Representatives committee, when it comes to tax matters, is named "Ways and Means," suggesting that agency is often going to be the focus of constructed dramas when the topic is tax policy.)

Scene

Those calling for action to address the nation's decaying infrastructure might choose to stress the scene—near-collapsing tunnels and bridges, pot-holed highways, antiquated railroad lines, water lines that leak water and leech lead). The stress would not be on who is to fix the problem or even the precise fixes; rather, it would be on what the dire situations look like.

Purpose

Those calling for reformed policing behavior might well stress how their goal is social justice. This purpose would dominate their discourse, not the specific means by which policing behavior might be reformed. If choosing to stress purpose, the discourse would not dwell on instances of police brutality or racism (acts); rather, it would emphasize a purpose that one would hope a large group might embrace.

The emphasis, then, affects how the discourse comes across. Stressing one element over another, then, can be a strategic decision on the part of the rhetor. In the last case mentioned, a rhetor, knowing that he or she is dealing with a volatile topic, might choose to stress a value that many would embrace. The goal would be to get more people behind police reform by citing a principle than by pointing the finger at instances that suggest action is necessary. Getting more people behind a call, in Burkean terms, increases how many are made consubstantial by the persuasive effort and led beyond division and guilt.

Burke also suggests that certain combinations are especially interesting, so a critic should not just point to the one term that seems to dominate the drama. Rather, one should try to find the pairing. In the case of the drama offered by FDR, it was act and scene. In the case of the 9/11 drama presented by Bush, the dominant pairing was probably scene and purpose: Catastrophic destruction was visited on American places to dispirit us and make us fearful, but that destruction will not so succeed.

Method

Texts do not always offer up their drama on the surface. So, the first step a Burkean critic must take would be to extract the drama and then analyze it in pentadic terms, asking what is the act, etc. Then, the critic's important task is determining what term or pair of terms dominate the drama as presented by the text. Now, if the analysis were to stop there, then the critic would have offered a description of the drama but not really a critical analysis of it. The missing step is asking why—to what end—is the drama being presented as it is. FDR wanted his audience to see what (act) has been done at Pearl Harbor on a peaceful Sunday morning (scene) so that the audience would be angry enough to agree with him that a state of war now existed between the United States and Japan. If you know your history, you know that there was considerable isolationist sentiment in the United States at the time. FDR wanted to get the nation beyond that isolationism and into a war that he had long thought was necessary. Bush wanted his audience to see the results (scene) of what had happened on a peaceful Tuesday morning, and he wanted his audience to understand why the terrorists had acted as they did so that his audience could emphatically say no to their goal of producing fear. In his speech, he declared that, the next day, America would be open for business—in other words, back to normal, not driven into hiding in fear. Pinpointing why the rhetor constructs the drama as he or she does is a crucial part of what a Burkean critic does.

Application: Point Lookout, Maryland

As noted in earlier chapters, rhetorical critics have increasingly paid attention to public memory sites on the assumption that they deliver messages and that these messages are oftentimes not as neutral as granite and marble might suggest.

A relatively unknown but fascinating memory site is in extreme southern Maryland, at the point where the Potomac River enters the Chesapeake Bay.[2] In the early nineteenth century, the site featured—in chronological order—a lighthouse, a fort (to keep the British from sailing up the Potomac), a modest resort, and an innovatively designed hospital. But, during the Civil War, the rather narrow peninsula held Fort Lincoln, a prisoner-of-war camp for captured Confederate soldiers. The conditions at Fort Lincoln were poor; then, typhoid fever hit. The consequence was that thousands died there.

The first attempt to memorialize the dead was a very modest obelisk erected by the state of Maryland at the site of a mass grave. In 1938, several miles north of the actual prison site, the federal government built a larger obelisk. On it are engraved the names of the known Confederate dead. At that time, Maryland moved its smaller funereal obelisk to this new site, since erosion had necessitated the relocation of the mass grave site. (The new grave site was miles south of the federally funded obelisk.)

Most of Point Lookout became a Maryland state park, featuring boating, swimming, fishing, and camping. Perhaps because family recreation and a Civil War prisoner-of-war camp did not mix well, the state did very little if anything in the park to note Fort

Lincoln's site. Then, new, fancy roadside markers appeared at the beginning of the twenty-first century. Construction began on a replica of the fort, although only a gate and a few sections of wall were completed. Given how limited parking is near this replica, few people view the memory site.

Just north of the state park's entrance and a few miles south of the federal memorial is where the mass grave was relocated. At that very point, in 2007, a Baltimore group, sympathetic to the plight of Confederate soldiers, built still another memory site. This one is a giant bean pot with a Confederate soldier standing atop it—suggestive of the poor diet the prisoners were fed. Surrounding it is a brick pavilion on which the names of the Confederate dead are listed. Surrounding that are stations at which visitors can read letters written by inmates (and a few guards). Surrounding that are a ring of flags representing the Confederate states the deceased had fought for. Prominent among these flags is the controversial Confederate battle flag.

So, we have three competing memory sites within a few miles of each other. Let's consider them from a dramatic perspective.

The federal obelisk (with the small Maryland one nearby) does not convey much meaning. In dramatistic terms, the act is dying, the actors are the named Confederate dead, the agency is the prison (although we know nothing about the conditions there), the scene is several miles south (although we are not told this), and the purpose behind their death is not addressed.

Act and actor seem equally stressed. The funereal architecture signals dying, and we do know most of the names of those who died. What is interesting about the site is that the agency, scene, and purpose elements in the drama are so very weakly present. It is almost as if those who erected the federal site did not want visitors to have that information. One could argue that the federal authorities wanted to commemorate the dead Americans (although rebels) but wanted to suppress almost all information about their deaths.

The roadside signs and the replica fort flip the drama. Dying *per se* is not stressed as much as the conditions of the soldiers' imprisonment. The soldiers are not named, so the actor is suppressed along with the act. How the soldiers died—by disease—is stressed. The scene is much more stressed, for we are at the fort's very site and can see its boundary lines, as well as a gate and few walls. The purpose behind the soldiers' death is almost as vague here as at the federal site. There, they just died; here, they died because of the typhoid epidemic.

At this site, the drama stresses the scene. You can stand where they stood; you can see Virginia across the Potomac as they did. Also stressed but not as much is agency, but note what the agency is—disease, not anything Union forces in the war might have been responsible for. Even the way disease is presented is interesting. Evidence suggests that there were many diseases rampant in the prisoner-of-war camp, most of them rooted in the unsanitary conditions the Union maintained and the poor diet the Union fed the southern prisoners. Diseases that might be linked to poor Union treatment are not stressed; rather, it is an epidemic—implicitly just somehow appearing on the scene—that swept the camp and killed thousands.

The pro-Confederate site offers the richest drama of the three. The act commemorated is the prisoners' deaths. The actors are not just named (as at the federal site), but their stories are heard. These stories, confirmed by those of guards, tell of their poor treatment at Fort Lincoln. So, in this drama, their demise was due to a combination of poor treatment and disease that was probably rooted in, or at least exacerbated by, their unsanitary living conditions and poor diet. The scene is not that of the fort but that of their nearby mass grave. Purpose, the last element in the dramatistic pentad, is still not treated fully, but there are suggestions in the soldiers' words that their poor treatment and their eventual deaths were punitive. They were being punished as rebels—kept starving just a very difficult four-mile swim from their beloved southern homeland. That they could see it, four miles across the Potomac, added to their anguish.

Because the drama here is richer, the ratios help one discern the drama's emphases:

Act: Actor – Actor(s), whose stories we read
Act: Agency – Agency, with blame attached
Act: Scene – Scene, the imagined prison, the nearby mass grace, and the nearby Virginia shore
Act: Purpose – Purpose (slightly), a punitive one on the part of the Union
Actor: Agency – Both, the prisoners and what killed them
Actor: Scene – Actor(s), the prisoners we hear more than the scene they inhabited
Actor: Purpose – Actor(s), the prisoners we hear more than why they were treated poorly
Agency: Scene – Agency, the poor treatment more than the specific place
Agency: Purpose – Agency, the poor treatment more than why
Scene: Purpose – Both, the place and the punitive goals are tied together

What do the ratios tell us? First, that the actors are stressed, but, second, that the agency (i.e., the means by which they suffered and died) was also stressed. At the federal site, we receive virtually no information about agency in the drama offered. At the in-the-park site, we receive information about agency, but we're told it's typhoid. At the pro-Confederate site, we receive far richer information about agency. From both the bean pot and the soldiers' words, we learn about the wretched lives these prisoners of war lived before disease overcame their weakened bodies. Many who have studied the Civil War have heard of Andersonville, the notorious prisoner-of-war camp that housed captured Union soldiers. Well, the pro-Confederate memorial makes it very clear that the Union maintained a prisoner-of-war camp in Maryland that was equally wretched.

The dramas offered by the three Point Lookout sites are very clearly not the same. In terms of persuasion and identification/consubstantiality, they have very different effects. The federal story brings viewers together as they remember dead Americans, soldiers who are named but not closely associated with any cause. That the memorial was built by the U.S. Office of Veterans Affairs perhaps explains the stress on those who have served, regardless of the cause. The in-the-park story brings viewers together as they remember (a version of) history. This group is more likely to be Civil War tourists than visitors with a particular ideology. They will appreciate all the information on the roadside markers (information on more than just Fort Lincoln), and they will especially appreciate the marking of the fort's site and the reconstruction of a few of its pieces. That this site is located within a tourist spot (the state park) perhaps explains the stress on touristy stuff. The pro-Confederate site brings viewers together as they remember what was done to *their* boys here. Maryland was, of course, not part of the Confederacy, but there was considerable sympathy for the South in the state as well as many Marylanders who crossed the Potomac and fought for the South. These sympathizers are brought together by the pro-Confederate site. At the same time, one should note that this memory site also, as it produces identity/consubstantiality among one group, has the potential to produce a heightened divide between that group and those who read the pro-Confederate site as a pro-slavery one. The prominence of the Confederate battle flag at the site almost guarantees that there will be a sharp divide between two groups encountering the memorial. One group will embrace it; another will shun it.

Strengths and Limitations

Those who use dramatism as a lens through which to view texts would probably admit that doing so is easier for some texts than others. At Point Lookout, something happened—there was a drama that three different visual texts recall. In other cases, applying the theory is easy because the rhetor chose to give his or her text a dramatic spin. A legislator, talking about healthcare, may choose to stress how people will suffer if care is inadequate; a memorial designer may choose to stress a revered hero's actions, not just erect a statue of the person (perhaps on a horse) with name and birth/death dates on the pedestal's side. But the rhetor may also not choose to proceed in a dramatic direction. In these cases, applying dramatism will be more difficult. In addition, doing so may seem to be adding a dramatic dimension to a text that really does not have one. A Burkean critic, believing that all texts are a dramatic display of human motives, would perhaps be comfortable doing so; however, a less committed critic might hesitate and want to find a lens more appropriate for the text in question.

So, dramatism may not always be the best critical approach to use. But, when the approach is applicable, it can reveal a great deal. An often-cited and reproduced example of what this approach can reveal is David A. Ling's discussion of Massachusetts Senator Edward M. Kennedy's apology after a tragic incident on Chappaquiddick Island in 1969.[3] After a barbecue the Kennedy Family had thrown for the late Robert Kennedy's staffers, Senator Kennedy drove himself and a female aide to the late senator off a bridge and into a pond, where she drowned. Many blamed Edward Kennedy; many questioned why he was alone with the aide and if he was sober. His apology offered the drama of that fateful night in considerable detail. An analysis of that drama revealed that Kennedy stressed the scene: It was dark, the road was curved, the bridge lacked railings, the pond water was murky. Ling's argument was that this drama was so offered to deflect blame from Kennedy onto the scene. One can, of course, argue about whether the strategy worked (Kennedy was reelected to the Senate but never to the presidency), but it is difficult to dispute what the dramatistic analysis revealed: that the speech was intended to shift blame, to the extent possible, from Kennedy to the scene. A dramatistic analysis also reveals that Kennedy did not eliminate the actor. Rather, he positioned the actor (himself) in the dominant scene in a manner that suggested that he was overwhelmed by the scene. Does one want a president so easily overwhelmed? The assumption that many would answer no to this questions is cited by those who believe the speech, although it saved Kennedy's political career, may have cost him the White House.

Exemplars

Birdsell, David A. "Ronald Reagan on Lebanon and Grenada: Flexibility and Interpretation in the Application of Kenneth Burke's Pentad." *Quarterly Journal of Speech* 73, no. 3 (August 1987): 267–79.

Brummett, Barry A. "A Pentadic Analysis of Ideologies in Two Gay Rights Controversies." *Central States Speech Journal* 30, no. 3 (1979): 250–61.

Peterson, Tarla Rai. "The Meek Shall Inherit the Mountains: Dramatistic Criticism of Grand Teton National Park's Interpretive Program." *Central States Speech Journal* 39, no. 2 (1988): 121–33.

Tonn, Mari Boor, Valerie A. Endress, and John N. Diamond. "Hunting and Heritage on Trial: A Dramatistic Debate Over Tragedy, Tradition, and Territory." *Quarterly Journal of Speech* 79, no. 2 (1993): 165–81.

Suggested Applications

Speech Applications

- After 9/11/2001, President George W. Bush gave several speeches. One led our nation into military action against Iraq by arguing that Iraq possessed weapons of mass destruction. Analyze this speech's drama.

- Unable to address the U.S. Congress directly, women's rights activist Carrie Chapman Catt delivered a speech at the Poli Theatre in Washington, DC, in which she pretended to address Congress. She creates a drama, but she also presents important social and political dramas. Analyze Catt's speech using a dramatistic lens.

Non-Speech Applications

- The memorial carved into the Dakota Black Hills, Mount Rushmore, presents one or more dramas. What are they and how are they presented as part of the monument's persuasive message(s)?

- Pick an episode of the popular Netflix drama *House of Cards*. What argument is offered about politics in America? In making the argument compelling, how is the drama presented?

Notes

1. Burke, Kenneth. *A Grammar of Motives*. Berkeley, CA: University of California Press, 1969. xv.

2. Hyden, Carl T., and Theodore F. Sheckels. *Public Places: Sites of Political Communication*. Lanham, MD: Lexington Books, 2016.

3. Ling, David A. "A Pedantic Analysis of Senator Edward Kennedy's Address to the People of Massachusetts, July 25, 1969." *Central States Speech Journal* 21, no. 2 (1970): 81–86.

Figure credit

Fig. 5: Copyright © Wystan (CC by 2.0) at https://www.flickr.com/photos/70251312@N00/8525983904.

The Students for a Democratic Society (SDS), who campaigned against much that characterized American in the 1960s, inspired student anti-war demonstrations late in the decade.

CHAPTER 6

"Fantasy Theme" Analysis

The fantasy theme approach responds to audience dynamics that are important to recognize. These dynamics create views of the world and how it and its smaller components ought to operate. The successful rhetor can play off these socially constructed views to persuade. As its developer Ernest Bormann notes, the term "fantasy" is a technical term, one that does not suggest the unreal. Far from that, fantasy themes are very real for the people who have created them to define their social realities.

Bales and Bormann

The approach has its origins in the work of social psychologist Robert Bales. He studied groups and how they function. He was not especially interested in groups that had tasks to perform; rather, he explored groups that offer members support, groups such as Alcoholics Anonymous. He found that storytelling characterized these groups' meetings. More important, he found that stories were built bit by bit. Someone in the group would make an observation; others would jump in, adding and elaborating. Bales referred to this observable group process as "chaining": group members would keep adding links.

Along the way, two things would happen to the story. First, it would become substantial—not a vague plot line but a story with details that members would nod yes to. Second, it would become the property of the group, not the person who may have initiated the chain.

Communication is inherently an interdisciplinary enterprise. Social psychology is interested in how groups work; so are communication scholars who hope to improve the group work that increasingly characterizes the work place. Ernest Bormann was an early communication researcher with an interest in groups. He saw in Bales's work something that he could apply to his exposition of what groups do. As Bales had observed groups developing shared stories, so did Bormann. But, whereas Bales perhaps saw the stories primarily as establishing group identity, Bormann also saw the stories as establishing a basis for those outside the group to connect with those within. These stories are termed "fantasy themes."

Bormann speaks about both the themes and the process of convergence that creates them in a seminal article that appeared in the *Journal of Applied Communication Research:*

> Convergence refers to the way, during certain processes of communication, two or more private symbolic worlds incline towards each other, come more closely together, or even overlap. If several or many people develop portions of their private symbolic worlds which overlap as a result of symbolic convergence, then they have the basis for communicating with one another to create community, to discuss their common experiences, and to achieve mutual understanding. But symbolic convergence means more than an intellectual coorientation in which people come together to have the same logical and rational interpretation of symbols. Symbolic convergence also explains how people come to have an emotional investment and commitment to the symbols they live by—how it is that people can sympathize, empathize, and identify with one another.

A fantasy theme consists of a dramatizing message in which characters enact an incident or a series of incidents in a setting somewhere other than the here and now of the people involved in the communication episode. Fantasy themes are often narratives about living people or historic personages or about an envisioned future. The term "fantasy" in the symbolic convergence theory is a technical term and should not be confused with another common usage of the term which is of something imaginary, not grounded in reality. Quite to the contrary, fantasy within this theory is the way that communities of people create their social reality and employs a meaning much closer to another common usage of the term: the imaginative and creative interpretation of events that fulfills a psychological or rhetorical need.[1]

Bormann termed these stories fantasy themes because they were often aspirational. They represented what the group wanted to be true, just as much as what it might be in their view. Consider the many social movements that have characterized American history. Each had a fantasy theme. Organized labor developed a story or theme featuring the triumph of the worker; those demonstrating against the War in Vietnam developed a story or theme featuring both the end of the conflict and the downfall of all politicians who had supported it; those who have fought fascism globally for decades, known as "Antifa," developed a story or theme featuring both the resurgence of fascist ideology and the use of many means, including violence, to suppress it. These are big fantasy themes. Smaller groups develop smaller themes, and larger groups—let's say the American population at large—develop still larger themes such as the American dream that anyone, no matter how humble his or her roots, can succeed in this nation.

In academe, a group of faculty may meet. If cynics, they may create a fantasy theme that characterizes forces above them at their school as unresponsive and dictatorial and characterizes themselves as the truth tellers who must alert their colleagues. Is the fantasy true? Perhaps to a degree, but its truth or falsity does not matter from the perspective of persuasion. This fantasy theme is what this group believes and, therefore, one who wishes to persuade them must recognize and deal with this theme. Also in academe, a group of Greek letter organizations may gather. One person tells of how the administration has tried to crack down on its parties. Others jump in. What may have been a few actions by campus police to stop underage drinking without bringing criminal charges suddenly becomes—through a process Bales had termed "chaining"—a conspiracy to end the entire Greek system. True? Probably not, but, once created, the fantasy theme has a power of its own that can impede or facilitate persuasion. Note I said "impede or facilitate."

Bormann's approach had its moment of popularity; then, fewer and fewer critics turned to it. Perhaps the term fantasy theme was part of the problem: It suggested untruth to many. However, the concept of social constructionism has gained dominance in the social sciences—and beyond. The basic idea is that what we think to be real may well be a constructed reality. Gender, for example, may be a socially constructed reality. There are few biological reasons those deemed masculine act one way and those deemed feminine act another. Rather, society has defined gender, and, thus, gender definitions vary from culture to culture and from time to time. The family is socially constructed; marriage is socially constructed; education (i.e., how it is structured, what it entails) is socially constructed; the state is socially constructed.

The social constructionist perspective is not easy for some to accept. Some will argue that we, here in the United States or in the Western world, define marriage correctly or the state correctly. Despite this resistance—and cries that social constructionism will promote value-less relativism—the perspective dominates academe today. Its dominance may give Bormann's fantasy theme approach new life, for what Bales and Bormann were identifying decades ago is really social construction.

Another take on essentially the same phenomenon is the concept of rhetorical communities. This concept posits that different groups are rhetorically different. They have different assumptions and are likely to accept certain arguments and reject other arguments. One could think of political conservatives and political liberals as rhetorical communities, but let's parse the variable audience in different ways. Consider World War II veterans and anti-Vietnam War activists back in the late 1960s and early 1970s. They saw American involvement in Vietnam differently. Consider KKK members and Civil

Rights crusaders. Striking differences. Even within the Civil Rights Movement back in the 1960s, consider the NAACP, the Southern Christian Leadership Conference (SCLC), and the Student Non-Violent Coordinating Committee (SNCC), groups that, although similar, are arguably different rhetorical communities. The NAACP preferred acting through traditional means such as legislative and judicial actions; SNCC eventually advocated violence, departing from the non-violent SCLC, which had created SNCC as its youth wing.

Such communities may not have unifying stories or themes front and center, but they are present. In the 1960s, African-American audiences were rallied by Dr. Martin Luther King, Jr. and by Malcolm X. They told somewhat similar stories about what had happened in America, but, at a point, the stories diverged, leading the two to envision very different resolutions. Dr. King offered a dream where all would sit down at the same table; Malcolm X offered separation and, perhaps, violence. Both men attracted followers who shared their visions. These were two very different rhetorical communities. A white speaker might have a difficult time reaching either, but King would also have a difficult time with those who had embraced Malcolm's fantasy theme and Malcolm would have a difficult time with those who had embraced Dr. King's. There was much common ground, but the different fantasy themes created a barrier between the two groups.

The Rhetorical Critic's Task

Critics who embrace this approach typically take two courses. The more common one is to discern what the socially constructed fantasy theme might be. This task is basically trying to find out what, rhetorically, makes a group tick. The other task assesses attempts by rhetors to persuade members of these rhetorical communities by tapping these members' fantasy themes. The latter task is similar to what critics do when ascertaining whether a rhetor gets a persuasive message through the terministic screen that can separate rhetor and audience (discussed in Chapter Four). Sometimes the two tasks merge, for texts that persuade may then become texts that embody, since social construction is an on-going process.

Method

A fantasy theme critic is using an idea developed by small group communication researchers. Thus researchers—not rhetorical critics—would be interested in observing how, through chaining, a group creates a fantasy theme. The rhetorical critic arrives on the scene later and is interested in two tasks: first, discerning a group's fantasy themes by examining its texts; second, seeing how successful an outside rhetor is in reaching a socially constructed group by playing to its fantasy themes.

To undertake the first task, a critic must closely read the group's texts. These texts could be speeches, but they are just as likely to be written documents, and might even be memory sites the group erects. Fantasy themes usually take the form of a narrative, so the critic looks for the stories and then analyzes the stories in terms of plot, characterization, setting, and the like. The critic's goal is to truly grasp the stories, especially why they are compelling. So, the question, "Why does this story or do these stories have the power to bring the group together?" needs to be focused on. Answering it may require the critic to get into the minds of the group members. This task is often not easy to do, especially if the group members' experiences differ greatly from those of the critic. For example, prisoners might socially construct fantasy themes. How would a typical college undergraduate understand their perspective? Research, including interviews, might help. But, the difficulty in getting into the minds of those who have developed the themes should suggest to the critic that he or she may be better off considering groups not too far removed from his or her experience. For example, I would probably be able to grasp the fantasy themes of sports fans or left-leaning political groups but not those of recovering alcoholics or religious groups outside the Christian tradition.

The second task, discerning how well a given text persuades those holding a particular fantasy theme requires an understanding of the theme and then a close examination of the text in question. The goal is to see if it matches, and it probably needs to match in terms of plot, characterization, setting, etc., for if there is dissonance on any of these counts, then persuasiveness will probably suffer.

As is the case with all rhetorical critical projects, there should be a good reason to undertake the tasks. A critic might do well to end his or her exploration by pointing to these reasons. In the first instance (i.e., examining a group's fantasy themes), the importance of the task is usually tied to the importance of the group. We perhaps do not need to know how a minor group has socially constructed its reality, but, for major groups, knowing means that we can explain what they do and what they don't do. People will, of course, disagree on what groups are major, so the critic needs to be prepared to make the case for the chosen group's significance. In the second instance (i.e., seeing if texts succeed in persuading a group), the importance is either the persuasion that occurs or the persuasion that does not occur. Consider, for example, Hillary Clinton. Curiously, in 2008, her message resonated with working class voters. In the Pennsylvania primary that year, she defeated Barack Obama because whatever she was saying or doing was arguably matching the fantasy themes of these voters. However, in 2016, Clinton's message did not resonate with this group, whereas Donald Trump's did. The puzzle may well be solved by discerning precisely what themes those Pennsylvania voters, meeting in union halls and restaurants and taverns, in places such as Johnstown and Allentown, developed through chaining and, then, seeing how Clinton's texts in 2008 matched (at least better than Obama's) and how Clinton's texts in 2016 failed to match (at least as well as Trump's). This case is a fascinating one involving persuasion and the absence of persuasion. A fantasy theme critic examining Clinton's campaign discourse would be well advised to end his or her analysis by highlighting what crucial dimensions of campaign communication the examination of the case revealed.

Application: The Port Huron Declaration

Those who lived through the 1960s and 1970s may remember the era as being dominated by protests against the War in Vietnam. But that was not the only front on which young people were challenging their elders. There was, at that time, a broad-based counter-culture movement that was raising questions about not only the war, but matters of gender, race, and class. Although the movement was not without problems of its own, it tried to remake American society along lines radically different from those that defined it coming out of the "happy days" of the 1950s.

One group that we associate with this counter-culture movement is the Students for a Democratic Society (SDS). The group was prominently present in Grant Park in Chicago during the tumultuous 1968 Democratic National Convention. At that point, its radicalism was turning more and more violent. But, earlier, it was both more peaceful and, perhaps, more visionary.

The group met in 1962 in Port Huron, Michigan. Its goal was to define its purpose and thereby define its identity. Out of that meeting came the multi-page "Port Huron Statement." On the assumption that the SDS, as a rhetorical community, socially constructed this document and its vision, a critic might examine it to see what fantasy themes characterized the group.

> We are people of this generation, bred in at least modest comfort, housed now in universities, looking uncomfortably to the world we inherit.
>
> When we were kids the United States was the wealthiest and strongest country in the world; the only one with the atom bomb, the least scarred by modern war, an initiator of the United Nations that we thought would distribute Western influence throughout the world. Freedom and inequality for each individual, government of, by, and for the people—these American values we found good, principles by which we could live as men. Many of us began maturing in complacency.
>
> As we grew, however, our comfort was penetrated by events too troubling to dismiss.

*****

Students for a Democratic Society, Selection from Port Huron Statement. Copyright © 1962 by Students for a Democratic Society.

We would replace power rooted in possession, privilege, or circumstance by power and uniqueness rooted in love, reflectiveness, reason, and creativity. As a social system we seek the establishment of a democracy of individual participation, governed by two central aims: that the individual share in those social decisions determining the quality and direction of his life; that society be organized to encourage independence in men and provide the media for their common participation.

*****

Tragically, the university could serve as a significant source of social criticism and an initiator of new modes and molders of attitudes. But the actual intellectual effect of the college experience is hardly distinguishable from that of any other communication channel—say, a television set—passing on the stock truths of the day. Students leave somewhat more "tolerant" than when they arrived, but basically unchallenged in their values and political orientations. With administrators ordering the institution, and faculty the curriculum, the student learns by his isolation to accept elite rule within the university, which prepares him to accept later forms of minority control. The real function of the educational system—as opposed to its more rhetorical function of "searching for truth"—is to impart the key information and styles that will help the student get by, modestly but comfortably, in the big society beyond.

*****

From 1960 to 1962, the campuses experienced a revival of idealism among an active few. Triggered by the impact of the sit-ins, students began to struggle for integration, civil liberties, student rights, peace, and against the fast-rising right-wing "revolt" as well. The liberal students, too, have felt their urgency thwarted by conventional channels: from student governments to Congressional committees. Out of this alienation from existing channels has come the creation of news ones; the most characteristic forms of liberal-radical student organizations are the dozens of campus political parties, political journals, and peace marches and demonstrations. In only a few cases have students built bridges to power: an occasional election campaign, the sit-ins, Freedom Rides, and voter registration activities; in some relatively large Northern demonstrations for peace and civil rights, and infrequently, through the United States National Student Association whose notable work has not been focused on political change.

*****

First, the university is located in a permanent position of social influence. Its educational function makes it indispensable and automatically makes it a crucial institution in the formation of social attitudes. Second, in an unbelievably complicated world, it is the central institution for organizing, evaluating, and transmitting knowledge.

*****

These, at least, are facts, no matter how dull the teaching, how paternalistic the rules, how irrelevant the research that goes on. Social relevance, the accessibility to knowledge, and internal openness—these together make the university a potential base and agency in a movement of social change.

1. Any new left in America must be, in large measure, a left with real intellectual skills, committed to deliberativeness, honesty, reflection as working tools. The university permits the political life to be an adjunct to the academic one, and action to be informed by reason.

2. A new left must be distinguished in significant social roles throughout the country. The universities are distributed in such a manner.

3. A new left must consist of younger people who matured in the post-war world, and partially be directed to the recruitment of younger people. The university is an obvious beginning point.

4. A new left must include liberals and socialists, the former for their relevance, the latter for their sense of thoroughgoing reforms in the system. The university is a more sensible place than a political party for these two traditions to begin to discuss their differences and look for political synthesis.

5. A new left must start controversy across the land, if national policies and national apathy are to be reversed. The ideal university is a community of controversy, within itself and in its effects on communities beyond.

6. A new left must transform modern complexity into issues that can be understood and felt close-up by every human being. It must give form to the feelings of helplessness and indifference, so that people may see the political, social, and economic sources of their private troubles and organize to change society. In a time of supposed prosperity, moral complacency, and political manipulation, a new left cannot rely on only aching stomachs to be the engine of social reform. The case for change, for alternatives that will involve uncomfortable personal effects, must be argued as never before. The university is a relevant place for all of these activities.

*****

To turn these possibilities into realities will involve national efforts at university reform by an alliance of students and faculty. They must wrest control of the educational process from the administrative bureaucracy. They must make fraternal and functional contact with allies in labor, civil rights, and other liberal forces outside the campus. They must import major public issues into the curriculum—research and teaching on problems of war and peace is an outstanding example. They must make debate and controversy, not dull pedantic cant, the common style for educational life. They must consciously build a base for their assault upon the loci of power.

As students for a democratic society, we are committed to stimulating this kind of social movement, this kind of vision and program in campus and community across the country. If we appear to seek the unattainable, as it has been said, then let it be known that we do so to avoid the unimaginable.[2]

Anti-Vietnam protests so dominate our memory of the late 1960s and early 1970s that many might label SDS as a leading anti-war group. It was, but, as the statement makes clear SDS, was a group that predated the anti-Vietnam War protests and had a broader vision.

The statement seems to have four parts: an initial part where it reflects on the situation faced by university students in 1962; a second philosophical part calling for broad changes in all areas of society; a third, more practical part, calling for specific courses of actions that might be pursued more immediately; and a fourth, which establishes the centrality of the university in the vision SDS presents. A quick summary of each should suggests the fantasy theme or socially constructed vision SDS had.

Part One presents a university world characterized by a large measure of prosperity and comfort but also by profound, largely suppressed worries (about nuclear war, for example) and apathy. The apathy has resulted in many university students playing "the game" that the schools have institutionalized—focused on getting a good-paying job and a nice, upper middle-class lifestyle. What is lacking are both ideas and values. Part Two argues that certain values must be embraced. At the core of SDS' vision is how we see humans and how we humans structure society. SDS says, "We regard men [sic] as infinitely precious and possessed of unfulfilled capacities for reason, freedom, and love." Once this definition is recognized and embraced by universities, then SDS calls for a rethinking of democracy that truly embraces all who are members of the community and a rethinking of the economy that truly embraces the needs of all who are members of the community. At present, according to SDS, the political and economic realms are dominated by elites. Those in society who have complacently accepted this reality must change. They will be led by students. And in order for students to do so, both educational institutions and the students themselves must change. Institutions must stop trying to control, and they need to make education relevant (i.e., connected to real-world problems, connected to the communities universities are in). Furthermore, university students must confront and abandon their apathy.

SDS, then, has a clear philosophical vision and a strong sense of what that shared vision means in terms of human relations and political/economic structures. More specifically, in Part Three, SDS points to six areas in which the vision can be operationalized:

1. The Civil Rights Movement. Embracing it and helping extend it to include voting rights.

2. The peace movement. Moving it from corners of the university and society into mainstream institutions.

3. Organized labor. Increasing its power by shifting control from elites to the rank-and-file and expanding minority involvement.

4. The Congress. Creating a meaningful liberal presence there.

5. Universities. Encouraging the growth of liberal-radical organizations and helping them build "bridges to power."

6. The Democratic Party. Resolving the contradiction between liberalism and racism in the party in favor of the former.

SDS is a student group. So, in the final part of the statement, the group talks about "a new left" rooted in a very different university. Students need more control of its programs; those programs need to be more connected to world and community problems. "[R]eal intellectual skills" must be taught so that the university ceases being a place featuring rote learning and research that is either empty or in service of what later radicals would term "the man" and becomes a "community of controversy."

Undoubtedly, in 1962, many who read the "Port Huron Statement" rejected, if not its premises, then many of its specific suggestions. Some rejected by calling the agenda idealistic and impractical; others rejected by nodding condescendingly but then refusing to surrender any power to the students that SDS represented. This rejection points to that fact that the vision was largely that of the group. One observing the gathering in Port Huron might have even noticed chaining, as those present developed the fantasy the document presents. What occurred fits Bormann's conception well, for it is a socially constructed view of how the world should be, which united SDS members. Identifying this vision is one task a rhetorical critic might undertake. Seeing how it functions in persuading or not persuading an SDS audience is another.

Early one morning (at something like 2:00 a.m.) at the height of anti-Vietnam War protests, President Richard Nixon decided to leave the White House and go talk to demonstrators camped near the Lincoln Memorial. Many of these demonstrators, if not SDS members per se, certainly shared much of the fantasy theme articulated in 1962 by the "Port Huron Statement." How successful do you think Nixon was getting through to these demonstrators? Did Nixon embrace, even partially, their vision of love, democracy, peace, controversy, and power to the people? Probably not. Given his statements on the war at the time, he probably tried to argue that peace was, of course, the goal but it could only be achieved by responding strongly, militarily to Viet Cong rebels and North Vietnamese forces in the short term. He would probably have added that his approach would ultimately reduce American casualties, even if it increased them in the short term. Nixon probably would have counseled these young people to trust in the judgment of their elders, who were serving in elected and non-elected government offices. In other words, Nixon would have likely totally missed the mark because he did not try to appeal to this audience's fantasy theme. Nixon was first elected in 1968. In that election, he was opposed by then Vice President Hubert H. Humphrey, whose position on Vietnam was somewhat unclear because he had dutifully supported Lyndon Johnson's expansion of the war. But, before the general election, there were the Democratic primaries, during which anti-war candidates Senator Eugene McCarthy and Senator Robert Kennedy campaigned. Both attracted large numbers of young volunteers. Why? One suspects that their messages did connect with at least some of the elements of the fantasy theme articulated by SDS in the "Port Huron Statement." Their messages were probably not radical enough to attract all; thus, there remained a sizeable anti-war presence outside the Democratic Party, but they did do a better job creating a degree of consonance between their positions and those being taken on many college and university campuses.

Application: The National World War II Memorial in Washington, DC

Rhetorical criticism, as noted frequently throughout this textbook, began with the analysis of speeches. In considering the "Port Huron Declaration," we have already departed from this tradition. It is a written text, but, because it was non-literary (and therefore not "owned" by literature scholars) and because it was so very political, considering it would not have been considered that much of a stretch for the rhetorical critic.

More of a stretch would be the more recent move many rhetorical critics have made to consider public places. The assumption is that places are not neutral: They are designed to send messages, to persuade. This is true of places such as corporate headquarter buildings. Consider, for example, Apple's headquarters in California. Google it. Even a quick examination should suggest that Apple was trying to project a certain image of itself by the building's very design. The building then is designed to persuade. If this is true of buildings such as corporate headquarters, it is even more so of structures designed to memorialize—to bring back into the viewers' minds the events and the people of the past.

The National Mall in Washington, DC, is the most prestigious place to build a memory site, but those who regulate it desire to keep it as open as possible. They do so that "the Mall" remains the people's and so that the grand vistas among the US Capitol Building at its East end, the Lincoln Memorial at its West, and the Washington Monument (almost) in the middle remain. The Mall, it may surprise some, is not a grand promenade that goes back to the beginnings of the nation. Rather, it emerged as a Depression-era work project in the 1930s. To come into existence, swamp land needed to be reclaimed, a creek needed to be buried, north-south railroad tracks had to be relocated, structures had to be demolished, and trees had to be hewn down. By 1940 or so, the Mall had its basic present-day shape and openness. Structures were added after 1940, but they were carefully placed off to the sides to preserve the people's open promenade and the vistas. Some of the most recently added structures have been buildings: new Smithsonian museum buildings and the National Gallery of Art's East Wing, for example. Others were memory sites, be they museums (Holocaust, American Indian, African American History and Culture) or memorials (Vietnam Veterans', Franklin D. Roosevelt). All have been placed, to varying degrees, off to the side.

Far from off to the side was the World War II Memorial dedicated in 2004. It sat dead center on the Mall, just west of the Washington Monument. It broke up the promenade, but, fortunately, it preserved the vistas by being, to a large extent, built down into the ground.

When one thinks of memory sites in Washington, DC, one probably thinks first of the grand ones—the Washington Monument and Lincoln Memorial on the Mall and the Jefferson Memorial just south of it. They represent a phase of memory-site building that seemed to pass after the Jefferson Memorial was dedicated in 1943. Then, there was a gap in memory-site building; then, there was Maya Lin's strikingly different design for the Vietnam Veterans' Memorial. Among the striking dimensions was its openness to multiple interpretations. Some thought this openness, termed "**polyvalence**," would be the new trend.[3] There were imitations, but the Vietnam Veterans' Memorial also evoked a backlash. It led to additions to the memory site—in order to lead viewers to the acceptable interpretation. It also led to both narrative designs for newer memory sites and a return to the monumentality of old.

We see both the narrative design and the monumentality in the World War II Memorial. From the street, one walks down into the memorial. On the north, there is a grand colonnade, along which are engravings telling the story of the Atlantic campaign. On the south, there is a second grand colonnade, along which are engravings telling the story of the Pacific campaign. The colonnades consist of pillars, named in rather random order after the states and territories. Midway along each colonnade is a grand turret, in which rests an oversized eagle. At the point to the West where the colonnades rejoin is a pool, above which sits a field of stars, each star representing a certain number of American casualties in combat.

It is difficult to remain objective in describing the World War II Memorial, for it has proven to be a design that one either loves or hates. These reactions are partially inspired by the design elements. For example, some find the field of stars either difficult to interpret or impersonal, especially when compared to the names of real people on the nearby Vietnam Veterans' Memorial's black marble wall; some think the eagles are far too large for the space they are placed in, making them looked trapped or caged.[4] However, these diverse reactions are also inspired by how the memory site does or does not match the fantasy themes held by those reacting.

So, what fantasy theme does the World War II Memorial present? It tells of American heroism. As one walks through the Atlantic pavilion, one reads how U.S. troops liberated Europe. The involvement—and the losses—of our allies are not mentioned. As one walks through the Pacific pavilion, one reads how Japan attacked the United States without provocation and then how U.S. troops defeated the Japanese Empire. Curiously, our dropping of two atomic bombs is not mentioned.

Responses to the World War II Memorial do not fall simply into two categories, but there is a measure of truth to the observation that World War II veterans respond one way and those nurtured on anti-war sentiments in the 1960s and 1970s another. World War II veterans, ever decreasing in number, flock to the site. They delight in it. Why? Because the site's stories are in agreement with their socially constructed fantasy theme about the war. They, of course, do not create this fantasy theme on site. They come with it. Oftentimes, it has been forged through conversations in VFW halls. If one were present for these conversations, one would observe the chaining as the fantasy theme was being socially constructed. (Comments at the Memorial would undoubtedly sustain this theme.) Many baby boomers, however, find the memory site horribly flawed. Where are our allies? Yes, this is America's World War II Memorial, but are we so egotistical as to think we alone were the victors in Europe? Where are Hiroshima and Nagasaki? Why are we hiding from view how we ended the war but also brought horrible destruction to two Japanese cities and nuclear weaponry into warfare? These baby boomers, put simply, do not have the same fantasy theme as the veterans and, undoubtedly, others who lived through the World War II era. These critics may also have a fantasy theme that has emerged in their shared reactions to the George W. Bush Administration. They see the Bush Administration as pursuing wars without justification, using fighting terrorism as an excuse and using patriotism as cover. In these critics' views, the Bush Administration is using the World War II Memorial to promote the patriotism. The critics thus have constructed a fantasy theme about the Bush Administration and use that theme in reading the memorial in a negative manner.

The World War II Memorial also exhibits a way in which fantasy themes often do their rhetorical work. The memorial attracts a certain audience because it presents a story that corresponds with the fantasy theme this group has socially constructed. However, it then re-persuades the group that their fantasy theme is correct. The memorial both reflects a social construction and reinforces it. One can see this by listening in on how veterans reach to the place. (One can also discern this process by listening to the skeptical remarks the skeptics make. They note the omissions, and they note how George W. Bush put his name on the memorial, something no previous president ever did.)

The view that veterans hold is very real to them and very important to them. That others disagree should not diminish their contribution to the war or discredit the validity of their view. The term fantasy, then does a disservice to them by suggesting how un-real their view is. To them, it is both quite real and quite important. Thus, it is the case with most of these socially constructed themes: Although others may fault the views, they are both real and important to those who hold them. It is because of this realness and this importance that they can often function powerfully in the communication situations rhetoricians study. Those who find fault with the memorial also strongly hold their view of Bush and, perhaps, more broadly on government. They see, in the World War II Memorial, an example of how government (not just Bush) uses patriotism to justify military action when more substantive justifications are not available.

Strengths and Limitations

Persuasion is necessarily tied to how one's audience views the world. This critical approach recognizes how the view is socially constructed and how persuasion occurs when the rhetor tries to play off that view. The approach can highlight rhetorical success as well as rhetorical failure. There are undoubtedly attempts at persuasion, perhaps even somewhat successful ones, that ignore the audience's fantasy themes. This approach, then, does not explain all successes and all failures; rather, it can explain some very powerful successes—for example, why Malcolm X's rhetoric was as effective as it was for certain audiences; and it can explain some rhetorical disasters—for example, why, in 1968, Maryland Governor Spiro T. Agnew's address to black leaders during the April riots in Baltimore caused most to walk out.[5] The approach can also explain texts that both work and don't work. Nixon, at the height of anti-Vietnam War demonstrations, gave a speech at a conservative youth rally being held in the campus of the University of Tennessee. The speech provided him with an opportunity, like his 2:00 a.m. visit to the Mall, to speech to what he termed "the youngsters." It is possible that the conservative youth gathered there responded positively to his message—because their view of the world harmonized with Nixon's. However, more radical youth (who were not there) reacted negatively because their socially constructed view was significantly at odds with Nixon's—and they didn't like being referred to as "youngsters."

This critical approach, then, is quite explanatory, but it does explain only one, big picture dimension of a rhetorical moment. There are many, many elements in a text that this approach glosses over. In some instances, the harmony or disharmony between socially constructed themes may well be *the* factor that is crucial in arriving at an understanding of a text's persuasiveness. In these instances, this critical approach is quite valuable. But there are many texts that require approaches that embrace more of a text's dimensions.

As in other chapters, then, what we see here is an approach that is sometimes a good choice, but, in other instances, a limiting one. That we do find that the fantasy theme approach has considerable value should at least get one beyond its misleading name and to the point where one sees its applicability in a world where groups do indeed socially construct divergent realities.

Exemplars

Benoit, William L., Andrew A. Klyukovski, John P. McHale, J. P., and David Airne. "A Fantasy Theme Analysis of Political Cartoons on the Clinton-Lewinsky-Starr Affair." *Critical Studies in Media Communication* 18, no. 4 (December 2001): 377–94.

Bishop, Ronald. The World's Nicest Grown-Up: A Fantasy Theme Analysis of News Media Coverage of Fred Rogers. *Journal of Communication* 53, no. 1 (March 2003): 16–31.

Bormann, Ernest G. "A Fantasy Theme Analysis of Television Coverage of the Hostage Release and the Reagan Inaugural." *Quarterly Journal of Speech* 68, (May 1982): 133–45.

West, Mark, and Chris Carey. "(Re)Enacting Frontier Justice: The Bush Administration's Tactical Narration of the Old West Fantasy After September 11." *Quarterly Journal of Speech* 92, (November 2006): 379–412.

Suggested Applications

Speech Applications

- Campaigning as an independent in 1912, former President Theodore Roosevelt delivered a "New Nationalism" speech in Kansas. How might fantasy theme criticism illuminate it?

- In the early 1950s, Maine Senator Margaret Chase Smith spoke to her colleagues in the United States Senate and, rather quietly, condemned the anti-communist activities of Wisconsin Senator Joseph McCarthy. She clearly envisioned politics differently than McCarthy. What was her fantasy, one she hoped others shared?

Non-Speech Applications

- Consider the Indigo Girls song "Love of My Life." What shared fantasy theme do Amy and Emily evoke?

- Consider the almost-sacred Texas memory site at the Alamo in San Antonio. What shared fantasy theme or themes does the site play off of to evoke strong responses from Texas visitors?

Notes

1. Bormann, Ernest. "The Symbolic Convergence Theory of Communication: Applications and Implications for Teachers and Consultants." *Journal of Applied Communication Research* 10, no. 1 (1982): 50–61.

2. Hayden, Tom. *Port Huron Statement*. June 15, 1962. Political Manifesto, Students for a Democratic Society, Port Huron, MI.

3. Blair, Carole, Marsha S. Jeppeson, and Enrico Pucci, Jr. "Public Memorializing in Postmodernity: The Vietnam Veterans Memorial as Prototype." *Quarterly Journal of Speech* 77, no. 3 (1991): 263–88.

4. Balthrop, V. William, Carole Blair, and Neil Michel. "The Presence of the Present: Hijacking 'The Good War.'" *Western Journal of Communication* 74, no. 2 (2010): 170–207.

5. Sheckels, Theodore F. *Maryland Politics and Political Communication, 1950–2005*. Lanham, MD: Lexington Books, 2006.

Figure credit

Fig. 6: Source: https://www.loc.gov/resource/g3844p.cw0257000.

A northern Minnesota taconite mine, much like where Lois Jensen, the central figure in the book *A Civil Action* and the film *North Country*, experienced sexual harassment, leading to her landmark civil suit.

CHAPTER 7

Narrative Criticism

Communication has, since its inception as an academic discipline, borrowed insights from cognate fields. These are usually starting points from which theorists, regardless of their area, pursue a communication-specific course. Such is the case with narrative criticism. It has roots in anthropology and its study of folklore, and it is enriched by what literary studies have explored through the years. However, narrative criticism poses a question that neither anthropology nor literary studies do: What makes a narrative persuasive?

Roots in Anthropology

Anthropologists have long observed that humans are storytelling animals. That may well not be the defining trait (that might be symbol using), but stories seem to have been part of the human experience from close to the beginning. Stories were used to explain natural phenomena; stories were used to share history; stories were used to convey religious beliefs. At some point, our storytelling ancestors undoubtedly discovered that storytelling was also entertaining for both the teller and the told-to.

Anthropologists are quick to note that stories exist in a purer form in more primitive societies. By "purer," they don't mean better; rather, they mean more clearly serving some social need such as explaining nature, sharing history, and inspiring religious beliefs. As societies became less primitive, the stories were still there, but they became embellished by sophisticated additions designed to both teach and delight. An anthropologist would have to dig the core stories out, not just record them.

Rhetorical Twist

Rhetorical critics recognized these social functions of stories, but they also discerned that stories did much more. In the 1980s, President Ronald Reagan was fond of telling audiences the story of an America that was "a shiny city on a hill," and, in 1984, New York Governor Mario Cuomo countered by telling the story of the other city, the one Reagan does not see, in the keynote address Cuomo delivered at the Democratic National Convention. In the 1960s, when Dr. Martin Luther King, Jr., told us his dream, he was telling a hopeful story. It followed, in that very famous 1963 speech, a less satisfying one of being stuck with a "bad check." In the 1970s, President Richard Nixon told stories about North Vietnamese incursions into Cambodia and about his White House's involvement in Watergate. In the 1990s, President Bill Clinton told audiences about his story that began in "a place called Hope," and a decade later Barack Obama began telling audiences his personal story that offered all hope. Now, President Donald Trump is telling stories about how America will be great again, while his ardent opponents are telling stories about how the rich are getting richer in contemporary America.

Some of these stories sound like stories. One might say in response, "Did you hear that story Obama told?" But others are story-like structures implicit in prose that may not seem, on the surface, to be a story at all. One might say, in response to someone offering such prose, "So, what's your story?" One might, if skeptical, ask another, "So, what's his story?" Even a policy-focused address that offers four reasons (lined-up 1-2-3-4) for supporting a legislative initiative probably implies a narrative.

So, if there are explicit narratives and implicit narratives, then there are a lot of narratives. They are not just explaining why the leaves turn brown in autumn. They are advocating for health care, tax reform, social justice, gender equity. It is the recognition of how ubiquitous stories or narratives are that gave rise to what was referred to, back in the 1980s, as "the narrative paradigm." The theorist who inspired this paradigm was Walter Fisher.

Fisher's motivation to develop a narrative perspective or paradigm is important to understand. He believed that what he termed a "rational world paradigm," which perhaps has a place in certain arenas such as science and law, had intruded into realms where strict rationality was inappropriate. In these realms, people affirmed arguments based on the offering of what Fisher termed "good reasons," and these good reasons mixed matters that might be labeled logical with other compelling elements outside strict logic or strict rationality. People so affirmed arguments in the way that came to them naturally, whereas, within the "rational world paradigm," people would have to learn rules of logic to make or assess an argument. This, in Fisher's view, made argumentation under that paradigm less genuinely human. Fisher believed that these good reasons were best discerned within a narrative frame because people are, inherently, storytellers and, within that frame, offer and assess what they find persuasive.

Here is how Fisher explains that frame or paradigm:

> The presuppositions that structure the narrative paradigm are: (1) humans are essentially storytellers; (2) the paradigmatic mode of human decision-making and communication is "good reasons" which vary in form among communication situations, genres, and media; (3) the production and practice of good reasons is ruled by matters of history, biography, culture, and character; ... (4) rationality is determined by the nature of persons as narrative beings—their inherent awareness of narrative probability, what constitutes a coherent story, and their constant habit of testing narrative fidelity, whether the stories they experience ring true with the stories they know to be true in their lives. ...[1]

The terms Fisher uses will be explained shortly. Before moving from theory to praxis, one should grasp a fundamental point Fisher insists on. He is not simply saying we rely on narratives. Rather, he is saying we rely on good reasons in our decision making and that these good reasons, varying among genres and varying among cultures, are most easily discerned if we, in recognition that humans are inherently storytellers, consider arguments as if they were presented and thought of in narrative terms.

Three tasks then faced those who embraced this paradigm. First, they had to find the narrative. This is an easy task when it is explicit, not so easy when implicit. Second, they needed to explore the narrative to make sure they understood all its dimensions. Third, they needed to assess if and why a text, described in narrative terms, was persuasive. Put another way, they needed to assess if a text embodied good reasons.

Implicit Narratives

In his 1965 address to Congress demanding the passage of voting rights legislation, President Lyndon Johnson tells a story about teaching in a poor Hispanic school in Texas. It's easy to spot that as a narrative, but what's the larger narrative in his famous speech? There is no "once upon a time," but Johnson talks about the promise of equality in our nation's foundational documents, about the specific terms added to the Constitution after the Civil War, about how a century had passed with certain states finding increasingly ingenious means to ignore those terms and deny voting rights to African Americans, and about the weak legislative efforts to address problem thus far. That's a narrative.

In recent times, political figures are sharing more of their personal stories. So, it is easy to find moments when we get Barack Obama's story, Hillary Clinton's story, John McCain's story, and Marco Rubio's story. But let's go back to 1961, to President John F. Kennedy's famous inaugural. There are no personal stories in it, but there is nonetheless a story. The story is of a nation with new leadership that is waking up from the "happy days" of the 1950s to embrace international challenges. The story is of a nation and its people ready to conquer a "new frontier." More recently, House Minority Leader Nancy Pelosi delivered an eight-hour speech protesting a federal budget extension that did not address DACA. Pelosi offered colleagues the stories of dreamers, children of illegal immigrants most of whom had lived almost all their lives in this country. If one were to assemble all of what Pelosi shared into a single narrative, one would have a narrative ready to be analyzed and assessed.

Once an implicit narrative is identified, before moving forward, it is useful to think it through in narrative terms. For example, who the characters are in JFK's narrative. Well, the protagonists are a "new generation born in this century." So, does that mean those sixty-plus are not part of the story? And who is the narrator in LBJ's larger voting rights story? LBJ, right? Is he a reliable narrative when talking about the South, since, after all, he is a southerner? Is he a reliable narrator when talking about what the Congress had done on civil rights in 1957 and in 1964, since he played a role in both cases? And what kind of language does Pelosi use in telling the dreamers' stories? That they are called dreamers is itself a metaphor with multiple reverberations in a country that has embraced both the "American Dream" and the dream Dr. Martin Luther King, Jr., talked about in August 1963. These are narratological questions concerning plot, narrative perspective, and figurative language, and they should be posed of narratives, whether explicit or implicit.

Narratological Questions

Here is where literary studies can help the narrative critic along.

For convenience, let's put the possible probes into six categories: narration, characters, setting, plot, type of narrative, and language. The goal in asking these questions is making sure you, the critic, fully understand the narrative that is in front of you before you do your primary job, which is to assess its role in persuasion.

Narration

In the middle of the twentieth century, students of literature would learn that there are three kinds of narration: first person, third-person omniscient, and third-person limited. Well, Wayne C. Booth's landmark *The Rhetoric of Fiction* (1961) proved that tripartite untenable, and, since he wrote, literary critics have been much more interested in the question of the narrator's reliability. And there are many ways one can be unreliable: You may be consciously lying or you may be deceiving yourself, for example. And there are many reasons why one might be unreliable, ranging from insanity to a bad memory, to being too personally invested in how the story is evaluated. Narration is far more complex than choosing one of the three possibilities students of literature learned about in the 1950s.

Characters

Among the major characters, who are the protagonists and who are the antagonists? They are easy to identify in an explicit narrative but often veiled in an implicit one. If the identities are veiled, why? Is the rhetor deliberately trying to not name names? Are any minor characters not as minor in reality as the narrative suggests? For example, why does much pro-civil rights rhetoric authored by white politicians put African American leaders in minor roles until the mid-1960s? Racism? Probably not. The real answer might be that these civil rights leaders were perceived by the mainstream audience as dangerous radicals—probably communists. Best to keep them off to the side in narratives if you want to persuade that mainstream audience.

Setting

Setting is an important dimension of a narrative when one is writing. The writer has many choices to make. One can choose to depict a scene realistically or not, fully or not. One can choose to emphasize any one of a number of elements in the setting. For example, in discussing the opioid epidemic in this nation, one could offer a narrative that vividly depicts the victims. One could set their vivid story in urban Detroit, in suburban Philadelphia, or in rural West Virginia. The setting can alter what the narrative is thought to be about—whose sad story and whose dire problem is being presented.

Plot

Plot may seem to be the most straightforward of the narratological elements, but it is complicated considerably by the distinction between story and **diagesis** made by structuralist critics and many afterwards. Story is what happened, timed-out as it happened—no gaps, no speed-ups, no slow-downs; diagesis is the rendition given that story by the narrative in question. As already suggested, three diagetic elements have the potential to distort the story. First, there can be gaps. If not interrogated, they may seem unimportant, but they could make a difference. Without the gaps filled in, the story may not be complete. Second, there may be speed-ups (i.e., places where the narrative zooms past certain events, signaling that they are unimportant). Well, they may indeed be important. Third, there will undoubtedly be slow-downs (i.e., places where whoever has constructed the diagesis wants attention to be riveted). But is that attention justified?

It is important to note that there will always be a diagesis; thus, there will always be gaps, speed-ups, and slow-downs. In debating a bill to address America's growing infrastructure problem, liberals are likely either not to mention costs (a gap) or speed by them (speed up), whereas fiscal conservatives will slow down and dwell on them. When it comes to U.S. foreign relations with a strategic nation rife with human rights violations, liberals are likely to slow down and dwell; conservatives might skip or zoom. Within reason, these are diagetical differences that go with politics. You should be alert to them. More importantly, you should be alert to a degree of diagetic "massaging" that truly misleads someone who is not being a careful consumer of messages. Those in politics will, of course, give to a message their emphases, but there is a difference between emphasizing and deceiving.

Types of Narration

When a narrative is implicit, the audience typically creates one that exhibits what narratologists term "formal realism," in which events proceed as if they were really occurring. Explicit narratives can sometimes possess elements of other types. One may need to filter these elements out. For example, a narrative might have elements of speculative (or science) fiction, which projects a current trend into the future. One needs to filter out—or at least clearly identify—elements that are truly guesses. Or, a narrative might have elements of romance, which might enhance emotional responses. Again, one needs to note the excesses, either filtering them out or clearly labeling. The goal is to get to the core narrative without the conventions of particular types of popular writing getting in the way.

Language

Poetry heavily uses figurative language such as metaphors and symbols; it also typically uses aural devices such as assonance (heavily using a vowel sound such as "eee"), consonance (heavily using a consonant sound such as "t"), and rhyme. These language devices do not play as much of a role in narrative, but may appear. Declaring a war on poverty, as Lyndon Johnson did, was using a metaphor powerfully. Depicting the advances of terrorists with words heavy in what are termed "back vowels" (made in the back of the mouth) can associate the enemy with deep, ominous sounds.

The goal of analyzing a narrative as if one were in a literature class is to get the full narrative, in all its intricacies, before the critic. Although a major thrust of literary criticism, doing so is a preliminary step in rhetorical criticism. The step assumes that all narratives are crafted. Obviously, a published one is more crafted than narratives that one might find in speeches or in public memory sites, but consider two texts, Donald Trump's 2017 inaugural and the proposed Dwight D. Eisenhower Memorial. Trump tells the story of an America plagued with problems. Written primarily by Steve Bannon, the address climaxes as Trump tells his audience that the "carnage" stops now. Why so bleak a narrative? How, in constructing it, was Bannon selective in highlighting certain traits in 2017 America and ignoring others? Why the very evocative word "carnage"? The Eisenhower Memorial, in the planning stage for many years, will be a narrative memorial such as the one for FDR. But what in Eisenhower's long career will be stressed? An early design stressed his wholesome boyhood growing up in Kansas. Family members thought that stress was overdone, and they wanted his military career and his presidential career to be equally emphasized. Will one be stressed more than the other? And what about his stint as President of Columbia University? Should it be ignored? The designers—and family members and politicians—are making narratological decisions that will affect how future visitors read the memorial.

Narratological matters, then, are not unimportant, even in public documents and public places. But the core of narrative criticism is assessing if a narrative, explicit or implicit, is persuasive.

Narrative as Persuasive: Coherence

Walter Fisher—and those who have embraced his narrative approach—argue that, to be persuasive, a narrative, whether explicit or implicit, must exhibit **narrative coherence** (or probability) and **narrative fidelity**.

Narrative coherence means that the pieces of the narrative hold together. We understand how a story gets from point a to point b. There are no unexplained events, no loose ends. With an explicit narrative, this test seems to be an easy one: Either the story does or does not make sense. But, with implicit narratives, we sometimes enter realms that do not offer a simple story. Let's take tax reform. The narratives offered on all sides involve tax provisions, many of which are arcane; the narratives also play off predicted scenarios that are offered by those who understand the dynamics of the economy better than the mainstream audience member. Often, these scenarios make assumptions that those arguing do not explicitly offer. In a case such as this, it might be easy for one to think he or she understands how a specific proposal or story gets from a to b to c when he or she really does not. How does trickle-down precisely work?

So, before moving onward, make sure that what seems coherent is truly so. "That sounds good," voiced too quickly, can lead one to judge as warranting persuasion a narrative that ought to be called into question because it lacks the detail to make it truly coherent.

Narrative as Persuasive: Fidelity

Fisher's works on the narrative paradigm are sometimes misunderstood. He devotes a great deal of attention to discussing values, and some have wondered about that. Some have even suggested that it was no more than a quirk. What these mis-readers of Fisher do not get is that, to have fidelity and thus be persuasive, a narrative must be faithful to the listener on the level of plot, characters, and values.

Plot fidelity basically means that the listener believes that the events narrated could happen, that they are plausible. Whereas coherence deals with whether it is clear how a plot gets from a to b to c, fidelity deals with whether that movement is believable. In other words, a very clear progression (i.e., one that has coherence) could lack fidelity if listeners say "That just couldn't happen." Let's apply the principle to tax reform. Some narratives assume that tax breaks given to the wealthy will trickle down to others. But if one has lived through times when that just didn't happen—when the wealthy held on to money, not reinvested it, then one might doubt the plot fidelity of the argument.

Character fidelity basically means that the listener believes that people (or institutions) in a narrative exist and act as described. Let's consider the very controversial topic of sexual harassment in the military. Calls for a crack-down that would involve hearing charges outside the military justice system might be premised on a narrative that told the stories of abusive officers and boys-will-be-boys judges. But what if an audience member simply did not believe the officers ever conduct themselves in the manner described? Then, for that audience member, the narrative lacks characterological fidelity. People believe all sorts of things about political actors: Some believe that Donald Trump can do no right; others believe he can do no wrong. Stereotypes get in the way here, too.

Audience members may believe that all people of a certain sort act a certain way and have difficulty accepting a character who acts contrary to this stereotype.

It should already be clear that fidelity is, to some extent, in the eyes—or ears—of the audience members. This fact makes assessing whether a text is persuasive or not difficult. What may be persuasive for you may not be persuasive for me because we hold different standards of plot fidelity and character fidelity.

Value fidelity makes the issue still worse. Narratives imply values. In dealing with North Korea, President Trump has tried to be tough. The narratives explicitly and implicitly in his discourse exhibit strength. If strength is valued, then the narratives have value fidelity. But what if someone thinks strength is dangerously foolish when nuclear weapons are in the picture? Then, the narratives lack value fidelity. In the late 1990s, Hillary Clinton, then just first lady, led a U.S. delegation to a women's conference in Beijing. She delivered one of her most famous and effective speeches there, a speech that saluted human rights and linked women's right to them. Many cheered loudly: They agreed with the value Clinton had placed on human rights. But what if you think a global standard of human rights is inappropriate given the cultural differences that exist from place to place? Or what if you think foreign policy needs to be based on cold, hard facts and that mushy considerations, such as human rights, just get in the way? Then, Clinton's address lacked value fidelity. More recently, high school students (and sometimes younger ones) have marched against gun violence. The narrative they are offering values safety—in school and in general. But, what if one values the Second Amendment right to bear arms more? Then, the students' march lacks value fidelity, for, in one's hierarchy of values, an alternative value outweighs safety.

Fisher's approach, then, is not one that explains why a text containing a narrative or is transformable to a narrative is always persuasive or not. Rather, it is an approach that explains why a text is persuasive for some listeners or readers. Given that auditors and readers have not only different experiences of the world but different values, one cannot expect an approach to do more.

Method

The method a narrative critic uses should already be clear, but, before looking at a book/film combination through the lens of narrative criticism, let's review what the critic must do. First, identify the narrative, easy when it is explicit but involving some effort when the narrative is implicit. Second, fully describe that narrative, paying attention to key story elements and how they appear in narratives of various sorts. Here, the list of narration, characters, setting, plot, type of narrative, and language is useful as a heuristic. It helps the critic acquire a thorough understanding of the narrative under consideration.

Third, assess narrative coherence and narrative fidelity. When considering the latter, look at plot fidelity, characterological fidelity, and value fidelity. And don't neglect the last, for it is often the type of narrative fidelity that makes a difference between persuasion and the absence of persuasion.

The rhetorical critic should keep in mind that his or her focus is on persuasion. Narratives are being examined by this approach because the narrative frame is thought to be the best one for seeing the good reasons that sway an audience. The critic's goal is not to illuminate the narrative as narrative but, rather, to discern what in the narrative was persuasive.

Application: *Class Action* and *North Country*

Class Action is a piece of non-fiction chronicling the quest for justice by Lois Jensen, worker on the iron range in northern Minnesota. In the 1990s, the mines were a male-defined realm, but, beginning then, women were being hired. The first women to take the jobs, very good union jobs, were not especially welcome. Lois Jensen, one of them, was subjected to sexual harassment and sexual assault, and, initially, not even the other women working at the mining company were willing to support her.

Eventually, she cobbles together a class action suit. It was novel, the first time a class action suit was ever brought in federal court for sexual harassment. Against the odds and after several years, she eventually wins. Although the settlement she received was modest, her victory was symbolically very important. Clara Bingham and Laura Leedy Gansler told the story in *Class Action*, which proved to be a national best-seller.

Here are excerpts from Clara Bingham and Laura Leedy Gansler's *Class Action*. The first is part of the narrative they offer; the second is from the court decision they quote:

> Lois, Rubenstein, and her assistant, Jackie, moved from the crusher to the concentrator to the pellet plant quickly with Erickson and Raich huffing and puffing beyond them, trying to keep up. Ever since filing the complaint, Lois, at Rubenstein's suggestion, had been snapping clandestine photographs of the most sexually explicit graffiti. She also started keeping detailed notes—almost like a daily diary—in a green six-by-nine-inch spiral notebook that Rubenstein told her to label "work product," so that it would be protected under lawyer-client privilege. To Lois's great relief, most of the things she told Rubenstein about were still visible.
>
> First stop was the crusher. Raich walked into the building and pointed out the freshly painted walls. He pushed the elevator button and explained that the company had recently installed stainless-steel panels in order to prevent graffiti. But when the elevator doors opened, the word cunts stared the group in the face. It was scratched in ten-inch-tall letters on the stainless-steel interior elevator wall. Raich hurried to stand in front of the graffiti.

Clara Bingham and Laura Leedy Gansler, Selection from *Class Action: The Lankmark Case that Changed Sexual Harassment Law*, pp. 130-132, 384. Copyright © 2003 by Penguin Random House LLC.

As they walked through a tunnel leading to the Mexico building, the group found "I eat cuntz and lots of it" scrawled in large white letters along the black walls. On the wall of the tunnel between the crusher and the concentrator no one could miss a primitive sketch of a man sticking his finger up the anus of a bent-over woman. Raich's eyes lit on the drawing at the same time as Helen Rubenstein's; it was not very large, he said, and besides, he couldn't be expected to catch everything. They walked into the foreman's office in the concentrator and found a nudie calendar hanging from the file cabinet and a pin-up of a naked woman on the foreman's desk, pressed under a piece of Plexiglas. Erickson quickly whisked the group out of the room.

Outside the women's dry, the bulletin board still contained a photograph of the back side of a female fitness instructor who had her legs apart doing jumping jacks. Someone had drawn a large penis pushing between her open legs. After viewing the graffiti, Rubenstein turned to Jackie, who was busy scribbling notes, and said, "Be prepared, you may have to testify that you saw this stuff."

"But … I can't say these words out loud on the stand," said Jackie."

With each new discovery, Raich's fury increased. The pellet plant proved to be the only building on the tour with clean walls because the foreman there had actually followed Raich's orders, whereas the foremen in the crusher and the concentrator had defied him. Rubenstein had been warned about the content of the mine's graffiti, but she was not prepared for the arrogance of the mine's management. Even the threat of a $1 million fine had not scared them into cleaning up their act. The tour drove home the point to Rubenstein that the mine just didn't care. "Their attitude was, What is *she* going to do to *us?*" Helen recalled.

Two days after Rubenstein's tour, Pat Kosmach came to work on a Saturday morning. LeRoy Stish, the concentrator foreman, walked up to her in a fit of laughter. Kosmach knew Stish better than she would have liked. Stish had a big metal locker in his foreman's office in which he stored supplies. On the inside door of his locker he taped a large poster of a nude woman lying on her back, legs apart, spreading her labia with her fingers. Stish liked to make fun of Pat in front of the whole crew; he'd open his locker door and say "Don't look, girls!" When Pat first saw the poster she suggested that Stish take it home and pin it up on the wall of his living room so his wife and daughter could enjoy it as much as he dd. The poster remained in place after the filing of the state complaint. Stish told Pat that the company couldn't force him to take it down.

Pat therefore wasn't surprised, that Saturday in July, when Stish said that the guys were doing some retaliating of their own. He suggested that she take a look at the company bulletin board. Pat strolled down the hallway past the lunchroom and the women's dry. The company bulletin board was a locked glass case that housed shift schedules, crew lists, and job postings. But today, the bulletin board also contained a sign that read: "SEXUAL HARASSMENT IN THS AREA WILL NOT BE REPORTED[;] HOWEVER, IT WILL BE GRADED."

It should be obvious that the callous pattern and practice of sexual harassment engaged in by Eveleth Mines, and the mental anguish of the women was clear. The emotional harm, brought about by this record of human indecency, sought to destroy the human psyche as well as the human spirit of each plaintiff. The humiliation and degradation suffered by these women is irreparable. Although money damage cannot make these women whole or even begin to repair the injury done, it can serve to set a precedent that in the environment of the working place such hostility will not be tolerated.

Narratological Matters

The book's acclaim led to a motion picture contract and the film *North Country* (2005). As is often the case, the movie and the book are different at points. Most strikingly, the duration of the court case is shortened and a dramatic, climactic courtroom scene is added. It is rather clearly a scene that could not possibly occur in a courtroom given the rules that govern such spaces. Despite these and other differences, the movie captures the spirit of the Bingham and Gansler book.

The book was co-authored by a lawyer and a journalist, both very sympathetic toward Jensen's case; the movie has a few voiceovers. So, rather clearly, we are getting the narrative largely from the perspective of the victim. Does this mean that we are getting a biased account? Does it mean that the perspective of the company—or the men at the mine—is not being presented as they would like it to be? Or fairly? A similar question might be asked about characters. Is the portrayal of Lois and the women who eventually support her overly sympathetic? Is the portrayal of the various men who victimize Lois overly unsympathetic?

Some critique the book and the film, especially the film, for how quickly characters change their attitude. Lois's father thinks his daughter is a slut because she had a child out of wedlock and could not even name the father; then, he rises to her defense at a union meeting. Lois's high school boyfriend lies in court to discredit her; then, he melodramatically changes his testimony and confirms her story of rape. There are other instances of quick changes. These suggest that perhaps the initial negative presentation of conditions at the mine may also have been a bit overdrawn.

The differences between book and movie alert us to diegetical elements—gaps, hurry-ups, slow-downs. Of the three, the hurry-ups may have the most effect. We do not see how long Lois endures negative treatment in the film. This may detract from sympathy for her: She seems to be more hazed as a new employee than victimized by sustained sexual harassment and assault. We also do not see how long the legal proceedings take. Again, the hurry-up (in the film) may detract from sympathy because we do not realize that this class action suit represents years of Lois's life marked by many trips from Duluth down to Minneapolis and St. Paul and many hearings and much tension, as well as many setbacks.

In the book, but especially in the film, the setting is quite realistic, fitting for texts that certainly exhibit formal realism. The realism, in this case, reinforces that this story, presumably in all its aspects, is a true one. Its language is spare. In reading the book, one can detect the objective style of the journalist and the precise style of the lawyer. The tone of the film is more melodramatic—after all, it is a feature film, but it retains much of the objective, precise style.

Narrative Coherence

The matter of narrative coherence really ought to be moot: This is a true story; a did lead to b and to c. If narrative coherence is a problem, then it is so because of the time constraints a feature filmmaker operates under. When events and character development have to be compressed to fit a film's ninety-some minutes, some viewers might find elements difficult to believe. But, since they did indeed occur, the doubt is probably moot.

Coherence is also helped along by the fact that the book's authors are a lawyer and a journalist. The presence of legal expertise suggests that the legal dimensions of the narrative are probably right; the presumed presence of journalistic objectivity suggests that the facts have probably been checked out with some care.

Narrative Fidelity

The matter of narrative fidelity is far more complex. One might recall that these events in northern Minnesota roughly coincide with the confirmation hearings for Clarence Thomas as an associate justice of the Supreme Court. In a postscript to those hearings, Anita Hill (once his administrative assistant) accused Thomas of sexual harassment and, then, Thomas vehemently defended himself, calling a second set of hearings "a high-tech lynching for uppity blacks." Interestingly, at the time the matter surfaced, males overwhelmingly believed Thomas, while females overwhelmingly believed Hill.[2] Could a similar split occur among readers/viewers of Lois Jensen's story? Might males simply not believe Lois's account of events as well as Lois's characterization of the men involved?

It would seem, at first blush, difficult to reject the values inherent in the book and film. They call for decent, equal treatment in the workplace and for justice in the courtroom. It would seem to be difficult to reject these values. However, not impossible. Lois did threaten both a male-defined workspace and men's jobs (necessary to support wives and children). Lois also threatened what seems to be well-defined (and long-held) gender norms in her community. Might someone find another set of values implicit in the men's position to set against those embodied by Lois? What if hiring women such as Lois reduced productivity at the mine? What if the hiring resulted in men not being hired and their families suffering?

When published and when filmed, *Class Action* and *North Country* evoked cheers, but these may have arisen from the same quarter that believed Anita Hill in 1991, ran for Congress in 1992, and made that political year the "Year of the Woman." But perhaps there is another quarter who find the artifacts' story exaggerated, its characters distorted, and its values out of sync with alternative values rooted either in sound business practices or the way communities—and the families in them—have functioned for many, many decades.

The narrative perspective, then, does not prove that these two artifacts were persuasive. Rather, it shows how and why they were persuasive with certain audiences. The perspective also alerts us to the possibility that, with other audiences, the artifacts may have failed to connect. Personally, I hope the narratives in the book and film did persuade, but, as a narrative critic who, first, tries to discern elements of narratology and, second, assess matters of coherence and fidelity, I must grant that the narratives may not be effective with some readers/viewers for reasons that I can surmise.

Strengths and Weaknesses

The narrative approach and the dramatistic one outlined in the previous chapter are similar insofar as they are premised on persuasion being either implicitly narrative or implicitly dramatic. In both cases, many texts clearly are, and, for those texts, the approaches reveal interesting and important dimensions of persuasion.

The possible weakness of the two approaches may be apparent when a text that seems non-narrative is read as narrative. Let me briefly consider two Washington, DC texts. Both are neither speeches nor treatises, but statues. (Rhetorical criticism is increasingly considering such memory sites, so turning to these texts is very much in line with what rhetorical critics now do.) The first has, arguably, enough information for an implicit narrative to be developed and the narrative approach used; the second lacks it.

The first is the rather difficult-to-find Garfield Memorial statue.[3] It is located in a small traffic circle at the intersection of Maryland Avenue and First Street NW at the southwest corner of the U.S. Capitol grounds. It is a modest memorial. Atop is a lifelike depiction of the assassinated U.S. president. Clinging to the pedestal are three allegorical figures. Based on their attire, one can link them with Garfield's three careers as educator, soldier, and statesman. The lifelike statue is depicted reading a speech. So, one can argue that the modest statue tells Garfield's story: an educator who fought (and led troops) in the Civil War and then became a legislator (served in the House, was elected to the Senate) noted for his oratory. An accurate story, although one lacking any references to his assassination and very short (six months, three of which were bed-ridden) presidency.

The statue is on the House of Representatives side of the Capitol grounds, and it faces west, more or less toward the White House. So, one could read the text as suggesting his movement from service in the House to service as president, but that seems to be pushing the visual evidence a bit. But, even without that last piece, we have a story that would seem to persuade one of Garfield's noble service in three very different realms—education, military, government. We do not have much specific information, so it is difficult to be highly persuaded. Curiously, we do not have the fact that he was shot and then died while president, so we are not, by this text, asked to honor him as martyr. What perhaps makes the statue rhetorically effective in honoring Garfield is the narrative's stress (although vague) on achievement in not one, not two, but three different arenas.

The second statue is Andrew Jackson's. It is in the middle of Lafayette Park, just north of the White House. It depicts him in military garb on horseback. The horse has reared on its two hind legs. On the pedestal are Jackson's name and a toast he delivered to honor Thomas Jefferson in 1830: "Our federal union must be preserved." He delivered it on Jefferson's birthday at a time when talk of nullification of federal law by states (South Carolina, to be specific) was threatening the Union. But, note, it was thirty years before the outbreak of the Civil War. A bit later, four Spanish canons were placed at the statue's four corners.

What narrative can one create from this text? The inscription tempts one to develop a story that has something to do with preserving the Union; the military attire tempts one to develop a story that has something to do with the War of 1812, which is the one Jackson fought in; and the four canons seem to be nothing more than a distraction. Those who have attempted to create a narrative have ignored all these elements and focused on another—that the horse has only its two rear legs on the ground. That fact, evidently important in the history of statue-making, has been read in numerous ways, all of which seem to be no more than guesses.

The Jackson statue is striking. It is a well-done piece of memorial art. However, forcing a narrative on it seems to be just that—forcing. A critic would probably be better off finding a lens other than narrative theory to discern the rhetoric of the Jackson statue. The narrative approach helps one understand what the Garfield statue says about the man and why it persuades one of his nobility. The narrative approach seems not to help with the Jackson statue.

The example should suggest that narrative criticism might be pushed too far when applied to texts not overtly narrative. Robert C. Rowland suggests as much in two critiques of Fisher's approach in the journal *Communication Monographs*.[4] Rowland felt that narrative was being defined so broadly by Fisher to be almost useless as a critical concept. The approach drew other critiques. Bruce Gronbeck thought Fisher was turning an enthymimetic form (i.e., one mixing arguments and stories) into a purely mimetic one and, thus, displacing arguments and the standards used to assess them.[5] Barbara Warnick tended to agree, finding Fisher's dismissal of the "rational world paradigm" as excessive. Fisher was clearly onto something in identifying the importance of narrative in persuasion.[6] However, the published critiques suggest that he first hit a nerve in indicting the "rational world paradigm," and second may have pushed theory and method too far.

Exemplars

Deming, Caren J. "*Hill Street Blues* as Narrative." *Critical Studies in Mass Communication* 2, no. 1 (1985): 1–22.

Garner, Ana, Helen M. Sterk, and Shawn Adams. "Narrative Analysis of Sexual Etiquette in Teenage Magazines." *Journal of Communication* 48, no. 4 (1998): 59–78.

Osborn, Michael, and John Bakke. "The Melodramas of Memphis: Contending Narratives During the Sanitation Strike of 1968." *Southern Communication Journal* 63, no. 3 (1998): 220–34.

Salvador, Michael. "The Rhetorical Genesis of Ralph Nader: A Functional Exploration of Narrative and Argument in Public Discourse." *Southern Communication Journal* 59 (1994): 227–39.

Suggested Applications

Speech Applications

- Consider President Franklin D. Roosevelt's famous speech declaring that a state of war exists between the United States and Japan. What narrative does FDR offer? How does it work in persuading Congress and the people to go to war?

- Consider Barack Obama's keynote address at the 2004 Democratic National Convention. How does it use narrative?

Non-Speech Applications

- The Franklin D. Roosevelt Memorial in Washington, DC is organized along narrative lines. Analyze the narrative and assess its effectiveness.

- Subaru has long run a commercial in which a couple turns keys to their Forrester over to their daughter. As the father readies the car, he pulls out items that remind him of various points in the daughter's—and the Forrester's—life. Analyze this narrative and how it is used to sell an automobile.

Notes

1. Fisher, Walter. "Narrative as Human Communication Paradigm: The Case of Public Moral Argument." *Communication Monographs* 51, no. 1 (1984): 1–22.

2. Thomas, Dan, Craig McCoy, and Allan McBride. "Deconstructing the Political Spectacle: Sex, Race, and Subjectivity in Public Response to the Clarence Thomas/Anita Hill 'Sexual Harassment' Hearing." *American Journal of Political Science* 37 (1993): 699–721.

3. Sheckels, Theodore F. "'Oft' Remembered, Oft' Forgotten: Remembering James Garfield." In *Haunting Public Memories, Rhetoric, and the U.S. National Mall.* Lanham, MD: Lexington Books, 2018: 207–217.

4. Rowland, Robert C. "Narrative: Mode of Discourse or Paradigm." *Communication Monographs* 54, no. 3 (1987): 265–82. and Rowland, Robert C. "On Using the Narrative Paradigm: Three Case Studies." *Communication Monographs* 56, no. 1 (1989): 41–54.

5. Gronbeck, Bruce. "Storytelling as a Mode of Moral Argument: A Response to Professor Fisher." Conference Proceedings, NCA/AFA Alta Conference on Argumentation, 1983. 463–69.

6. Warnick, Barbara A. "The Narrative Paradigm: Another Story." *Quarterly Journal of Speech* 73, no. 2 (1987): 172–82.

Figure credit

Fig. 7: Copyright © Bjoertvedt (CC BY-SA 3.0) at https://commons.wikimedia.org/wiki/File:Mountain_Iron_taconite_mine_IMG_1481_Minnitac.JPG.

Coober Pedy, South Australia, the largely underground opal-mining town where the performers in *The Adventures of Priscilla, Queen of the Desert*, received their most hostile audience response.

CHAPTER 8

Genre Criticism

The concept of genre is probably familiar to most through their study of literature. In literature courses, students learn the basic division of the field into poetry, prose, and drama, but they soon learn that each of these areas of artistic endeavor can be further subdivided. Thus, when it comes to poetry, there are sonnets, odes, elegies, epics, etc. All these are genres in the sense that they are a recognizable type of expression with recurring characteristics. To meet this definition, a would-be genre does not have to be so tightly defined that all examples fit the bill absolutely perfectly. Far from that: A genre can admit a fair amount of variety, especially since literary artists like to play with the genre they are working in. They will, for example, write a tragedy, but not focus on a noble character whom the whole nation knows but rather on a common man. (That playing gave us Arthur Miller's classic, *Death of a Salesman*.)

Campbell and Jamieson

Some of the most fruitful work on genre in the communication discipline has been done by Karlyn Kohrs Campbell and Kathleen Hall Jamieson.[1] They have theorized genre—perhaps saving it from other critics who thought it mechanical or simple. In an important journal article in 1980, they outline their assumptions, shared with other critics, about genre criticism based on what others had written:

Despite their variety, there are certain noteworthy constants: 1) Classification is justified only by the critical illumination it produce[s], not by the neatness of a classificatory schema; 2) Generic criticism is taken as a means toward systematic, close textual analysis; 3) A genre is a complex, an amalgam, a constellation of substantive, situational, and stylistic elements; 4) Generic analysis reveals both the conventions and affinities that a work shares with others; it uncovers the unique elements in the rhetorical act, the particular means by which a genre is individuated in a given case.[2]

They made it clear that genre is complex and useful as a critical lens only if it illuminates texts. They also draw attention to how genre criticism is designed to reveal how a text both does and does not fit into a given genre.

They have also, through careful empirical work, defined a large number of genres used in the political realm. In 1990, they authored *Deeds Done in Words*.[3] In preparation for this important book, they examined all the presidential oratory that might fit into a number of categories or genres: inaugural, state of the union, apologia, war message, veto message, others. For each category, they derived from the extant body of presidential oratory a definition of what the genre is. For some genres, such as the inaugural, they could come up with a fairly tight definition, for incoming presidents have been doing much the same things in the address ever since George Washington delivered the very first. The same would be true for the presidential farewell offered by many outgoing chief executives, with Washington perhaps getting even more credit for establishing that genre, too. For other genres, such as the state of the union, the definition is more fluid. One reason is that that particular genre has changed over time—from written to spoken, from spoken to Congress to spoken on television, to the American public, from delivered by itself to accompanied by a brief response by the opposition party. Another reason for genre variability is that, sometimes, there seem to be optional strategies available, not a single path. There are, for example, many strategies that a president might use to "apologize" (i.e., explain something that has or seems to have gone awry). That some genres are tight and others are loose is not a problem for the critic; rather, the variability means that the critic must be clear in establishing his or her starting point. Do we expect the president to be doing thus and so, or do we know what the menu is and wait to see which items will be served up?

Noting that some genres are tight and some are loose is important. So is the principle that Campbell and Jamieson establish of basing genre, not in either guesses or in some idealized notion of what a type of speech might be, but in the large body of extant work that constitute the genre. What they did with presidential genres should be what any genre critic does with any genre. Also crucial is how the definitions, once posited, are used. They are not checklists. A critic should not be listening to Donald Trump speaking in January 2017 ready to tick off the things he does and then point out the things he does not do in his inaugural. Rather, the critic should use the genre definition as a guide to discussing how a rhetor uses a genre. So, Trump tries to unite the nation, which is a crucial characteristic of the genre. But how does he try to do so? FDR unites the nation as people without fear; Reagan as heroes. On what basis does Trump try to pull the nation together after a very divisive election? Trump does not seem to express his awareness of the limits on his power, another inaugural trait. He doesn't mention the Congress, the Constitution, the people, or even time as limiting factors. Why? Does he not know these limits exist? Is he trying to project strength without bounds on the assumption that the people want this kind of leader? Is he approaching the presidency on the assumption that the office is much like that of a corporate CEO who can simply say "do it"? Trump's style is not especially grand, and inaugurals, as a genre, are typically delivered in a manner that one would describe as eloquent, even ornate. Why did Trump (or his speechwriter) choose a more straightforward style?

Other Genres

Campbell and Jamieson updated their 1990 work when they reissued *Deeds Done in Words* in 2007 under a different title.[4] It introduced emerging presidential genres, such as the signing statement in which the president expresses how he interprets the law he is signing. Along the way, others have proffered definitions of other political genres, such as the convention keynote or the defeated candidate's concession speech.[5] Still others have broadened their view and considered a debate on the floor of Congress as a genre or the proceedings of a Congressional committee as a genre. As with single speeches, the critic's goal is to note how a debate or a hearing matches up with expectations and, very importantly, how it departs. Some of the most interesting moments in the Senate are what we loosely term "filibusters." Why are they so interesting? Because they violate the norms of the debate genre in order to make a point loudly and clearly. The House of Representatives does not, by the way, permit filibusters. However, recently, Democrats, led by Georgia Congressman John Lewis, staged a sit-in on the House floor, demanding that the Speaker bring to the floor a vote on gun control legislation. The action violated the norms for the genre of a floor debate, and that violation made the sit-in rhetorically interesting.

Among the genres that Campbell and Jamieson consider are *apologia* and *elegy*. There are indeed times the president must explain things that have gone wrong, and there are indeed times when he or she must lead the nation in mourning. However, these genres extend well beyond the presidency: many mourn, many must explain or even say "I'm sorry."

The latter genre, the *apologia*, has a long history. And it also appears in arenas other than politics. For example, most organizations experience moments when things go wrong and someone needs to explain. The organization might be at fault (e.g., the

Exxon-Valdez oil spill in Prince William Sound off Alaska in 1989); the organization might not (e.g., the tampered-with Tylenol bottles in Chicago in 1982). Either way, the organization will often offer an *apologia*. I mention these organizational examples because, for the genre *apologia*, there is interesting work being done by communication scholars who see themselves as organizational communication specialists, not rhetorical critics. And, dealing with the *apologia*, there has also been a group of scholars whose work is difficult to pigeon-hole. Back in the 1970s, Ware and Linkugel outlined strategies a rhetor (or organization) might use to apologize.[6] A longer list is offered by Benoit in *Accounts, Excuses, and Apologies* (1995).[7] There, Benoit surveys a large body of image restoration literature that extends far beyond the work of rhetorical critics. Several have used Benoit's list of strategies—or others—in case studies. For example, *Repairing the Athlete's Image: Studies in Sports Image Restoration*, edited by Blaney, Lippert, and Smith, considers *apologia* in sports, looking at how golfer Tiger Woods, NBA star Gilbert Arenas, and many others have explained what had gone wrong.[8]

The work on genre considered thus far has dealt with speeches and, in organizational contexts, oral performances, such as news conferences, and written performances, such as press releases. Genre, however, goes beyond the spoken and the written. Many visual products fall into genre categories. Consider television entertainment. Through the years, we have seen westerns, doctor shows, lawyer shows, crime dramas, etc. And television news has genres too, such as the "meet the press" format that began back in the 1950s with the original *Meet the Press*. Consider motion pictures. We have horror films, sci-fi films, westerns, *film noir*, and others. Some of these visual genres are tight, such as the western; some are loose, such as sci-fi, which seems to have several variations. And, in many instances, the genre has been well-enough understood that serious departures and comic departures have been possible and recognized as just that, departures from a generic norm. The television series *Bonanza* and the Mel Brooks movie *Blazing Saddles* would not have struck viewers as they did without the norms of the western being so widely known that they would see *Bonanza* as an interesting dramatic departure featuring the stories of a widower and his three sons and *Blazing Saddles* as a hilarious parody of the genre.

There are even generic norms when it comes to public places. If you've been in enough museums, you know how they operate—enough to know that the Holocaust Museum in Washington, DC departs from the norm insofar as it compels—not suggests—a path through the experience. If you have walked around in the nation's capital, you've probably encountered enough equestrian statues to come up with a definition of that form of memorial. The same would be true if you visited structures such as the Washington, Lincoln, and Jefferson memorials. They are all big, they are all in a style termed "stripped classicism" (i.e., using forms from classical antiquity without paying much attention to how they were precisely used long ago), they all celebrate an individual, and they all contextualize that individual's story within the story of the nation. Then, along came Maya Lin's very different design for the Vietnam Veterans' Memorial. It was not especially large and was dug into the earth, making it less imposing. It was not stripped classicism, the long-preferred style, because its grandness suggested importance. It celebrates the many who died, by name. And, at least in its original form, it left all matters of interpretation, including what the war meant to the nation, ambiguous so that those encountering the memorial could think it through. The Vietnam Veterans' Memorial, then, represented a major break from genre norms, and a rhetorical critic should explain both how and why it departed.

The Goals of Genre Criticism

Genre criticism is sometimes criticized as mechanical. Why? Because some do little more than use a definition of a genre as a checklist. Jimmy Carter's 1977 inaugural? There are—let's say—seven traits an inaugural should have. Carter does five, but not two. End of analysis. The problem, of course, is that there really wasn't much analysis. How did Carter meet the norms he met? How and why did he depart?

Carter's address was, arguably, not in the "high style" of most such speeches, such as John F. Kennedy's very famous one in 1961. Why? Well, despite being a highly trained nuclear engineer, Carter portrayed himself as a Georgia peanut farmer. Despite being "James Earl," he introduced himself as "Jimmy." He even—shocking at that time—appeared at public events wearing blue jeans! The less-formal-than-usual inaugural was, then, part of a pattern, part of a common man trope that Carter had used throughout his rather long march to the White House. Now, the absence of high style may have weakened the speech—and that's worth noting. However, much analysis is absent unless one asks why he proceeded as he proceeded.

Let me continue with Jimmy Carter for just a minute. The inaugural, as a day, might be considered as a genre. There are certain events that have come to be expected. For example, the outgoing and incoming president ride together and alone from the White House (where they and spouses had breakfasted) to the Capitol. After the ceremony, the outgoing president is whisked away—these days, by Marine One and Air Force One—while the incoming president lunches with Congressional leaders and then travels back up Pennsylvania Avenue where he or she reviews the inaugural parade. Jimmy Carter broke from this day-long genre as well. He stopped his limousine near the intersection of Second Street and Pennsylvania Avenue NW, got out, and proceeded to walk (with spouse Rosalyn) to the White House, shaking hands along the limousine/parade route. Why did he depart from the norm? Same reason as why he departed from high style in the address: to show that he was "Jimmy," in touch—literally—with the common man.

As the Carter story suggests, departures from the generic norm are what make genre criticism both non-mechanical and fascinating. In fact, rhetorical critic (primarily of literary texts) John Schilb has devoted a book-length study, *Rhetorical Refusals* (2007), to studying texts that depart—and why.[9] The rhetorical critic, however, needs to remember that how a text conforms can also be fascinating—not the fact that the text conforms, but how it conforms. In the late 1990s, President Bill Clinton offers a number of *apologia* for his sexual misconduct with White House intern Monica Lewinsky. In the last, at a prayer breakfast, he earnestly confesses his sins. Prior to that he uses a variety of strategies. One can just go text by text and list the strategies Clinton uses, or one can step back from them and ask why is he mixing things up as he does. The latter critical strategy points to a pattern: that, while gradually admitting fault, he unrelentingly both counter-attacks and asks that all (politicians and public) move on to important matters of governance. What then does one make of a strategy that seems a tad contradictory insofar as Clinton sounds very partisanly political in attacking special prosecutor Ken Starr while rather non-partisanly political in asking all to join him in addressing the nation's issues? One theory would concentrate on the matter of focus. Where does Clinton want the focus to be? On his unprincipled accusers and on the nation's business. More important, where does he not want the focus to be? On himself. So, in asking how Clinton engaged in *apologia*, we get beyond listing what he did and get at what may have been a concerted strategy to survive. Some might join him and shift attention to accusers; others might join him and shift attention to the nation's business. The number then paying attention primarily to Clinton's behavior thereby shrinks. It is important to see how genres are used for purposes as crucial as political survival.

Method

Some genre critics engage in the task of defining a genre. In doing so, they need to proceed much as Campbell and Jamieson did in *Deeds Done in Words*: gather many, many examples of the supposed genres and identify what the common traits are. This kind of work, however, usually precedes where the rhetorical critic enters the picture. He or she tends to use definitions of genres that have already been developed by others.

Not all these others will proceed 1-2-3-4 through a set of genre characteristics. One reason is that they do not want to initiate critical practice that follows a checklist. But, a rhetorical critic using a genre lens does need such a list. So, if the literature establishing a genre does not offer a clear sense of a genre's traits, then the critic must create one. In doing so, the critic needs to be careful not to turn a characteristic common in a genre into one that must be present, and the critic needs to be careful not to present a trait that should be defined with some variability into a more narrowly stated one.

With a list of traits before him or her, the critic needs to consider how the text under consideration matches up against the traits on the list. The critic should not use the list as a checklist. Rather, the critic should ask how the text illustrates a trait if it does or how and why a text departs from the generic norm if it does. Criticism that says, quickly, that, yes, a text is a member of a genre is boring. What is interesting in generic criticism is how a text embodies a trait and how and why a text goes in a different direction. In the latter case, the critic's goal is not just to elaborate on the departure. Rather, the task is, based on the assumption the rhetor knows what he or she is up to, to figure out what the rhetor's game is.

Application: *The Adventures of Priscilla, Queen of the Desert*

In 1997, when Stephan Elliott's Australian film *The Adventures of Priscilla, Queen of the Desert* debuted, it was hailed as outrageous, more so than offensive. In Australia, it is said that audience knew the three major performers—Terrence Stamp, Guy Pearce, and Hugo Weaving—were heterosexual, and, thus, the Aussie audience did not react in a homophobic manner to the movie. However, there was much in the film that could have provoked ugly feelings in an Australia not at that time known for tolerance, for the three main characters are two gay transvestites and one transgendered woman (once Ralph, now Bernadette). They are all nightclub performers; wearing outrageous female costumes, they dance and lip-sync popular tunes, including, in the finale, Abba's "Mama Mia."

The film was also popular in the United States, so much so that Back Row Productions transformed it into a musical that played worldwide, including in Sydney, London's West End, and New York City's Broadway Palace Theatre for eleven months. The relatively brief run was probably due to a problem with the show and a problem with the audience. What was added to the film as it went to the musical theatre stage not only did not fit especially well but arguably detracted from the film's serious point (for it does have one). The audience, on the other hand, appreciated the show's campiness, but was not sure what to make of it. It was often described as bizarre. Even LGBT audiences were uneasy about the play, for, unlike *Rent*, which depicted gay and lesbian New Yorkers as ordinary people, *Priscilla* played-up stereotypes the same way many gay-lesbian parades did.

A useful critical lens to apply to the film is genre theory. Earlier, I listed a number of well-known film genres, but that list was only partial. A missing genre with many examples is something movie-makers and film students refer to as the "road movie." If you Google the term, you'll find many lists of examples, including some that offer what are supposedly the top twenty-five or the top one hundred. *Priscilla* is high on these lists.

I've introduced the central characters. Now, the plot. One day, one of the performers, Anthony/Mitzi gets a telephone call from his wife (yes, wife) in Alice Springs in the hot, dry center of the country. She is managing a casino night club there, and the resort needs an act to fill the seats and the coffers. She asks her husband to come and help. He recruits two fellow performers, the brash Adam/Felicia and the older Ralph/Bernadette. Adam buys a bus, he christens it "Priscilla, Queen of the Desert," and they go off on the long road trip from Sydney (on the nation's east cost) to Alice Springs. They do reach "Alice," and they do perform, but the real plot unfolds as they head westward on the road.

A road movie is a rather loose genre, but one can point to a number of traits that might be used in analyzing a film such as *Pricilla*. First, it features a relatively small number of characters—two or three, more often two males. Second, they go on the road—usually prompted by some problem. Third, along the way, there are episodic adventures. Fourth, through them, they learn a great deal—usually about themselves. Fifth, by the end of the road, they have changed or matured and are thus ready to return home.

So, how does *Priscilla* fare when walked past these traits?

First, there are three characters, although for the last bit of the trip, they are joined by a lonely older man named Bob. The cast is, however, far removed from the motorcycling male duo we have in *Easy Rider* (1967) or the convertible-riding female duo in *Thelma and Louise* (1991). Rather clearly, the film-makers are twisting the formula by giving us a gay transvestite, a gay transvestite who was once—we presume—bisexual, a transgendered woman, and then heterosexual Bob. Why the twist? Arguably, to get us well out of comfortable sexual orientation categories so that we recognize that there are very diverse others trying to make their way through our shared community.

Second, they go on the long road. Adam/Mitzi's wife's call is a motivating factor, but there are hints that all is not all that well in Sydney. Crowds are not responding to the act as well as they once did, perhaps because the act has become stale. Bernadette is in mourning because her presumably bisexual husband—a man nick-nicknamed "Trumpet"—has suddenly died.

Third, there are episodes, and these are important. Stop one is Broken Hill, a country town in western New South Wales. They are not welcomed, but, when Bernadette drinks a hefty local woman under the table in the pub, she wins applause. Thinking they made friends, the three awaken the next morning to find anti-gay graffiti spray-painted on Priscilla. Stop two is somewhere outside Port Augusta in South Australia. On an unpaved shortcut, their bus breaks down. After being shunned by some who pass by, they eventually are helped by auto mechanic Bob. When he finds out they are female impersonators, he excitedly invites them to perform at the local pub. Their performance evokes ugly grumbles, not applause, and the day is saved (for them) only when Bob's mail-order wife performs her rather obscene striptease there.

Bob stops her mid-show, she gets angry and leaves him, and Bob decides to go along to Alice Springs with the trio in case Priscilla breaks down again. Their next stop is an aboriginal encampment, where they perform to accepting cheers. Then, the largely underground mining town of Coober Pedy in northern South Australia. There, Adam/Mitzi is almost beaten to a pulp because, high on drugs, she visits an all-male beer-swilling party out at the old drive-in and flirts with the men. After Coober Pedy, Priscilla is back on paved roads, and it's on to the northern territory and Alice.

The crew is welcomed in Alice Springs, and their show receives polite applause, but, en route, we see the hostility toward the gay (and, by extension, LGBT) community steadily increase. The lesson we then learn about Australia is how much intolerance there is once one leaves the relatively safe enclaves of the major cities—except on the part of the aboriginals, also victims of prejudice. The movie is comic, but the Australian audience does not get a very pretty picture of itself.

So, fourth, the characters learn about their country (and, although not much is made of it, their common ground with another oppressed group, the aboriginals). However, the characters also learn a great deal about themselves. Anthony/Mitzi comes to terms with his past, embodied by his wife and his young son (yes, he has a son, too); Ralph/Bernadette decides that love and companionship may trump all and decides to stay with Bob in Alice Springs. Adam/Felicia learns that he's both juvenile and a jerk. Oddly, playing with Adam/Mitzi's young son helps Adam/Felicia begin to grow up.

Here's an excerpt from late in the film. In it, Anthony/Mitzi talks with his son:

ADAM:	So, what's it like to finally have a father?
BEN:	It's okay.
ADAM:	Sorry about last night. I don't always dress up in women's clothes. I mean don't get the wrong idea. I do lots of different stuff—you know, like Elvis and Gary Glitter and. …
BEN:	Abba? I'm not supposed to know about the Abba show, but I'd really like to see it. Would you do the Abba show for me?
ADAM:	Sure. You know what I am, don't you?
BEN:	Mum says you're the best in the business.
ADAM:	Well, your mum was always prone to exaggerate.
BEN:	Will you have a boyfriend when we get back to Sydney?
ADAM:	Maybe. Come on!
BEN:	Where are we going?
ADAM:	We're going to unleash the best in the business.[10]

So, in line with the fifth trait, Anthony/Mitzi takes on responsibility. To give his long-suffering wife a holiday, he takes his highly tolerant son with him back to Sydney. Adam/Felicia begins to grow up. Ralph/Bernadette may have overcome her bitterness at life and found a new home with Bob. So, Priscilla leaves her behind and uneventfully

Stephan Elliott, Selection from *The Adventures of Priscilla, Queen of the Desert.* Copyright © 1994 by Gramercy Pictures.

returns to Sydney where, in the film's last scene, Mitzi and Felicia do Abba with Anthony/ Mitzi's young son working the lights.

The film, then, meets the criteria for a road movie, but, given its twists, it has a different feel. Moreover, it raises different issues than the usual road movie. Accepting responsibility, growing up, accepting responsibility, and moving on with one's life are not uncommon themes in a road movie, but intolerance against the LGBT community is. Road movies, with some exceptions, such as the feminist *Thelma and Louise*, rarely raise what we might term social issues. The films tend to be more about personal growth. *Priscilla* then goes against the genre norm a bit by raising the matter of intolerance.

The importance of raising that issue perhaps escaped the Broadway audience. Australia has a long history of intolerance—and worse. Sexism is still rampant, with evidence that a rape culture persists.[11] Australia has a long history of racism: Down through the decades, its native people have been forcibly relocated, driven to alcoholism, systematically murdered. In many parts of the nation, mixed-race children were kidnapped from their aboriginal mothers so these children could be raised to assume menial jobs in white society. And Australia, despite the many who line the streets of Sydney to watch the annual gay-lesbian Mardi Gras parade, has a very macho-male culture and a long history of discrimination and harassment directed against members of the LGBT community. The film was intended to confront the Australian audience with this ugly truth. The film's use of the road movie genre, how it is used, and how it departed from the genre's conventions played a major role in getting the uncomfortable message across.

The American reaction was probably different. As noted earlier, it was the campiness of the film (and musical) that audiences noted first. They responded to *Priscilla* much as they had to Australian Jim Sharman's *Rocky Horror Picture Show*, which debuted in 1975 but had a long life as a midnight movie in urban theatres across the country and, then, a television rendition in 2016. It was campy; it was outrageous; end of story. The social commentary that *Priscilla* offered may not have especially struck the American viewers. But, whether as social commentary or campy comedy, *Priscilla* departed from the norm of the road movie.

Strengths and Limitations

If practiced well, genre criticism can be a very useful lens. It takes the critic from looking at an entire text to examining very specific aspects. The critical approach truly acts as a lens insofar as it focuses attention on specific, arguably important dimensions of a text. The key to realizing the approach's strength is using it well. Genres should not be thought to be carved in stone. One using genre as a lens should not use its common traits as a checklist. The critic must always ask how the rhetor is fulfilling a trait and, if departing, why.

The previous statement implies many of the approach's limitations. Genre criticism can be practiced mechanically. There also is a tendency to force texts to fit a genre's traits. The critic assumes the text, as an example of a particular genre, must do such and such, and then find a way to make the argument that it does. A fledgling genre critic needs to be reminded frequently that departures from a genre are what are really interesting, not the fact of compliance.

Not all texts fit genres, so this approach is not universally available. And the critic must resist the temptation to create genres where there really is not a yet a body of texts with recurring traits. It is indeed an important moment in rhetorical criticism when a new genre seems to be emerging, but it is rare. In 1957, President Dwight Eisenhower ordered federal troops to intervene in Little Rock, Arkansas, to compel the integration of its schools. He spoke to the American people about his action. In 1962, President John Kennedy ordered federal troops to intervene in Oxford, Mississippi, to compel the integration of the University of Mississippi, and he spoke to the American people. Kennedy's speech is strikingly similar to Eisenhower's. Both say how reluctant they are to take action, both note how they are doing so in accordance with their duty to enforce federal court decisions. Both argue that the problem of racial discrimination is not just a southern problem, implying that their actions should not be construed as anti-southern. Then, in 1963, Kennedy intervened once more—at the University of Alabama, and he spoke to the American people about it. In this speech, he does many of the same things Eisenhower and he had done in 1957 and 1962. But, he also departed from the pattern by arguing that civil rights was a moral issue. Are we dealing with a genre here that JFK interestingly departed from? I once thought maybe; now, I'm inclined to say that two speeches are not enough to establish a genre. One, then, needs to be careful both in defining a genre and in analyzing a text as an example of a genre. One should not declare that a genre exists prematurely, and one should focus on how a text exhibits a genre's traits and how—and why—it departs.

Exemplars

Achter, Paul J. "Narrative, Intertextuality, and Apologia in Contemporary Political Scandals." *Southern Communication Journal* 65, no. 4 (2000): 318–33.

Benoit, William L., Paul Gulliform, and Daniel A. Panici. "President Reagan's Defensive Discourse on the Iran-Contra Affair." *Communication Studies* 42, no. 3 (1991): 272–94.

Bostdorff, Denise. "George W. Bush's Post-September 11 Rhetoric of Covenant Renewal: Upholding the Faith of the Greatest Generation." *Quarterly Journal of Speech* 89, no. 4 (2003): 293–319.

Rodgers, Raymond S. "Generic Tendencies in Majority and Non-Majority Supreme Court Opinions: The Case of Justice Douglas." *Communication Quarterly* 30, no. 3 (1982): 232–36.

Suggested Applications

Speech Applications

- President Bill Clinton, on August 31, 1998, finally confessed to inappropriate sexual behavior with White House intern Monica Lewinsky. Assess this speech as an example of the genre.

- Donald Trump was certainly an unusual presidential candidate in 2016. So, it should not surprise anyone that he might offer an unusual inaugural address. Analyze that inaugural speech as an example of the genre.

Non-Speech Applications

- In the late 1970s, CBS debuted the television show *All in the Family*. It was a situation comedy, but it was, in a number of ways, unlike the situation comedies that preceded it. Analyze it as a departure from a genre.

- Mount Rushmore is not the only monument or memorial in the United States to be carved out of a mountain, but Mount Rushmore—and other mountain carvings—did represent a departure from how heroes were usually memorialized (i.e., with big, classically inspired structures). Analyze Mount Rushmore in terms of the genre of presidential memorials.

Notes

1. Campbell, Karlyn Kohrs, and Kathleen Hall Jamieson. "Form and Genre: Shaping Rhetorical Action." *Philosophy & Rhetoric* 13, no. 3 (1980): 217–19.

2. Campbell and Jamieson, "Form," 218.

3. Campbell, Karlyn Kohrs, and Kathleen Hall Jamieson. *Deeds Done in Words: Presidential Rhetoric an dthe Genres of Governance.* Chicago, IL: University of Chicago Press, 1990.

4. Campbell, Karlyn Kohrs, and Kathleen Hall Jamieson. *Presidents Creating the Presidency: Deeds Done in Words.* Chicago, IL: University of Chicago Press, 2008.

5. Miles, Edwin A. "The Keynote Speech at National Nominating Conventions." *Quarterly Journal of Speech* 46, no. 1 (1960): 26–32. and Corcoran, Paul E. "Presidential Concession Speeches: The Rhetoric of Defeat." *Political Communication* 11, no. 2 (1994): 109–31.

6. Ware, B. L., and Wil A. Linkugel. "They Spoke in Defense of Themselves: On the Generic Criticism of Apologiae." *Quarterly Journal of Speech* 59, no. 3 (1973): 273–83.

7. Benoit, William. *Accounts, Excuses, and Apologies: A Theory of Image Restoration Strategies.* Albany, NY: State University of New York Press, 1995.

8. Blaney, Joseph R., Lance R. Rippert, and J. Scott Smith, eds. *Repairing the Athlete's Image: Studies in Sports Image Restoration.* Lanham, MD: Lexington Books, 2012.

9. Schlib, John. *Rhetorical Refusals: Defying Audiences' Expectations.* Carbondale, IL: Southern Illinois University Press, 2007.

10. *The Adventures of Priscilla, Queen of the Desert.* Directed by Stephan Elliott. Performed by Terence Stamp, Hugo Weaving, and Guy Pearce. Australia: Gramercy Pictures, 1994. Film. http://www.awesomefilm.com/script/priscilla.text.

11. *Change the Course: National Report on Sexual Assault and Sexual Harassment.* Report. Australian Human Rights Commission. http://www.our-work-sex-discrimination/publications/ change-course-national-report-sexual-assault-and-harassment.; also pertinent is Graham, Ben. "Around 30 Students Sexually Harassed Every Day in Australia." *News.com.au,* April 28, 2018. https://www.news.com.au/lifestyle/real-life/news-life/around-30-students-sexually-harassed-every-day-in-australia/news-story/49573f4ce7b4c662be651c15ae2a740d. It focuses on Australian universities but offers general observations on the wider culture that supports sexism on campuses.

Figure credit

Fig. 8: Source: https://commons.wikimedia.org/wiki/File:Coober_Pedy_-_The_Big_winch_lookout.jpg.

Iconic folk singer and Nobe[l] laureate Bob Dylan, who voiced (and appeared in) the third of the Chrysler Superbowl commercials.

CHAPTER 9

Mythological Criticism

Mythological criticism has, through the years, been far more popular in literary studies than in communication studies. Although texts of all sorts undoubtedly reflect mythological stories, the assumption has been that literature, because it is an imaginative creation, is more likely to reflect mythology, which is also considered an imaginative creation. Consider the mythological story of the phoenix rising from the ashes of its immolation. Might it not be reflected when a policy issue, thought to be dead, resurfaces? Consider the story of Icarus, whose ambition caused him to fly too close to the sun. Might it not be reflected in a political story? To be fair to both parties, this mythological story seems reflected in the 1950s story of Wisconsin Senator Joseph McCarthy, a republican. His anti-communism crusade worked, but only to a point: He flew too close to the sun. He began that crusade making accusations that were plausible, but, eventually, his accusations became reckless, causing his U.S. Senate colleagues to repudiate both him and his cause. And the same mythological story seems to be reflected in the 1980s story of Colorado Senator Gary Hart, a democrat, whose strong presidential campaign was destroyed when he dared the *Miami Herald* to follow him to check on the rumors of his marital infidelity. The newspaper found him, young girl sitting on his lap, aboard a pleasure boat named "Monkey Business." He also got burned—and bumped out of the presidential sweepstakes. A man who could have become president thought he was invulnerable: His behavior could not bring him down; the media could not bring him down. But he was proven wrong.

Mythological criticism fits realms far from the literary because myths are, by definition, patterns found in human life turned into stories because the stories—because they are more memorable—have explanatory power. The explanatory power was greater in ancient times, when the stories were widely believed to be true. But, even today, the patterns have explanatory power. We do not believe in the tale of Icarus, but we do believe that men and women often become so proud that they do the real-world version of flying toward the sun and getting very badly burned.

Classical Myths and Folk Tales

The myths referred to in the previous paragraphs come from the richest reservoir of such stories in the Western tradition, Greek and Roman—or classical—mythology. They have found their way into literature from antiquity through the present day. Some of the stories are sufficiently popular that they find their way into discourse more generally. Any rhetor who plays off a myth must ask how many in the audience will get it. The Trojan horse? Persephone's annual return to Hades? Hercules's labors? Sisyphus's eternal task of rolling a stone uphill? My guess is that the first has far more resonance than the other three. Mythological critics, however, do not restrict themselves to the conscious use by rhetors of material such as these tales. This use would be labeled a **classical allusion**. But mythological critics believe that the patterns embodied by the tales find their way into texts without the rhetor necessarily being aware. They believe that these patterns run deep in the human experience, and they surface in a wide variety of texts and play a role in making these texts persuasive. Myth, then, is an undercurrent that texts reflect, not just something a rhetor might quite consciously allude to in order to give a text depth or the rhetor's ethos a boost by suggesting how learned he or she is.

There are many mythologies. As already noted, the body of stories we label classical mythology play a major role in our Western culture. Another influential body is the folk tales that show up in different guises in the many European countries. Folk tale scholar Vladimir Propp tried to give some regularity to this body, classifying them across cultural or national lines as specific "tale types."[1] One familiar type is the one we are most likely to know as "Little Red Riding Hood." At its core, it is the story of an innocent who, not heeding an elder's advice as well as necessary, falls prey to a wolf in disguise. That tale's pattern, without references to red riding hoods or even wolves, can undergird any number of texts dealing with matters far removed from a basketful of treats. Consider foreign policy. A nation may well not recognize a genuine enemy because that enemy is disguised as a friend, despite warnings issued by either senior officials or an allied nation. In warning a nation against the disguised enemy, a rhetor might well evoke this tale type, maybe even referring to the enemy as a wolf—or a bear—in the woods.

Monomyth

Propp's work was encyclopedic: He tried to embrace all folk tales and classify them. Another avenue pursued by students of mythology is to find a single myth that explains it all, with other myths being but subparts of it. Joseph Campbell, for example, saw the journey of the hero as such a single or monomyth. In his famous *A Hero with a Thousand Faces* (1949), Campbell traces this journey through phases that show up in a wide range of cultures.[2] When Campbell's work was very popular and very influential in literary and cultural studies, textbooks were published that went phase by phase, offering snippets from the writing of European, Asian, Latin American, and African sources. Name a religion. These texts would illustrate how its stories fit into this monomyth. The texts were usually literary, but they need not have been, for much of what the rhetorical critic routinely examines can be linked to this monomyth's phases. Abraham Lincoln, for example, in his famous and very brief second inaugural evoked at least three of the phases Campbell charts—tests or trials, the dark night of the soul, rebirth.

Perhaps more influential in literary studies—and potentially in rhetorical studies— would be the work of Canadian scholar Northrop Frye. Frye's lectures on Shakespeare at the University of Toronto were routinely packed, but his work went well beyond Shakespeare. In exploring the mythological roots of literary expression, Frye ranged through many literatures with a special emphasis on classical texts and the Bible.

Northrop Frye

In this chapter, we will explore how Frye's approach to mythological criticism can inform the rhetorical examination of texts. Frye explains the thinking behind his approach in *Fables of Identity: Studies in Poetic Mythology* (1963):

> It is clear that criticism cannot be systematic unless there is a quality in literature which enables it to be so, an order of words corresponding to the order of nature in the natural sciences. An archetype should be not only a unifying category of criticism, but itself part of a total form, and it leads us at once to the question of what sort of total form criticism can see in literature. Our survey of critical techniques has taken us as far as literary history. Total literary history moves from the primitive to the sophisticated, and here we glimpse the possibility of seeing literature as a complication of a relatively restricted and simple group of formulas that can be studied in primitive culture. If so, then the search for archetypes is a kind of literary anthropology, concerned with the way that literature is informed by pre-literary categories such as ritual, myth and folktale. We next realize that the relation between these categories and literature is by no means purely one of descent, as we find them reappearing in the greatest classics—in fact there seems to be a general tendency on the part of great classics to revert to them. This coincides with a feeling that we have all had: that the study of mediocre

works of art, however energetic, obstinately remains a random and peripheral form of critical experience, whereas the profound masterpiece seems to draw us to a point at which we can see an enormous number of converging patterns of significance. Here we begin to wonder if we cannot see literature, not only as complicating itself in time, but as spread out in conceptual space from some unseen center.

The myth is the central informing power that gives archetypal significance to the ritual and archetypal narrative to the oracle. Hence the myth *is* the archetype, though it might be convenient to say myth only when referring to narrative, and archetype when speaking of significance. In the solar cycle of the day, the seasonal cycle of the year, and the organic cycle of human life, there is a single pattern of significance, out of which myth constructs a central narrative around a figure who is partly the sun, partly vegetative fertility, and partly a god or archetypal human being.[3]

We will start with the monomyth that Frye posits and then how Frye moves from that conception to a theory of genres and conventions. We will then consider other backdrops to mythological criticism one might find useful.

The Monomyth

In *The Anatomy of Criticism* (1957), Frye's classic text, he argues that the cycle of the seasons (reflecting the cycles of both day and life) is the essential monomyth. He argues that this cycle creates four mythoi that we can associate with spring, summer, fall, and winter. Frye acknowledges that we see these four mythoi, in pure form, only in literature closer to primitive times, when explaining why nature dies only to be renewed was a crucial concern. In our times, the mythoi are displaced. This means that the mythoi are more often than not buried in texts, perhaps pushed off to the side as texts bring more sophisticated ideas to the fore. In other words, in classical times we encounter the tale of Persephone's annual descent into the underworld and her mother's mourning. In our times, a pattern of death and eventual rebirth may well be present but buried in a story that draws immediate attention to other matters—in, perhaps, an account, such as those offered by Ronald Reagan, of how the nation, weakened militarily, is now becoming strong again.

The Mythoi

The initial mythos is that of spring. It is associated with the broadly defined genre of comedy. In this genre, there is often a young couple. Their desire to marry is blocked by representatives of the older order, but they are helped along in the romantic quest by an often middle-aged helper and, in the end, triumph. Marriage, celebrated with strong hints of future fertility, is often celebrated at the work's end.

These precise plot elements are, however, not essential. Consider, for example, humankind's story as represented in the Bible. We have a couple in a garden, but they fall from grace and therefore must experience a nature that entails pain and death. This fate is, of course, not just that of Adam and Eve, but that of humankind. Humankind will suffer through a kind of winter for a long, long time, but eventually there is redemption and rebirth. Instrumental in bringing it about is the thirty-three-year-old Jesus. In the end, there is no marriage per se, but there are, in the New Testament books, many references to both marriage and rebirth, even to Jesus as a kind of bride. Humankind has, through the intercession of Jesus, made it back to the garden. So, structurally, the Bible is a comedy. Comedy in Frye's terms does not mean a lot of laughs; rather it is a structure.

The next mythos is that of summer. It is associated with the genre Frye terms romance. In this genre, the plot begins with trouble, trouble that seems irresolvable. The solution? The characters escape from the threatening world to a somewhat magical one where the troubles do not exist. Their escape is like going on a vacation, which, of course, is something people frequently do in our culture in the summer. The escape, like a vacation, is not permanent, but, upon return, the troubles quickly, often magically, vanish. If the account of this comedy makes you think of a Shakespearean comedy, this account should make you think of a Shakespearean romance such as *The Winter's Tale* or *The Tempest*. (Frye was, after all, a Shakespeare scholar!) In the former, problems galore are breaking out in Sicily, so the threatened characters escape to the pastoral island of Bohemia. It's an unreal place, as its being an island suggests (since the real Bohemia is land-locked), but it provides a respite until a return is possible, with magic even restoring those thought long-dead once the characters are back in Sicily.

Again, the precise plot elements are not crucial. Consider the well-known novel and movie *The Natural*. In both, more so in Bernard Malamud's book, baseball player Roy Hobbs is haunted by his past. He escapes from it by, out of nowhere, getting a delayed second chance at the game with the wretched New York Knights. His vacation is magical: he gets to start; he starts to slug; and the Knights rise to the top of the standings. But the vacation cannot last: The past catches up with Roy. Now, at this point, novel and film differ. In the novel, Roy ultimately fails. Its rhythm is not that of the romance. But in the film, Roy magically succeeds. Using a special bat named "Savoy Slugger" (replacing the equally magical "Wonder Boy"), he knocks the lights out in the ballpark, and he wins the game and fame and his long-lost love Iris. We last see him on the farm playing catch with his son. The movie is romance.

The third mythos is that of fall. It is associated with the genre of tragedy. Here, a central character, usually with some stature, falls from grace. He or she suffers, as does the audience vicariously. In the end, there is a slight suggestion that there is redemption ahead, not for the character but for his or her society. The suggestion is often faint, for spring is months away.

Any number of famous literary works fit this pattern: Sophocles's *Oedipus Rex,* Shakespeare's *Hamlet*, Milton's *Paradise Lost*. They all fit the pattern almost perfectly. But consider the Broadway classic *West Side Story*. It is a modern-day rewrite of Shakespeare's *Romeo and Juliet*. It is set in New York City, and the rival forces that threaten the love between Tony and Maria are the rival gangs the Polish-American Jets and Puerto Rican Sharks. In the end, Tony is shot dead. Maria verbally assaults both gangs, and, in the concluding scene, we see members of both gangs helping to carry Tony's body from the urban playground where he fell. There is clearly a fall, even though the musical's Juliet (Maria) lives, not dies. But, in the way the two gangs come together in the end, there is that moment of hope.

The final mythos is that of winter. The associated genre is what Frye terms "irony." It has a peculiar rhythm. Things are going wrong, but, then, it looks like all will be well, but no. This cycle is often repeated as the genre sinks deeper and deeper into despair. The uplifting moments are much like those scattered warm days in winter when you think that, at last, winter is over, only to be hit by a snowstorm. If you know the structure of Shakespeare's *King Lear*, it has this wintry feel. So does the fairly well known 1971 Peter Bogdanovich film *The Last Picture Show*, based on Larry McMurtry's 1966 novel. It is set in a dying Texas town and depicts the lives of the characters and the life of the town. Throughout, the viewer or reader experiences one downturn after another. There are, scattered in both book and film, moments when you think that, maybe, things will be fine, but, no, every moment of hope is squashed as the works enact what Frye's terms an ironic rhythm.

Phases

Another dimension of Frye's theory to be aware of is how he divided each mythos into four phases. So, one can talk of phase one comedy or phase three tragedy. The significance of this division is that Frye posits that there are borderlines between mythoi or genres where a work in one genre might, with a twist, become another. Consider the film *The Natural*. It was described previously as romance, but recall the novel version with a very different ending, which has Roy striking out. The romance then shifts to being a phase one tragedy. Consider the famous Broadway musical *Fiddler on the Roof*. One by one, the tradition-bound father Tevya sees his daughters abandon him. Meanwhile, the political situation in Anatevka is getting more and more dire. But there are moments of celebration, as well as moments where father and daughter almost come to an understanding. In Frye's terms, the work seems to be an example of irony. However, in the end, despite the forced removal of the Jewish people from the village, Tevya is reunited with his daughters. So, it turns from irony to phase one comedy: It crosses the borderline between mythoi/genres.

Conventions

One last piece of Frye's mythological theory. He posits that each mythos/genre often contains certain conventional, heavily symbolic events. They are clues as to what genre one is dealing with. More than that, these conventions convey some of the meaning—or at least the feel—of a mythos or genre. Marriage is conventional in comedy, giving the genre a celebratory tone and suggestions of rebirth. Magic is conventional in romance, taking the genre beyond the confines of the real. Death is conventional in tragedy, making it a rather ominous mythos/genre. Storms are conventional in irony, making the genre unstable, frightening. These are not the only conventions Frye notes. These conventions also need not be literally present, for we are dealing with displacement, here. So, mental instability might be the storminess; the end of traditional ways might be the death.

Goals of Mythological Criticism

Let's stick with literature for the moment. The goal of all literary criticism is to unpack the richness of the artifact before the critic. Seeing the mythological patterning adds to other riches one might have already noted. Mythological criticism does more, however, for it roots literature in larger human stories. It shows, among the many functions of literary expression, it is an anthropological one. Literature entertains, literature present important ideas, literature also reflects how we, as a people, have patterned our existence.

But what about the forms of discourse that rhetorical critics usually look at? The goals are much the same—to expose the richness of the text, whether it be a speech or an advertisement; to show how, besides all else these texts might do, there is a rooting in certain core patterns that we have constructed to explain our existence. We will consider a set of ads in a minute. Let's briefly consider a more traditional text—a speech. In the late 1970s, President Jimmy Carter gave a speech that most commentators think was famously unsuccessful. Although he never used the word "malaise," the speech is often referred to as his "malaise speech." The speech has two parts: The first is yet another presidential address on the energy crisis facing America; the second talks to Americans about how both the White House and the nation at large are suffering from a "crisis in confidence." The speech has an odd rhythm: Every time you think Carter is going to turn the corner and start outlining how to address these two problems, he returns to reflecting pessimistically on them. The speech exhibits the rhythm Frye terms irony—the mythos of winter. There are no literal storms in the speech, but both the energy picture Carter depicts and the no-confidence picture Carter offers are unsettled, stormy ones. Spring, of course, follows winter, so there is hope in that fact—delivered in Ronald Reagan's rather comic (in Frye's terms) inaugural in which he celebrates how fully all Americans, famous or not, are married to the concept of heroism. But, Carter's speech is wintry bleak.

Method

No matter whether the critic's goal is to find a monomyth such as Frye's or Campbell's in a text or some other kind of myth, such as one based in a nation's history or its popular culture (both discussed shortly), the starting point is the myth. It needs to be understood. Then, the critic must find the myth in the text under consideration. Since the text will probably offer the myth in a displaced version, finding the myth usually means looking deep into the work and getting past details that are extraneous to the mythological pattern.

The next step is seeing how the text embodies the myth. If using Frye's conception of a monomyth as one's critical lens, doing so means first identifying which mythoi is being offered (spring and comedy, summer and romance, fall and tragedy, winter and irony); second, placing the text with the possible generic range of the discovered mythos. If, for example, the text is thought to fit spring/comedy, then does it border winter/irony or summer/romance? The third step would be to see if any of the conventions of the mythos are present. Given that the text is displaced, as it likely is, the conventions will probably show up in unfamiliar guises. The literal death of fall/tragedy may be dire poverty or rampant crime or environmental degradation in policy addresses that fall under the mythos of fall.

One might well ask why a critic would want to do this kind of work. There are three answers. Some, such as Campbell or Frye, take delight in finding *the* story that informs human discourse, be it primitive folktales or great works of literature. They are, at heart, literary anthropologists. Others believe that all the ways texts are enriched should be noted if one is to understand and appreciate them. A mythological structure, for them, is an important enhancement, one that may increase the text's power and persuasiveness. Still others are interested in how myths have been transformed (e.g., how the ancient story of Icarus flying too close to the sun is re-represented in Lin-Manuel Miranda's Broadway hit *Hamilton* or how quest motifs find their way into many policy speeches about matters that will require many steps and many years to address fully). Discerning how a mythological pattern is used is akin to discovering how any rhetorical resource is used, and pointing to the use enhances and expands our understanding of rhetoric. No matter why, a critic's fourth step should be addressing the why. What do we learn from seeing the mythological pattern undergirding a text?

Application: Three Super Bowl Ads

Super Bowl ads are a big deal: They are expensive to launch; they are, by some, watched with more interest than the game itself. In two successive years, and then two years later, Chrysler offered the viewing public three memorable ads.

2011 Ad, Narrator Eminem

I got a question for you.
What does this city know about luxury, hmm?
What does a town that's been to hell and back know about the finer things in life?
Well I'll tell you.
More than most.
You see, it's the hottest fires that make the hardest steel.
Add work and conviction. And a know how that runs generations deep in every last one of us.
That's who we are.
That's our story.
Now it's probably not the one you've been reading in the papers. The one being written by folks who have never been here. Don't [know] what we're capable of.
Because when it comes to luxury, it's as much about where it's from as who it's for.
Now we're from America—but this isn't New York City, or the Windy City, or Sin City, and we're certainly no one's Emerald City.
This is the motor city—and this is what we do.[4]

2012 Ad, Narrator Clint Eastwood

It's halftime. Both teams are in their locker room discussing what they can do to win this game in the second half. It's halftime in America, too. People are out of work and they're hurting. And they're all wondering what they're going to do to make a comeback. And we're all scared, because this isn't a game.
The people of Detroit know a little something about this. They almost lost everything. But we all pulled together, now Motor City is fighting again. I've seen a lot of tough eras, a lot of downturns in my life. And, times when we didn't understand each other. It seems like we've lost our heart at times. When the fog of division, discord, and blame make[s] it hard to see what lies ahead. But after those trials, we all rallied around what was right, and acted as one. Because that's what we do. We find a way through tough times, and if we can't find a way, then we'll make one.
All that matters now is what's ahead. How do we come from behind? How do we come together? And, how do we win? Detroit's showing us it can be done. And, what's true about them is true about all of us. This country can't be knocked out with one

Born of Fire. Copyright © 2011 by FCA Group.
Matthew Dickman, Halftime in America. Copyright © 2012 by FCA Group.

punch. We get right back up again and when we do the world is going to hear the roar of our engines. Yeah, it's halftime, America. And, our second half is about to begin.[5]

2014 Ad, Narrator Bob Dylan

Is there anything more American than America?

'Cause you can't import original. You can't fake true cool. You can't duplicate legacy.

Because what Detroit created was a first and became an inspiration to the … rest of the world.

Yeah, Detroit made cars. And cars made America.

Making the best, making the finest, takes conviction. And you can't import the heart and soul of every man and woman working on the line.

You can search the world over for the finer things, but you won't find a match for the American road and the creatures that live on it.

Because we believe in the zoom, and the roar, and the thrust.

And when it's made here, it's made with the one thing you can't import from anywhere else. American Pride.

So, let Germany brew your beer, let Switzerland make your watch, let Asia assemble your phone.

We … build … your car.[6]

The first featured the voice—and eventually the person—of white rapper Eminem. The ad focuses on Detroit, as he drives through it, past a number of iconic structures and past a noticeably racially diverse collection of people. He ends up at a famous theatre where, presumably, he will front a well-known African American choir. The message is that Detroit is back *and* Chrysler is back.

The second featured the voice and person of actor/director Clint Eastwood. He is presumably in a stadium tunnel and tells his viewers that it's "halftime in America." He is not referring to the game, however; he is referring to the American automobile industry, specifically Chrysler. The images on the screen are not just of Detroit, but, no matter the location, they suggest a nation moving forward. It's not clear in the ad whether the home team is technically ahead or behind at halftime—behind seems more likely, but the nation, its industry, and Chrysler are close enough to the lead to be declared halfway to victory and, with perseverance during the second half, they will all get to that goal.

So far, we have a white rapper and a conservative-leaning entertainer famous for his law-and-order "Dirty Harry" cop role. The third ad brings us the very different person and voice of folk songwriter/singer (now, Nobel laureate) Bob Dylan. Perhaps his gravelly voice links Dylan to Eastwood, but there is very little else that links the two. Eastwood performed at the 2012 Republican National Convention, mocking Barack Obama who presumably sat in an empty chair next to Eastwood on stage; Dylan has delivered a long series of social and political protest messages at numerous concerts beginning way back in the early 1960s at the Newport Folk Festivals. They both performed politically, but with very different politics and messages. In the Dylan-narrated commercial, the visuals

America. Copyright © 2014 by FCA Group.

are of a wide variety of American scenes. One might even term the visual collage as "Americana." The message is that America, especially a traditional image of the nation, has value, is worth saving, and may—to a degree—have been restored. Buying America is not exactly the message, for the ad says we can buy our watches, our electronics, and our beer elsewhere. However, America makes cars, and we should buy our cars here—from Chrysler, of course.

The three advertisements can be treated separately or together. Either way, they offer what Frye refers to as the mythos of spring or comedy. Comedy borders irony, so the Eastwood ad edges in the ironic direction insofar as it suggests we're only at halftime. The Eminem ad, on the other hand, tells us Detroit and its automobile industry is back; and the Dylan ad tells us that a traditional America is back, led by its redeemed auto industry.

Comedy, in Frye's terms, does not mean lots of laughs. So, we should not expect to laugh at these Super Bowl ads. But they do not conform to the comic model in its purest form if that form is thought to necessarily feature young lovers, etc. But the purest form is, in Frye's view, about rebirth or redemption not thwarted young love. The young lovers represented potential fertility. As they overcome the obstacles in their path, they get closer and closer to the fertility celebrated in marriage. The Super Bowl ads are also about redemption. In the Eminem ad, Detroit (and Chrysler) are redeemed from not only an economic slump but also racial problems. The images shown mix white and black, and the concert the ad rises toward mixes white Eminem and the black gospel choir. When the racial subtext of the Eminem ad is considered, there is a sense of marriage implicit, marriage of two races that had been badly divided in Detroit.

In the Eastwood ad, Detroit and Chrysler are not quite there yet—it's halftime, we're in the rather dark tunnel. The ad edges away from comedy toward irony. In the Dylan ad, redemption—for a very traditional rendition of America—seems a *fait accompli*. Curiously, the images are heavily rural. So, is only part of America redeemed? This question becomes especially relevant when, in the ad's final words, several industries (watches, electronics, beer) are surrendered to foreign nations. Just as a cultural redemption seems limited to a part of America, economic redemption seems limited to automobiles. In Frye's terms, comic and ironic do border.

So, why would a critic want to point to the mythological pattern buried in these ads? Certainly, doing so is not the only thing one might want to do with this set of ads, but doing so gets at how we, as a people, seem to continually seek redemption, seek the spring and its greenness and fertility. The ads, however, locate this desire just in the United States. We, as a nation, need redemption or rebirth. The timing of the ads might then be relevant. Although the nation arguably escaped from economic collapse in 2008–09, matters were still not great by the years of these ads. Job growth was slow; economic progress was slow. These were also uneven, with places such as Detroit not seeing as much progress as other spots. The audience then desires the redemptive vision offered by Eminem and Dylan and wants to push the borderline ironic (winter) and comic (spring) vision offered by Eastwood clearly toward the victory of industrial rebirth.

Although the ads privilege certain places in the country over others, the ads do try to embrace a wide swath of Americans in the redemptive message. Chrysler probably could not have chosen spokespeople to use as different as Eminem, Clint Eastwood, and Bob Dylan. Arguably, Eminem, especially when coupled with a black gospel choir, appeals to a young, urban, heavily African American audience. Eastwood, on the other hand, appeals to an older and more conservative demographic. And, although many baby boomers, who grew up listening to Dylan, perhaps found Dylan's presence in the ad odd, his presence did appeal to those who, back in the 1960s and 1970s, were anti-establishment. This American need for redemption or restoration or rebirth (choose your term) is then something many different groups of Americans feel. A mythological critic would argue that discerning the mythological roots of the ads and then exploring them is a worthy rhetorical critical task. Doing so alerts us to a rhetorical power that extends beyond the three ads' particular images.

Other Bases for Myths

Campbell, Frye, and others who seek a monomyth are perhaps the most profound mythological critics, insofar as they believe there is a single human story undergirding all discourse. Less profound and less universal are those who explore national myths or popular culture-based myths.

National Myths

Many nations have stories that have been raised to myth status by a combination of exaggeration and reverence. Within nations, particular people may also have such stories and myths. For example, in the United States, the story that anyone, regardless of how humble his or her roots are, can grow up to be rich or president is a dominant myth often termed "the American Dream." Similar are the story/myth that the United States is a "shining city on a hill," exceptional in comparison to the rest of world in many respects, and the story/myth of Americans as conquerors of vast frontiers.

In Australia, the national myths are quite different. Because of the massive casualties suffered by the nation in World War I, a mythology has developed that venerates "the diggers," those men who fought and died in the war. A similar—a similarly bleak—myth involves exploration, for Australia is marked by the trails of those who tried to cross the continent north-south or east-west and failed. Major highways, rather ironically, are named after these unsuccessful explorers. Whereas the United States' national myths are ones characterized by success, Australia's are ones characterized by fatalism. In another similar country, Canada, the dominant myth, according to author/critic Margaret Atwood, is survival, for story after story involves barely getting by in battles against formidable forces, often those of nature. There is a fatalistic quality to this Canadian myth as well, for, according to Atwood, many of the stories of survival imply "until the next time."[7]

A critic, then, can assess a text from a particular nation—or culture—in the mythological terms that define that nation or culture. To do so, a critic must know what myths function in what places and among what groups. The critic must keep in mind that the myths of his or her nation or culture may not apply if a text from another nation or culture is being examined. Australians often talk of "a fair go," and they sometimes proudly—perhaps falsely—claim their society is class-less. Such talk, however, should not lead the critic to assume that the myth of "The American Dream" applies "Down Under." It is crucial, if a critic is going to consider texts outside her/his nation or culture to understand the mythologies they may be functioning there.

These national myths are much like the fantasy themes discussed in an earlier chapter. Those who developed the fantasy theme or symbolic convergence approach argued that groups socially construct stories or themes that come to define the group and play a major role in whether they accept or reject an argument. These national myths are also much like the rhetoric that constitutes a group's identity discussed in a later chapter on "constitutive rhetoric." So, a critic who connects a text to a national myth in assessing how it persuades may see his or her critical venture as falling into one of a number of categories. All that points to is how these categories of critical approaches are somewhat arbitrary ones designed to help the student of rhetorical criticism see the variety of approaches that are possible. That three approaches, arising out of different assumptions, lead to similar analyses does not totally eliminate what makes each approach philosophically different.

Popular Culture Myths

There may no longer be a sharp distinction between elite culture (what you learn about in the university classroom) and popular culture (what you explore on your own). Once upon a time, there were novels labeled "literature" and novels labeled "popular fiction." Bookstores even put them in different sections. The distinction began becoming blurred in the 1960s when academe began to realize how powerful popular culture was. It— novels, films, television programs—commanded attention, and, more relevant to our purposes, established a body of stories that could rise to the level of myth. What was necessary for popular culture to so rise was a high level of audience awareness of the story and a shared sense that the story was in some way "larger" than an ordinary one. There is still a distinction that might be made between that which has stood the proverbial "test of time" over centuries and that which might prove to be more transient. However, that which has been labeled popular does often have a power to inform texts that needs to be recognized if those texts are to be understood.

Examples may make the matter clearer. *Star Wars* will, over a period of decades, consist of eight films. Most have seen them; most understand references to "the Force," "the Dark Side," and the like. These films can then function as a mythological backdrop for texts. So, when during the Reagan presidency the president referred to the Soviet Union as the "evil empire" and others referred to the president's space-based Strategic Defense Initiative as "star wars," most saw Darth Vader or the Death Star in the backs of their minds. The Harry Potter books and films may work much the same way. If a text refers to "he whose name cannot be spoken," many will picture Lord Voldemort. Any popular culture text, be it film (*The Godfather* trilogy, *Jaws*), television program (*House of Cards*, *Game of Thrones*), or music (Pink Floyd's "The Wall" or Bruce Springsteen's "Born in the U.S.A.") could be resonating in the background of whatever a critic might be analyzing, giving it what might be termed a mythic quality.

It is almost impossible to predict how durable popular culture myths might be. The television show *Bonanza* was very popular in the 1960s. How many would find the phrase "like the Cartwrights" resonant today? Probably very few, yet references to Frank Capra's classic films *It's a Wonderful Life* and *Mr. Smith Goes to Washington* still might work. One might credit the resonance of the former to its repeated showings every Christmas season, but the latter still evokes some resonance even though it is rarely re-screened. *The Wizard of Oz* and *Gone with the Wind* have lived on; other artifacts from the same decades have not. Both the monomyths and the national myths discussed earlier may be more durable. However, this factor should not cause one to reject the power myths derived from popular culture might have in a text. After all, the rhetorical critic—unlike the literary one—often deals with texts that are situated in a particular time. Perhaps fifty years from now, a political figure's referring to himself as "like Rocky" might require a footnote. Maybe it even does now, but at the height of the popularity of the films featuring the Sylvester Stallone character Rocky Balboa, the reference evoked a myth that added several positive qualities to the political figure's appeal. (After all, tourists still flock to Rocky's statue outside the Philadelphia Art Museum, and tourists still replicate Rocky's triumphant run up the Museum's steps.)

Strengths and Limitations

There may well be a split among mythological critics concerning what they see themselves doing. Some look for mythological underpinnings on the assumption that these enrich a text and add to its persuasive power. Others believe they are discovering fundamental stories that define both who we are and what we think life consists of. Either way, critics are uncovering a dimension that adds to our understanding of a text.

One limitation is shared with other approaches discussed in this textbook: that the mythological undergirding may be only one dimension of a text and that focusing on it may result in ignoring other dimensions. Also shared with some other approaches is the possibility that the critic will be overly ingenious in searching for a mythological basis, whether a monomyth or a national myth or a pop culture myth. One of my graduate school friends was often criticized—in a joking manner—for being able to find a Christ figure in a Donald Duck cartoon book. The point of the joke was that, if one is intent on finding mythology, one can perhaps strain both the text and the reader's credibility in doing so. Put another way, not all evil empires are allusions to *Star Wars*; not all young lovers who overcome obstacles are evocations of spring.

An ardent myth critic might insist that mythologies are at the root of all human expression, literary or practical, novels or inaugurals. Most who embrace mythological criticism are not that ardent. They claim that mythologies are often present, more often than perhaps other critics grant. The critic's role, then, is often to point out that which others may overlook because what is overlooked can play a significant role in persuasion.

Exemplars

Carpenter, Ronald H. "America's Tragic Metaphor: Our Twentieth-Century Combatants as Frontiersman." *Quarterly Journal of Speech* 76, no. 1 (1990): 1–22.

Cooks, Leda M., Mark P. Orbe, and Carol S. Bruess. "The Fairly Tale Theme in Popular Culture: A Semiotic Analysis of *Pretty Woman*." *Women's Studies in Communication* 16, no. 2 (1993): 86–104.

Kelley-Romano, Stephanie. "Mythmaking in Alien Abduction Narratives." *Communication Quarterly* 54, no. 3 (2006): 383–406.

Rushing, Janice Hocking. "The Rhetoric of the American Western Myth." *Communication Monographs* 50, no. 1 (1983): 14–32.

Suggested Applications

Speech Applications

- Look at Bill Clinton's 1993 inaugural using Frye's approach to mythological criticism.

- In 1979, President Jimmy Carter told the American people they—and their leaders—lacked confidence. Discuss this speech in Frye's terms.

Non-Speech Applications

- The Harry Potter books and films may, in themselves, constitute a source for popular culture-based myths, but go deeper. Consider an episode and see what monomyths may lurk beneath it, making it more appealing.

- The Lincoln Memorial in Washington, DC tells both the story of the nation and the story of its sixteenth president. Consider these in mythic terms.

Notes

1. Propp, Vladimir. *Morphology of the Folktale.* Austin, TX: University of Texas Press, 1958.

2. Campbell, Joseph R. *The Hero with a Thousand Faces.* 3rd ed. New York, NY: New World Library, 2008.

3. Frye, Northrop. *Fables of Identity: Studies in Poetic Mythology.* New York, NY: Harcourt, Brace and Company, 1963. 480–83.

4. Chrysler. "Eminem Super Bowl Commercial." Advertisement. Arianna O'Dell. http://www.ariannaodell. com/2011/02/chrysler-eminem-super-bowl-commercial-imported.

5. "Halftime in America." Wikipedia. July 21, 2018. http://en.wikipedia.org/wiki/Halftime_in_America.

6. "Bob Dylan Stars in Super Bowl Ad for Chrysler 200." *Michigan Automotive News.* http://www.mlive.com/auto/index.ssf/2014/02/bob_dylan_stars_in_super_bowl.

7. Atwood, Margaret. Survival: *A Thematic Guide to Canadian Literature.* Toronto, Canada: House of Anansi, 1972.

Figure credit

Fig. 9: Source: https://commons.wikimedia.org/wiki/File:Joan_Baez_Bob_Dylan_crop.jpg.

Barack Obama, delivering one of his first major public addresses at the 2004 Democratic National Convention.

CHAPTER 10

Mikhail Bakhtin, Polyphony, and the Carnivalesque

Mikhail Bakhtin was a prolific theorist. He wrote his many works long before they became noteworthy among critics, largely because he was something of a lost figure off in Kazhakstan when he did his writing. A bit of biography is necessary to explain this rather odd story.

Bakhtin pursued graduate work in an area that, from our view many years later, seems to blend philosophy and linguistics and theology. American students need to keep in mind that the academic divisions we think of as departments or majors are human constructions, not set in stone anywhere. Academic divisions are different in Europe than they are in the United States, and academic divisions back in the 1930s were not what they are today. In other words, there was no communication department for Bakhtin to study in. Furthermore, at that time and in the institutions Bakhtin had associations with, rhetoric was not positively viewed. (More on that in a minute.)

There are quite a few controversies surrounding Bakhtin's academic career. Did he fake his credentials at one point—claiming degrees he did not have? Are some essays we routinely ascribe to him really written by others—perhaps by close associates? We're not going to resolve these matters here. Suffice to say that Bakhtin's writing gradually drifted in the direction of what we would term literary criticism. But, with his training in linguistics, Bakhtin retained his interest in the language writers used. During the post-World War II era, Russia's leader, Josef Stalin, was interested in some of the matters that linguistic scholars were. Language was not as politically neutral an issue as one might think. Well,

Bakhtin as a scholar found himself on the wrong side of a dispute with pseudo-scholar Stalin, and then Bakhtin found himself moved from Moscow, the center of Russian intellectual life, to remote Kazhastan. Not as bad as Siberia, but still pretty bad. There, Bakhtin, doing various jobs and suffering from poor health, continued to write, even though paper itself was scarce.

Bakhtin wrote a great deal, very little of it published during his lifetime. He also constantly revised previous works, and he left many texts in unfinished states. All this has created a great deal of work for those who have chosen to edit his works and make them available to present-day scholars. The texts that are available today present, arguably, very different pictures of who Bakhtin was and what he had to say. A critic, decades ago, opined that there were as many Bakhtin's as there were Bakhtinian scholars.[1] Now, that's an exaggeration, but there is some truth to the statement that there are many different takes on Bakhtin. I would suggest that the Bakhtin one creates depends heavily on where one begins his or her reading of the theorist. In some ways, this situation is not all that different from that of Kenneth Burke and Burkean critics. What one might point to as the essence of Burke will depend largely on what work by Burke you read first.

With Bakhtin, there seem to be four choices that communication scholars might take—and have taken. Late in his life, Bakhtin wrote an essay entitled "Speech Genres." Given that the word "speech" is in the title, some in communication gravitated to it. The problem here is that the essay is unfinished, deals with everyday genres such as how to greet someone, and has very little to do with rhetorical concerns as they are usually conceived. Throughout his career, Bakhtin used the Russian words translated as "dialogue" or "dialogic" a great deal. Therefore, communication scholars, mainly interpersonal and group communication scholars, interested in dialogue gravitated to a set of essays collected and published as *The Dialogic Imagination*. Two problems: First, the collection of rather disparate pieces creates the illusion of an over-arching theory that may well be more the creation of Bakhtin's editors than Bakhtin; second, the essays deal heavily with the novel, not interpersonal or group communication. Bakhtin is talking in them about a quality he likes to see in fiction and believes characterizes not only the best fiction but the best human discourse. Those using *The Dialogic Imagination* to illuminate dimensions of interpersonal or group human interaction may stumble a bit over Bakhtin's discussion of how the novel as a genre developed, wondering how this relates to the human dialogue they wish to stress.

A better way to get at this quality is to read *Problems of Dostoevsky's Poetics*, an important early work that Bakhtin returned to decades later to update. We will consider the core of this book in a minute. Off to the side is the fourth approach, rooted in a book-length study of French satirist Rabelais. Many go directly to this book and point to the essence of Bakhtin's thought as the "carnivalesque." We will get to that theoretical notion by first working through what Bakhtin has to say about discourse in the book on

Dostoevsky. The Dostoevsky book and the Rabelais book work together well, once one understands how Bakhtin places parody in the larger scheme he presents when discussing language use in the novel in general and in Dostoevsky in particular.

Polyphony

When you pick up *Problems of Dostoevsky's Poetics*, one surprise is how little the book talks about the Russian novelist. The book is more about discourse in general. Here are a set of excerpts:

> The life of the word is contained in its transfer from one mouth to another, from one context to another context, from one social collective to another, from one generation to another generation. In this process the word does not forget its own path and cannot completely free itself from the power of these concrete contexts into which it has entered.
>
> When a member of a speaking collective comes upon a word, it is not as a neutral word of language, not as a word free from the aspirations and evaluations of others, uninhabited by others' voices. No, he receives the word from another's voice and filled with that other voice. The word enters his context from another context, permeated with the interpretations of others.[2]

****

> Someone else's words introduced into our own speech inevitably assume a new (our own) interpretation and become subject to our evaluation of them; that is, they become double-voiced.[3]

[handwritten margin note: Univocal discourse and Polyphonic discourse]

Bakhtin makes it clear that other voices enter into much discourse. This leads to a core distinction that Bakhtin makes between **univocal discourse** and **polyphonic discourse**.

Univocal discourse in Bakhtin's story is the villain. He posits that words and phrases all have a history, and, when one uses a word or a phrase, previous uses come with it as entailments. Sometimes, the rhetor is aware of this; oftentimes, not. Discourse that tries to strip away all entailments, in Bakhtin's view, is discourse that denies the human dimension of language. This stripped discourse, insofar as it loses all voices but one, is univocal. It is the language of science, technology, law, government, and, as Bakhtin defined it, rhetoric. Opposed to univocal discourse is polyphonic discourse, which admits all these other voices and is thus fully human. This is the voice of literature, especially that of the novel. Thus, Bakhtin will talk of "novelizing" non-fiction discourse. By this he means bringing in more voices.

Polyphonic discourse is Bakhtin's hero. (Bakhtin actually uses the terms "villain" and "hero" in offering his theory.) It comes in four forms: **active unidirectional**, **passive unidirectional**, **active varidirectional**, **passive varidirectional**. Don't let the terms turn you off. The distinctions are pretty simple. Active polyphony is outside the rhetor's control: Echoes come into discourse without the rhetor's awareness; passive, on the other hand, presumes the rhetor's control: He or she chooses which voices to admit by doing things such as quoting, citing, and echoing. Unidirectional polyphony is characterized by the rhetor's voice and the other voices moving in the same direction (i.e., toward the same rhetorical goal). Varidirectional, on the other hand, assumes that the text and the subtexts may move in different directions. This kind of discourse is sometimes termed "double-voiced," but the directions can be more than two. (Some confusion enters into Bakhtin studies because a Russian word for "double" means both "double" and "more than one.")

Of interest to the rhetorical critic are the two varieties of passive polyphony. Most critics assume that a rhetor makes choices in order to persuade. So, this Bakhtinian lens alerts us to the ways a rhetor might bring in other voices to either support the overt message or to set up, beneath the surface, a second (or third) message. If a critic wants to abandon the assumption that the rhetor controls the text, which some postmodern critics do, then the two varieties of active polyphony become of interest as well.

So, in applying this Bakhtinian insight, what does the critic do? He or she explores a text, listening for the other voices. Is someone quoted? Is someone just named, but with the likelihood that his or her words might be recalled by the audience? Are the words or the style of someone else echoed? Bakhtin terms this **stylization**. Are words put in the mouths of characters such as in, "The American people are saying x"? This is the classical technique known as *prospopoeia*, which Bakhtin appropriates. There are other ways of bringing in voices. But, for our purposes, this short list should suffice.

Bakhtin talks about stylization and another possibility, parody, in the following passage from his book on Dostoevsky:

> Stylization stylizes another's style in the direction of that style's own particular tasks. It merely renders those tasks conventional. Likewise a narrator's narration, refracting in itself the author's intention, does not swerve from its own straight path and is sustained in tones and intonations truly characteristic of it. The author's thought, once having penetrated someone else's discourse and made its home in it, does not collide with the other's thought, but rather follows after it in the same direction, merely making that direction conventional.
>
> The situation is different with parody. Here, as in stylization, the author again speaks in someone else's discourse, but in contrast to stylization parody introduces into that discourse a semantic intention that is directly opposed to the original one. The second voice, once having made its home in the other's discourse, clashes hostilely with its primordial host and forces him to serve directly opposing aims. Discourse

> becomes an arena of battle between two voices. In parody, therefore, there cannot be that fusion of voices possible in stylization or in the narration of the narrator. ...[4]

The assumption in what this says about stylization (and narration) is that the voices brought into a text and the rhetor's voice are pursuing the same course—thus, unidirectional. But what of texts where added voices and the rhetor's voice do not coincide, as in the case of parody? Let's consider some examples. What if, in a U.S. Senate debate over judicial nominations, a senator speaking for a nominee quotes a constituent who argues that confirmation ought to be obvious and that, rather than waste time debating the nomination, the Senate ought to be doing something about raising the minimum wage. The introduced voice says something that pursues a different course than the rhetor. Different doesn't necessarily mean opposed; different means different. Or, what if in a speech on sexual harassment in the military, a senator, after citing examples of the problem, says, "Clearly, nothing to be concerned about" based on the Senate's inaction. This senator's comment, taken at face value, says that there must then be no problem, but, rather clearly, buried in his or her comment is the true voice saying the exact opposite and implying that Congress has too often suggested that there is not a big problem and therefore not acted. This criticism of Congress is a different message from the senator's overt argument that sexual harassment in the military is a major problem. These are both examples of varidirectional or double-voiced polyphony. In the first instance, there is no contradiction between the voices: They just take different courses, with the added voice bringing in a matter that the rhetor wants to insinuate into the discussion. In the second, there is a *seeming* contradiction. This, of course, is the nature of irony: The rhetor means the opposite of what he or she overtly says. Consider a make-believe ad for a new pharmaceutical, something you might see on the television show *Saturday Night Live* Let's say it makes all sorts of outrageous claims. Beneath its surface is the message that this ad, like many others, manipulates listeners or viewers. What the fake ad writers are doing is engaging in parody, where there is a surface message we are not to believe and a second message that we are supposed to get. The surface message is ironic. Parody is a particular use of the ironic, one which Bakhtin (and theorists of parody influenced by Bakhtin) explores at length when discussing varidirectional or double-voiced polyphony.

As these examples of irony and parody make clear, double-voiced polyphony is often used in a mocking manner. What is stated is mocked by the alternative voice beneath the surface. Bakhtin explores this rhetorical possibility so much because mockery was especially interesting to him—perhaps because he was fundamentally against many of the ideologies that were gradually being imposed by the Soviet system and could not overtly criticize them.

The Carnivalesque

This interest in mockery—and the power it might give those power-down in a society, perhaps explains Bakhtin's interest in French satirist Rabelais. Like many satirists, Rabelais mocked human pretension by reducing the presumptively rational human to the animal extreme. In Rabelais's case, the reduction was often to the grossly animal.

In Bakhtin's book on Rabelais, the critic likens what Rabelais was doing to the medieval carnival. This was a day-long festival or fair at which mockery of the elite—the nobility, the university, the church—was permitted, even encouraged. Typically held on the day before the beginning of Lent, it was considered an irreverent blow-out before the penitential season. The tradition continues with Mardis Gras in New Orleans or Carnivale in Brazil and on many Caribbean islands. On Trinidad, for example, it has long been traditional for calypso artists to perform from parade floats. What they performed were poems/songs mocking those who held various kinds of power. Some Calypso artists became quite famous for their mockery.

Bakhtin saw Rabelais working in this spirit. Those who have embraced Bakhtin's ideas do not insist on precisely the kind of mockery one might find in either Rabelais's sketches or the medieval carnival's satirical excesses. The carnivalesque will frequently make heavy uses of the physical—of the body, for stressing the body, especially its grosser aspects, has long been a way of mocking the pretentious. In the 1970s, for example, a popular college dorm room poster depicted President Richard Nixon sitting on a toilet with his pants down. That was a way of lowering Nixon to the level of all. However, mockery by this type of gross, physical depiction is not necessary in the carnivalesque. Recognizing this opens the definition of the strategy up a good bit.

Method

There are many ways to be a Bakhtinian critic. Two have been suggested by what has presented in this chapter. One might be interested in describing and assessing the impact of the polyphony a rhetor has created. In this case, the critic must closely read a text, looking for the voices that the text admits. As already noted, quoting, citing, stylizing, and creating prosopopoeia are common ways of inserting other voices into one's discourse. These would be tools used in constructing passive unidirectional polyphony. Also relevant are irony and parody, tools used in constructing passive varidirectional polyphony. Any ideas introduced through quoting, etc., that seem off to the side may also be used by a rhetor to create this kind of double-voiced discourse. So, the critic's task is, simply, to ask who is quoted, who is cited, etc.

Then, with a list of the other voices in a text before him or her, the critic should assess what, in general, the rhetor is up to. If the discourse in passive, then the rhetor is presumed to be in control and his or her rhetorical goals ought to be discernible. The critic's job is to pinpoint those rhetorical goals. Why has the rhetor created the polyphony he or she has?

Looking for and analyzing the carnivalesque is the second task. Here, a critic would select a moment of seeming irreverence. It could be as large as the demonstrations by women that filled the street on January 21, 1917; it could be as small as a parodic YouTube posting. The critic would then catalogue how the moment exhibits irreverence. What is done? What is said? Some carnivalesque moments are heavy on acts; others, on words. Then, the critic would clearly identify the target(s) of the irreverence. In the tradition of Rabelais, some Bakhtinian critics seem to prefer events that call attention to the body, especially its gross animal dimensions, sometimes even restricting the label "carnivalesque" to such moments. Most critics apply Bakhtin's concept more broadly. Either way, the critic should try to assess the effectiveness of the irreverence. In doing so, the critic may have to wrestle with an aspect of the carnivalesque that has often called into question its rhetorical effectiveness—that it is often irreverence that the targeted establishment has licensed. That was true of the medieval carnival that Bakhtin discusses; it may or may not be true of irreverent moments since.

I have talked about two tasks that a Bakhtinian critic might undertake (i.e., two methods he or she might use). As a consequence, one might think that there are indeed multiple Bakhtins—well, at least two. But these two are connected in Bakhtin's theory. In exploring passive varidirectional double-voiced discourse, Bakhtin is very interested in how other voices can be used to undermine authority. His interest in parody is but one manifestation of Bakhtin's interest in irreverence. He—I surmise—would see Rabelais's use of parody—and more broadly, satire—as but an extension of what he says in the Dostoevsky book about double-voiced discourse. In the case of carnival, the irreverence is perhaps more enacted and less verbalized, but the intent is the same. One reading Bakhtin needs to keep in mind that opposition very much characterized his work. There are many aspects of Soviet society (and modern society) that Bakhtin seems strongly opposed to. His sociolinguistic terminology and his suppression by Soviet authorities limit what he can say, but he clearly saw that words, with a life of their own, were tools that could be used by an opposition.

Application: Polyphony in Barack Obama's 2008 Election Night Address

President Obama celebrated his 2008 victory outdoors in Grant Park in Chicago. Thousands joined in the celebration, representing young and old, white and black. Obama said the kinds of things one would expect: He thanked supporters, he noted the fact that he had made history by being the first African American elected to the presidency, and he repeated the message of hope that he had sounded throughout the campaign. All very predictable. Here are some of his words:

> If there is anyone out there who still doubts that America is a place where all things are possible; who still wonders if the dream of our founders is alive in our time; who still questions the power of our democracy, tonight is your answer.

> *****

> It's the answer spoken by young and old, rich and poor, Democrat and Republican, black, white, Latino, Asian, Native American, gay, straight, disabled and not disabled— Americans who sent a message to the world that we have never been a collection of Red States and Blue States: we are, and always will be, the United States of America.

> *****

> It's been a long time coming, but tonight, because of what we did on this day, in this election, at this defining moment, change has come to America.

> *****

> But above all, I will never forget who this victory truly belongs to—it belongs to you. I was never the likeliest candidate for this office. We didn't start with much money or many endorsements. Our campaign was not hatched in the halls of Washington—it began in the backyards of Des Moines and the living rooms of Concord and the front porches of Charleston.
>
> It was built by working men and women who dug into what little savings they had to give five dollars and ten dollars and twenty dollars to this cause. It grew strength from the young people who rejected the myth of their generation's apathy; who left their homes and their families for jobs that offered little pay and less sleep; from the not-so-young people who braved the bitter cold and scorching heat to knock on the doors of perfect strangers; from the millions of Americans who volunteered, and organized, and proved that more than two centuries later, a government of the people, by the people and for the people has not perished from this Earth. This is your victory.

Barack Obama, Selection from Victory Speech on Election Night. Copyright © 2008 by Barack Obama.

*****

The road ahead will be long. Our climb will be steep. We may not get there in one year or even one term, but America—I have never been more hopeful than I am tonight that we will get there. I promise you—we as a people will get there.

There will be setbacks and false starts. There are many who won't agree with every decision or policy I make as President, and we know that government can't solve every problem. But I will always be honest with you about the challenges we face. I will listen to you, especially when we disagree. And above all, I will ask you join in the work of remaking this nation the only way it's been done in America for two-hundred and twenty-one years—block by block, brick by brick, calloused hand by calloused hand.

*****

Let us resist the temptation to fall back on the same partisanship and pettiness and immaturity that has poisoned our politics for so long. Let us remember that it was a man from this state who first carried the banner of the Republican Party to the White House—a party founded on the values of self-reliance, individual liberty, and national unity. Those are values we all share, and while the Democratic Party has won a great victory tonight, we do so with a measure of humility and determination to heal the divides that have held back our progress. As Lincoln said to a nation far more divided than ours, "We are not enemies, but friends … though passion may have strained It must not break our bonds of affection." And to those Americans whose support I have yet to earn—I may not have won your vote, but I hear your voices, I need your help, and I will be your President too.

And to all those watching tonight from beyond our shores, from parliaments and palaces to those who are huddled around radios in the forgotten corners of our world—our stories are singular, but our destiny is shared, and a new dawn of American leadership is at hand. To those who would tear this world down—we will defeat you. To those who seek peace and security—we support you. And to those who have wondered if America's beacon still burns as bright—tonight we proved once more that the true strength of our nation comes not from the might of our arms or the scale of our wealth, but from the enduring power of our ideals: democracy, liberty, opportunity, and unyielding hope.

*****

This election had many firsts and many stories that will be told for generations. But one that's on my mind tonight is about a woman who cast her ballot in Atlanta. She's a lot like the millions of others who stood in line to make their voice heard in the election except for one thing—Ann Nixon Cooper is 106 years old.

She was born just a generation past slavery; a time when there were no cars on the roads or planes in the sky; when someone like her couldn't vote for two reasons—because she was a woman and because of the color of her skin.

And tonight, I think about all that she's seen throughout her century in America—the heartaches and the hope; the struggle and the progress; the times we were told that we can't, and the people who pressed on with that American creed: Yes we can.

> At a time when women's voices were silenced and their hopes dismissed, she lived to see them stand up and speak out and reach for the ballot. Yes we can.
>
> When there was despair in the dust bowl and depression across the land, she saw a nation conquer fear itself with a New Deal, new jobs and a new sense of common purpose. Yes we can.
>
> When the bombs fell on our harbor and tyranny threatened the world, she was there to witness a generation rise to greatness and a democracy was saved. Yes we can.
>
> She was there for the buses in Montgomery, the hoses in Birmingham, a bridge in Selma, and a preacher from Atlanta who told a people that "We Shall Overcome." Yes we can.
>
> A man touched down on the moon, a wall came down in Berlin, a world was connected by our own science and imagination. And this year, in this election, she touched her finger to a screen, and cast her vote, because after 106 years in America, through the best of times and the darkest of hours, she knows American can change. Yes we can.[5]

Much of the speech is the predictable stuff one says when one wins. Obama, however, enriched the address by bringing other voices into it.[6] The voices are largely predictable, too. Given that his story is an African American one, he quoted Lincoln, who freed the slaves, and refers to Dr. Martin Luther King, Jr., who led one branch (the non-violent Southern Christian Leadership Conference) of the Civil Rights Movement. He also either quoted or echoed a string of U.S. presidents—Franklin Roosevelt, John F. Kennedy, Lyndon B. Johnson, and Bill Clinton. The common thread is, of course, that they are all Democrats. He told the story of an average American, an African American woman who voted for the first time in 2008—at the age of 106. Part of her story is how, through the years, many barriers had been placed in her way when it came to voting. So, the polyphony Obama created further celebrated his victory as an African American one and also made it clear that he is not a departure from Democratic Party tradition but a continuation of a line of progressively thinking Democrats.

Obama also declares that "it's been a long time coming." The polyphony here is complex. It echoes a Sam Cooke song often sung during the Civil Rights Movement, a song with roots in what was sung by slaves themselves. That line, I would suggest, also echoes the song "Long Time Gone," written by David Crosby and sung by Crosby, Stills, and Nash, with its often-repeated "It's been a long time coming" line. This could be coincidence; it could be relevant. Echoing Crosby, Stills, and Nash might evoke, in the mind of listeners, other politically tinged songs by the group—for example, their (with Young) 1970 lament "Ohio" written after four unarmed students were shot by Ohio National Guard troops at Kent State University or their 1968 ironic tune "Chicago." Let's consider the latter.

In 1968, the Democratic National Convention met in Chicago. Besides the goings-on at the convention hall, there were goings-on of several sorts by thousands of protesters. The media was covering the convention and protests equally. Chicago Mayor Richard

Daley did not appreciate the image of his city that was being shown, and so he ordered the police to charge the unarmed demonstrators and forcibly remove them from where they were demonstrating. Where were they demonstrating? Grant Park, the very same place Obama chose to give his 2008 speech.

Some, in 1968, termed the Chicago "police riot" (as a later commission termed it) the end of the dream. JFK had initiated this dream, and the media had termed it "Camelot"; Johnson tried to sustain it, calling it "The Great Society." But the Vietnam conflict, the government's inability to fund both the war and JFK-LBJ social programs, the protests against the war, and the violent reaction against the protests here in Chicago and elsewhere ended the dream. Mixed in with this ending was MLK's 1963 dream and how, with his death in April 1968, his peaceful dream was being replaced with often-violent activism. By speaking in Chicago's Grant Park and by echoing a song ("Long Time Gone") that recalled another song ("Chicago"), Obama may have been recalling what Grant Park was and then redeeming it from that 1968 past. He might be restoring that JFK dream, as well as confirming the possibility of another dream, the one spoken of by the "young preacher from Atlanta" that he evokes in the address.

Obama's speech, then, is richer than it first seems. It is rich in many ways. One is the way Bakhtin's theory of polyphony (in this case, passive unidirectional) illuminates it. Many who listen to texts, be they speeches, films, recordings, or ads, often will say, "I've heard that before." What they are hearing are the entailments that come along with words and phrases. According to Bakhtin, they just come, unless you consciously try to strip language of its life by, for example, writing/speaking "legalese" or technical jargon. But a rhetor can do more than just let the voices come. The rhetor can create an orchestration that enhances his or her performance. That is precisely what Obama has done in this instance.

A related concept that might be mentioned here is that of intertextuality. Those who talk about this concept usually cite the work of European linguist and literary critic Julia Kristeva. In essays such as "Word, Dialogue, and the Novel" (1966) and "The Bounded Text" (1967), Kristeva talks about how literary works evoke other literary works in ways that extend beyond literary allusions that the author, of course, is absolutely aware of. Kristeva believes that previous works of literature as well as previous uses of language can intrude into a text, even without the author being fully aware. In making her argument, Kristeva cites Bakhtin. The utility of the concept of intertextuality is that it alerts us to how, not just voices, but previous texts can be part of the orchestration a rhetor either knowingly (passive) or unknowingly (active) creates. In evoking Sam Cooke and in evoking Crosby, Stills, Nash, and Young, Obama would be exhibiting what Kristeva would term intertextuality.

Application: The Carnivalesque on the Floor of the US House of Representatives

Just to demonstrate that the carnivalesque need not involve the gross references to bodily functions such as drinking, eating, or excreting, let's go to the austere US Congress to explore an example of the carnivalesque.

Now, you might think that bills the members of Congress introduce all make their way through various processes (hearings and the like) and eventually come to the floor of the House of Representatives or the Senate for a vote. No. What gets to the floor is controlled by the leader of the majority party. So, in the House, that is usually the Speaker, whereas in the Senate it is the Majority Leader. Down through history, these leaders have typically let bills sponsored by either political party move forward. They would undoubtedly favor their party a bit, letting its legislation get to the floor more frequently and more readily, but they did not shut the opposition party down entirely. Lyndon B. Johnson, for example, when he was Majority Leader during the Eisenhower presidency, allowed legislation favored by the Republican president and his party to be considered. As Democrat Johnson saw the matter, Eisenhower had won and therefore deserved to have his ideas fully debated, whereas his job, as Majority Leader, was to provide a "loyal opposition." Johnson was as partisan as a politician can get, but he nonetheless did not see fit to shut the other party down.

Recently, however, the partisan atmosphere in the Congress has become so strong that leaders are indeed blocking all legislation they or their party do not like. In the current House of Representatives, for example, Speaker Paul Ryan will not allow a bill to come to the floor if it lacks majority support from the Republican caucus. Thus, a bill that might pass with strong Democratic support and some Republican support will not get an "up" or "down" vote on the floor.

In 2015, in the House, several gun control bills were introduced—in the wake of major tragedies involving firearms. The Speaker of the House was not allowing them to come to the floor for debate and a vote. So, what are the Democrats to do? How can they make the point that the Republicans, with the power to regulate procedural matters, are preventing even the discussion that ought to be a hallmark of democracy?

Well, Congressman John Lewis of Georgia, a leader of the Civil Rights Movement in his younger days, decided to launch a sit-in. During the Civil Rights Movement, sit-ins were a tactic frequently used by student members of the Student Non-Violent Coordinating Committee. In Greensboro, North Carolina, for example, students at a number of black colleges banded together, went to the downtown Woolworth's, sat down at the lunch counter, and intended to stay there until served. Back-ups were nearby to replace any demonstrators who grew tired, had a class, or were arrested. Evoking the sit-ins of the 1960s, Lewis led a number of legislators to the front of the chamber where they stood or sat, in theory refusing to move until there was a vote.

Here are Lewis' words:

> For months, even for years, through several sessions of Congress, I wondered what would bring this body to take action. What would finally make Congress do what is right, what is just, what the people of this country have been demanding and what is long overdue? We have lost hundreds and thousands of innocent people to gun violence—tiny little children, babies, students and teachers, mothers and fathers, sisters and brothers, daughters and sons, friends and neighbors. And what has this body done? Mr. Speaker, nothing. Not one thing. We have turned deaf ears—we have turned deaf ears to the blood of the innocent and the concern of our nation. We are blind to a crisis. Mr. Speaker, where is the heart of this body? Where is our soul? Where is our moral leadership? Where is our courage?
>
> Those who work on bipartisan solution[s] are pushed aside. Those who pursue commonsense improvement are beaten down. Reason is criticized. Obstruction is praised. Newtown, Aurora, Charleston, Orlando—what is the tipping point? Are we blind? Can we see? How many more mothers, how many more fathers need to shed tears of grief before we do something? We were elected to lead, Mr. Speaker. We must be headlights and not taillights. We cannot continue to stick our heads in the sand and ignore the reality of mass gun violence in our nation. Deadly mass shootings are becoming more and more frequent. Mr. Speaker, this is the fight. It is not an opinion. We must remove the blinders. The time for silence and patience is long gone. We're calling on the leadership of the House to bring commonsense gun control legislation to the House floor. Give us a vote! Let us vote! We came here to do our job! We came here to work!
>
> The American people are demanding action. Do we have the courage? Do we have raw courage to make at least a down payment on ending gun violence in America? We can no longer wait. We can no longer be patient. So today we come to the well of the House to dramatize the need for action—not next month, not next year, but now, today! Sometimes you have to make a way out of no way. We have been quiet for too long. There comes a time when you have to say something, we have to make a little noise, when you have to move your feet. This is the time to get in the way. The time to act is now. We will be silent no more. The time for silence is over.[7]

As the sit-in proceeded, sympathetic members of the Senate joined in. C-SPAN covers all House proceedings, so the sit-in was on live television until the Speaker, exercising his power, ordered the C-SPAN cameras turned off. What did the demonstrators do then? They used the video function of their cell phones (actually forbidden on the House floor) to record their sit-in. News networks picked up the video feed, and, ironically, C-SPAN, intent on covering the news, played the cell phone videos that the other news networks were showing. This sit-in lasted for fifteen hours.

The issue Lewis was raising was serious, but there were certainly moments of humor during the sit-in, as well as much camaraderie. It had very much the mocking feel of the carnival. It mocked the Republican leadership; it not so subtly suggested that that leadership was abusing its power. Although the Democratic members were as much members

John Lewis, Selection from Speech on Floor of House of Representatives, 2016.

of the elite as the Republicans in a broader social context, in the specific Congressional context, the sit-in was a power-down group using irreverent (i.e., against the rules) tactics to mock the power-up group for its abuses. No gross bodies; no toilet references, but it was nonetheless what Bakhtinian critics mean when referring to the carnivalesque. Such exhibitions have an irreverent tone, yes, but the essence of the carnivalesque is the power dynamic, how those in a down position use mockery to at least question the use to which those in an up position put the power they have. Now, it is of course true that the Democratic legislators were arguably members of a politically elite class, and it is also true that the rules that govern the House were set by both parties and, in theory, agreed to by all when they took office. But one can nonetheless be power-down if the rules are being used consistently to thwart one from performing his or her legislative duties. This is how the Democrats, who wanted gun control legislation to at least be debated felt. Bakhtin's notion of the carnivalesque, then, need to apply to irreverent protest by just those totally without power.

Strengths and Limitations

The Bakhtinian approach illuminates dimensions of communication that might be over-looked—or treated in passing. Premised on a theory about the very nature of language, the approach is alert to the voices that find their way into a text and thereby enrich it. Anyone who has studied speechwriting is well aware that, in planning public addresses, those wielding the pen are well aware of who they quote, who they refer to, and who they echo. The Bakhtinian approach helps illuminate the orchestration one finds in political discourse.

That orchestration, although important, is not the only aspect of a text that should be illuminated. Similarly, recognizing how a text may serve a carnivalesque role is not recognizing all that a text does. So, the Bakhtinian approach may, in its emphases on voices and dissent, overlook other important dimension of a text. The approach can also be overused by the ingenious critic who claims to find echoes where there may not be any. Bill Clinton talked about building a bridge to the twenty-first century. For a short period of time, other rhetors using the term "bridge" or phrase "building a bridge" were probably echoing Clinton. Is that still true? Even further back, Kennedy was evidently fond of the word "vigor." For a time, using the word echoed JFK. But today? So, the critic needs to be careful not to find echoes where there aren't any. This care may put the critic in the awkward position of contradicting Bakhtin's fundamental premise about words and phrases all having entailments. But, one may need to qualify Bakhtin's pronouncement by observing that, if few or no people hear the entailments, are they in any real sense there?

Bakhtin's concept of the carnivalesque also needs to be used with caution. Not all instances of irreverence are carnivalesque. Although there need not be gross references to bodily functions (as in Rabelais), there does need to be acts and/or words that reduce those in power to a lower level—common with or even below those using the carnivalesque. The carnivalesque is, in theory, a radical rhetorical tool, especially if it is seen as not permitted or not fully permitted. The concept becomes watered down and loses its power if any and all demonstrations are considered through this Bakhtinian lens.

Exemplars

Janack, James. "The Rhetoric of 'The Body': Jesse Ventura and Bakhtin's Carnivalesque." *Communication Studies* 57, no. 2 (2006): 197–214.

Jasinski, James. "Heteroglossia, Polyphony, and the *Federalist Papers*." *Rhetoric Society Quarterly*, 27 no. 1 (1997): 23–46.

McLean, Polly Bugros, and David Wallace. "Blogging the Unspeakable: Racial Politics, Bakhtin, and the Carnivalesque." *International Journal of Communication* 7 (2013): 1518–37.

Zulick, Margaret D. "Pursuing Controversy: Kristeva's Split Subject, Bakhtin's Many-Tongued World." *Argumentation & Advocacy* 28 (1991): 91–102.

Suggested Applications

Speech Applications

- John F. Kennedy's inaugural is often echoed in other speeches, but was Kennedy (and his speechwriter Ted Sorenson) echoing others? Investigate what voices Kennedy may have been trying to bring in as well as what words, put in the mouths of the nation, he was addressing.

- A filibuster in the U.S. Senate is not always as dramatic as the one depicted in Frank Capra's classic film *Mr. Smith Goes to Washington*. In fact, the term can be applied to any attempt to delay normal proceedings. Thus, on February 8, 2018, Kentucky Senator Rand Paul took the floor to criticize the legislation that would keep the U.S. government operating. Consider it as an example of the carnivalesque.

Non-Speech Applications

- The relatively new African American History and Culture Museum in Washington, DC, embraces many voices as it creates what Bakhtin would term "polyphony." Describe this polyphony and discuss why the museum's designers/curators chose the voices they did.

- The day after Donald Trump's inauguration, women took to the streets of Washington, DC and other cities to protest. Consider their demonstrations as carnivalesque.

Notes

1. Schuster, Charles I. "Mikhail Bakhtin as Rhetorical Theorist." *College English* 47, no. 6 (1985): 574–607.

2. Bakhtin, Mikhail. *Problems of Dostoevsky's Poetic.* Edited and Translated by Caryl Emerson. Minneapolis, MN: University of Minnesota Press, 1984. 202.

3. Bakhtin, 195.

4. Bakhtin, 193.

5. Obama, Barack. "Election Night Victory Speech." Speech. http://www.edition.cnn/2008/POLITICS/11/04/transcript.

6. For a fuller account, see Sheckels, Theodore, F. "Place, Genre, and Polyphony in Barack Obama's Election Night Address." *American Behavioral Scientist* 54, no. 4 (2010): 394–405; and Sheckels, Theodore F. "The Polyphonic Orchestration of Barack Obama, 2004 to 2012." *American Behavioral Scientist* 57, no. 12 (2013): 1716–30.

7. Lewis, John. Speech. http://www/democracynow.org/2016/6/23/let_us_vote_rep_john_lewis.

Figure credit

Fig. 10: Source: https://pixabay.com/en/obama-barack-obama-president-man-356133/.

Lin-Manuel Miranda, the creator and star of the Broadway musical *Hamilton*.

CHAPTER 11

Ideological Criticism

This chapter draws together a number of similar approaches. All deal with power. All deal with critiquing power relations that might not be immediately apparent to you, or perhaps to anyone else as well. The last clause is important. An assumption undergirding all these approaches is that there is a prevailing order. It regulates who can speak and how, who can act and how. Different theorists call it different things, but the precise term really does not matter. What matters is that the prevailing order is present but can easily be overlooked because viewers, listeners, readers assume the order to be normative. That's the way it is, right?

The problem with that assumption is that the prevailing order is not neutral. It assigns positions within power structures: some are power-up, some are power-down. With that assignment come rights, privileges, opportunities, resources. The prevailing order has tangible, material implications. It can also affect identity, for, if you are labeled low in the prevailing order, you may begin to identify as just that. There are many ways this can happen: You can be power-down and identify as low because of gender, because of race, because of immigrant status, because of sexual orientation, because of social class. The list goes on. And some may be doubly or triply down because they fall into more than just one power-down group. Much of these dynamics are not immediately discerned. The ideological critic tries to bring them into the open.

The ideological critic is inherently a radical critic. He or she engaged in a critique of the prevailing order, with an awareness of its costs, with an eye to changing it—perhaps dramatically. The critic's role following most traditional theories is to explain how persuasion occurs by looking at elements in a text. That role is exceeded by the ideological critic. He or she seeks to explain how a text instantiates the prevailing order *and*, through radical critique, overthrow that instantiation. Not all are comfortable with this role, but it is one of the most exciting ones rhetorical criticism has ever taken on. Here is how critic Raymie McKerrow puts the task. Although he refers to "critical rhetoric" *per se*, his description is applicable to all the approaches outlined in this chapter:

> In practice, a critical rhetoric seeks to unmask or demystify the discourse of power. The aim is to understand the integration of power/knowledge in society—what possibilities for change the integration invites or inhibits and what intervention strategies might be considered appropriate to effect social change.[1]

The prevailing order is an ideology—or, perhaps more accurately, a set of ideologies. The ideological critic attempts to expose and explode the ideology or ideologies and to replace it with one that better serves humanity by eliminating some of negative effects of the prevailing order.

In this chapter, we will consider Marxist critique and post-colonial critique. We will also consider the insights offered by theorists Michel Foucault and Jacques Derrida and queer theory. Lumping all these together may bother some readers, for there are, out there, ardent disciples of Foucault, for example, who think they have little common ground with a Marxist thinker such as Antonio Gramsci. Since this textbook introduces students to rhetorical criticism, I am hoping that the genuine differences among the approaches and thinkers brought together here can be set aside with a focus on the enterprise they share. The further explorations students might engage in can alert them to the important nuances that have caused critics to much prefer one person's insights—and terms—to another's. Students might then choose to embrace one approach over another because it rings truer with them than others. This is fine. For the moment, however, the focus will be on the enterprise shared by all who have chosen to challenge the dominant ideology.

One important critique is missing from this chapter. That is feminist critique. It is treated in a separate chapter because of, first, its long history; second, its impact in criticism; and third, its primary focus on a rather different power determinant, gender, than the other approaches.

Marxist Approaches

Notice the "s." There is not a single Marxist approach. In fact, Marxist approaches seem to have come in waves. Antonio Gramsci, Louis Althusser, Theodor Adorno (and the Frankfurt School), and Frederic Jameson are all names we associate with espousing a particular brand of Marxism. They all, however, focus on social class as the crucial determinant of who has power. In most basic Marxist theory, the power-holding class is the one that controls the capital in society (the factories, for example), and the power-down class is the one that is providing the labor but is not benefitting fairly from that labor. Most Marxist theorists, however, do not present the class division as simple as capitalists versus workers. That's a formulation that resonated decades ago, but, now, Marxism (and Marxist criticism) seems aware that the power that the dominant class has extends beyond the purely economic. Although this broader Marxism might, by some, be said to be new, Gramsci talked of **hegemony** long ago and wrote, from his prison cell, of more than just economics. Gramsci may not have been caught up in the intellectual swirling in Europe that had Frankfort School professors trying to merge many disciplines (economics, philosophy, psychology, sociology) all into a single critique, but the Italian was well aware of the power dynamics that he felt poisoned society. He knew hegemony. From his personal life, he not only knew oppression, but he knew how he was complicit in promoting and protecting the structures that guaranteed his own oppression. This complicity is a crucial dimension of hegemony: It is not simply oppression, but oppression that those oppressed are complicit in.

Recognizing who has and exercises hegemonic power is the crucial first step. Then comes the attempt to use the power inherent in the critical act to undermine this power. Let's consider the recurring debates in the U.S. Congress over taxes. Imagine a member offering a strong speech about how corporate tax rates must be lowered to boost the economy. The argument is premised on the assumption that, given more money, businesses will invest it, producing jobs and, thus, more money for people to spend on various goods. Now, this argument would probably be countered by others who would question whether businesses would actually invest, but let's assume the initial argument prevails, as it has at a number of points in our recent history. A Marxist critic would look at the argument in terms of how the tax policy distributes not just money but power. Consider the unemployed woman, waiting for the job to emerge. She is clearly disempowered insofar as she is dependent on how the business owners, who are the ones with power, choose to act. And nothing in the argument, as I presented it, restrains their power in the least. The Marxist critics' task would be to expose the power relations—in their fullness, expose the human consequences of those power relations, and advocate for whatever argument that would empower the unemployed woman as opposed to those who already possess both economic and social benefits. This empowering would not be easy. Why? Because power, in all sorts of ways, is held by those making the pro-business argument. They largely control the political processes through their donations, and they may largely control the media because, independent as the media might seem, they are owned by large corporate entities who have more in common with the capitalists than the proletariat. Hegemony is hegemony, after all, because of how far the power reaches.

One way to go beyond just exposing the effects of power is to promote discourse that runs contrary to the hegemonic order. As a literary critical movement, Marxist criticism has tried to valorize writing that reflects the lives and values of the working class. Such writing may have a very different style, one not thought to be literary. Marxist criticism insists that not only is this style just as valid but it may be preferred because it is more authentic. In England, for example, there was a group of writers in the middle of the twentieth century who literary historians refer to as "the angry young men." One of them, Alan Silitoe, wrote the novel *Saturday Night, Sunday Morning* (1958), with a working-class protagonist. The protagonist is presented, warts and all, and his English, slang and all, is used in the narrative. Silitoe also wrote the novella (turned into a feature film directed by Tony Richardson) *The Loneliness of the Long-Distance Runner* (1959). In it, a working-class character, given the opportunity for a posh education because of his athletic prowess, ultimately refuses to play the elite class's game. He refuses to be exploited. The Marxist critic would salute what Silitoe—and the other "angry young men"—were doing: Bringing non-elite characters, voices, and concerns into literature.

Rhetorical critics could make a parallel move. Rather than study—and, thereby, signal as significant—elite discourse, rhetorical critics could find and study that of the worker. Rhetorical critics often do not know where to locate such discourse—mainly because it's not in the anthologies of great speeches, but there are newsletters, posters, and memory sites that are not the product of the elite. Valorizing these would be one way to counter the prevailing power structure. The next chapter will mention how initially Karlyn Kohrs Campbell, and then many others, found the supposedly lost voices of many, many women speakers down through the centuries. A similar project would have to be undertaken to discover the voices of the working class, which are probably not as long gone as the elites would lead you to believe.

Academic institutions are sometimes attacked by political conservatives for a liberal bias. Many political liberals in academe are quite happy with the charge—because they think their perspective should be preferred. But even these faculty might be surprised by the extent to which they are entrapped within structures set up by the elite. To a large extent, what is read by students and what is studied by scholars is established by institutions such as mainstream publishers, the nation's most prestigious universities, and even the government. The discourse of the workers may, then, be difficult to find because mainstream publishers did not print it, because prestigious universities did not encourage the study of it, and because the government issued no grants to study it or established no archives or libraries to maintain it. A Marxist critic in an academic context, then, must be aware of how his or her context may well be part of the hegemonic structure.

Post-Colonial Approaches

Stuart Hall, often pointed to as the leading figure in cultural studies, is often credited with the term hegemony. (As already noted, Gramsci used the term as well.) Hall tends to talk about power differences less in terms of class and more in terms of culture, although class is not irrelevant. Other theorists also deal heavily with cultural dominance as well and, like Hall, they think in terms that involve colonization, for, now centuries ago, the nations of Europe colonized other parts of the world, creating power dynamics that still exist. So, in Africa, for example, a cluster of nations was colonized by France; another cluster by the United Kingdom; a few by Portugal; etc. Unlike the colonization of other places, such as the United States, Canada, Australia, New Zealand, and South Africa, this colonization did not entail transporting large numbers of people to the colonies. Rather, this colonization had more to do with resources, but it did involve transporting culture to these less-developed nations, so named at least by the "conquering colonizer." So, the colonial powers transformed the educational institutions so that they were more like what one would find in Paris or London or Lisbon; the colonial powers promoted European styles and standards for literary expression, supplanting many oral traditions; and the colonial powers imported Christianity, sometimes aggressively. What happened in Africa is the most dramatic example of this type of colonization, but it occurred in other places as well (e.g., British colonization of Hong Kong).

So, in terms of matters such as education, literature, and religion, the metropolitan center (i.e., London, Paris, Lisbon, etc.) exercised hegemonic control. That control extended to matters such as politics and economics, too. These colonized nations began to have political structures that were colonial copies of what was found in the European capitals, and, quite frequently, their economies were directed, not by their long-terms needs, but by what the metropolitan center needed. For example, in many African nations, colonial forces strongly encouraged soil-depleting cash crops (i.e., those that could be sold internationally) over food crops. These African nations, of course, did not see the lion's share of the profits from the cash crops, and then when the market for the cash crops collapsed, they were left with no food and poor soil—in other words, famine. The widespread famine in Sudan, for example, can be traced to British colonial policy that pushed soil-depleting cash crops there.

This is the story for places where the colonial influence did not involve a large influx of people. It is the typical African story because, in most African locations, colonists experienced a high mortality rate because of tropical diseases when they did take up residence. Within post-colonial studies, a curious tension exists involving the nations that were colonized by people, not just by their supposedly superior ideas. These people, living in places with a mix of indigenous and colonizing people, are victims. Their education, among other things, is dominated by the metropolitan center; their economic moves are often dictated by the needs of some European power. However, because they came from that center and perhaps served as instruments of that center's will, they may have been—and may still be—complicit to a degree in the colonizing process. More important, in all these cases, the colonizing, who often were poorly treated in the nations they fled, have treated the indigenous people in the places they came to in much the same oppressive way in which they were treated by the European power. Tragically, the oppressed turned into the oppressor. In the United States and Canada, the colonizers colonized the native North Americans; in Australia, the aborigines; in New Zealand, the Maoris; and in South Africa, the numerous African tribes that lived in the four colonies that formed the Union of South Africa after the Boer War in the early twentieth century. Because these colonizers acted in such a manner, many post-colonial theorists do not want to embrace them in the ranks of oppressed people that post-colonial criticism is designed to help. In literary studies, for example, some post-colonial critics refuse to grant Canadian or Australian writing by whites post-colonial status. In *The Empire Writes Back* (1989), Bill Ashcroft, Gareth Griffiths, and Helen Tiffin term these places "settler societies" and attempt to put their literature on an equal post-colonial footing with that from Nigeria or Keyna or even indigenous writers in these settler places. To a large extent, that attempt (by three Australians) has been rejected, leaving settler discourse in a curious neither-here-nor-there position.

The post-colonial picture, then, is complex. Two examples of what a rhetorical critic might do should make matters clearer. One involves African discourse; the other, Native American.

With reference to Africa, a rhetorical critic might consider how Europeans, in their discourse, talked about the African people they colonized. What did the Europeans say in the reports they issued on their travels? How did they describe the people and their customs? What did the European politicians back home say about the African continent as they carved it up and distributed it among themselves? Did they suggest that the people were so inferior they would not resist? Did they suggest that what they, the Europeans, were doing, was noble insofar as they were bringing the superior Western culture and the superior Christian religion to people labeled primitive?

The colonial enterprise in Africa was amazingly effective in changing education and politics there. Those Africans aspiring to status and power sought out European-style education and, politically, before and after independence, behaved in a European style. A critic might look at their discourse. To what extent did they behave rhetorically as if in Europe? To what extent did they try to mix European ways and African ways in their discourse? Are there any examples of African rhetors, explicitly or implicitly, thumbing their noses at the European ways? Among rhetorical artists such as South Africa's Nelson Mandela or Liberia's Ellen Johnson Sirleaf, both of whom felt they could not be as radical as Kenyan author Ngugi wa Thiong'o, who tried to totally reject the European? Mandela and Sirleaf, as political leaders, needed to work within governmental structures modeled after the European. They would occasionally acknowledge the constraint they were under, but they did not try to either abandon or destroy the structures. Ngugi, on the other hand, did try to reject the structures by rejecting both the colonial languages and the modes of writing London privileged.

In post-colonial Africa, an interesting tension developed between two writers—and two groups of writers—over this very question.[2] The situation of these writers and rhetors, caught up in a colonized and then post-colonized context, is complex. Ashcroft, Griffiths, and Tiffin explain it in *The Empire Writes Back*:

> Post-colonial literatures developed through several stages which can be seen to correspond to stages both of national or regional consciousness and of the project of asserting difference from the imperial centre. During the imperial period writing in the language of the imperial centre is inevitably, of course, produced by a literate elite whose primary identification is with the colonizing power. ... Such texts can never form the basis for an indigenous culture nor can they be integrated in any way with the culture which already exists in the countries invaded. Despite their detailed reportage of landscape, custom, and language, they inevitably privilege the centre, emphasizing the "home" over the "native," the "metropolitan" over the "provincial" or "colonial," and so forth.

*****

> The second stage of production within the evolving discourse of the post-colonial is the literature produced "under imperial license" by "natives" or "outcasts. ... "The producers signify by the very fact of writing in the language of the dominant culture that they have temporarily or permanently entered a specific and privileged class endowed with the language, education, and leisure necessary to produce such works.

*****

> It is characteristic of these early post-colonial texts that the potential for subversion in their themes cannot be fully realized. Although they deal with such powerful material as the brutality of the convict system ... , the historical potency of the supplanted and denigrated native cultures ... , or the existence of a rich cultural heritage older and more extensive than that of Europe ... they are prevented from fully exploring their anti-imperial potential. Both the available discourse and the material conditions for the production of literature in these early post-colonial societies restrain this possibility. The institution "Literature'" in the colony is under the direct control of the imperial ruling class who alone license the acceptable form and permit the publication and distribution of the resulting work. So, texts of this kind come into being within the constraints of a discourse and the institutional practice of a patronage system which limits and undercuts their assertion of a different perspective. The development of independent literatures depended

upon the abrogation of this constraining power and the appropriation of language and writing for new and distinctive usages. Such an appropriation is clearly the most significant feature of modern post-colonial literature. ...[3]

So, how do writers—and, by extension, rhetors—get beyond the power that arguably constrains them? Ngugi, as previously noted, totally rejected the European influence—to the point of refusing to write in English. His course would be very much in line with what Ashcroft, Griffiths, and Tiffgin say. Nigerian author Chinua Achebe, on the other hand, might disagree with their assessment, for he advocated blending the European and the African. In his famous novel *Things Fall Apart* (1958), he blends elements of classical tragedy with Ibo customs and folklore. He borrows his title from William Butler Yeats. Another Nigerian, Nobel laureate Wole Soyinka, writes plays that quite consciously merge cultures. *A Dance of the Forest*, a play he wrote to celebrate Nigerian independence in 1960, merges Yoruban lore with elements right out of Shakespeare's *A Midsummer Night's Dream*. Both Achebe and Soyinka believed they could sufficiently escape the metropolitan center while still accepting some of its terms, such as its language and its education. The post-colonial critic should, however, not choose between Ngugi and Achebe. Rather, the critic should valorize *both* the attempts to reject the impositions from the metropolitan center and be purely African *and* the attempts to blend what the metropolitan center says with what the particular African culture suggests. They are both ways of critiquing hegemony. The one is just a tad more radical than the other.

With reference to America, a rhetorical critic might consider how both government discourse and popular discourse depicted Native Americans in the nineteenth century. There were a few sympathetic portrayals, but most were not. Most—it might be argued—were in service of an agenda. If native Americans were depicted as ignorant, then the government was justified in directing their affairs—including directing where they might live. If they were depicted as savage, then the government was justified in waging war on them, acquiring their land in the process. The critic's goal would, of course, be to reveal what the government was up to in its discourse. The government was not, however, the only agent of hegemony in this case, for non-governmental sources also depicted native Americans in negative terms. This treatment extended well into the twentieth century. For example, how were native Americans depicted in motion picture westerns or television westerns? By the 1950s, the actual exploitation of native Americans was probably at an end: American colonialists had what they wanted by then. In the 1950s, then, we are dealing with a rhetoric that covered up what hegemonic forces had done. That rhetoric extended beyond movie and television westerns; even in academic history, scant attention was paid—until Dee Brown's landmark *Bury My Heart at Wounded Knee* (1971)—to the Indians' side of the story. He carefully examined the historical documents related to their post-Civil War history and offered a version of it that revealed hegemony at work.

A rhetorical critic would attend to that side. Native Americans voiced their sentiments throughout the nineteenth century. Are there nineteenth-century Indian documents associated with the "Trail of Tears" which forcibly removed Cherokees and others from the American Southeast to Oklahoma? Are there nineteenth-century Native American documents associated with the Indian Wars, documents that give us the voices of some of their heroes? These documents and voices should be valorized. And, as with African texts, their interplay between white ways and Indian ways should be investigated. Some Native American rhetors were, for example, masterful ironists, who would use white words ironically against what the colonizing whites were doing. They were engaging in counter-hegemonic discourse before it had a name.[4]

Critical Rhetoric

A Marxist critic and a post-colonial critic have very specific ideologies that they were reflecting in what they do with texts. But, the forces dominant in society are sometimes more general than the oppression of workers or the oppression of a to-be-colonized other. The theorist who may recognize this more general power structure is French thinker (no better term describes him) Michel Foucault.

Foucault uses the term "discourse" (translated as such from the French) in a very specific way. It is the set of dominant ideologies that define an era. These ideologies dictate, in ways those living in an era may be only dimly aware, how we educate, how we reason, how we assign value, how we live our lives, even down to personal matters such as our sexuality. There are, as Foucault saw matters, breaks that occur as we move from era to era, epoch to epoch, but these breaks are separated by centuries. One break was in the late Renaissance, and, with it, we moved into an era that highly values reason and insists on order. Perhaps all eras must enforce their discourse; however, this post-Renaissance one, with its insistence on order, truly needed to, for there was a very human, rather strong pull toward irrationality and disorder. Thus, the era develops many, many ways to regulate human words and human actions. As Foucault describes them in *Discipline and Punish* (1975), judicial and penal procedures are designed to regulate, and, in general, society is set up so that we all feel we are under a kind of surveillance. If we were aware of what the dominant discourse does, we might describe it as creepy; however, Foucault notes that most are unaware of what is going on. So, a rhetorical critic can make it his or her mission to expose the operations of the dominant discourse so that what is hidden becomes revealed, so that regulation—and oppression—have both visibility and a name.

Foucault also noted that there will be, especially when an era and its discourse seem to be changing to a new one, resistance to the dominant forces. He terms this resistance "counter-discursive," meaning that it challenges the dominant discourse. This counter-discursive activity, be it rhetorical or otherwise, will, of course, be resisted itself. The critical rhetorician here needs to salute the counter-discursive because it represents freedom. Discourse, although Foucault may seem to always stand in opposition to it, is not inherently bad, but, more often than not, because it does compel conformity and reduce freedom, it should be at least challenged. The critical rhetorician's activist position puts him or her in support of the challenge. So, just as ideological critics of other sorts valorize workers' genuine discourse or post-colonial people's genuine discourse, critical rhetoricians should valorize that discourse that interrogates and challenges.

Foucault's writings are fascinating, but they are dense, and many students find the leap between his discussion of penal institutions and sexual practices (in the multi-volume *History of Sexuality*) to what rhetorical critics usually do quite a leap. These students might advisedly turn to the work of contemporary rhetorician Raymie McKerrow. In a 1989 essay published in the journal *Communication Monographs,* McKerrow presents a critical rhetoric that, although influenced by post-colonial theorists and Foucault and others, cuts to the chase. He outlines both why one should use the liberating power of rhetorical criticism to challenge oppressive and general principles for doing so.[5] These principles are not a formula for enacting criticism. Rather, they are a set of assumptions or positions a critical rhetorician must embrace, among them a commitment to act based on the critical principles he or she would articulate.

Queer Theory

Queer theory emerges, in part, out of feminist criticism, so it might be more logical to treat it in the next chapter. However, queer theory has evolved in such a way that it is no longer as related to gender or sexual practices as it once was. The approach, very much in the spirit of Foucault, challenges all that those who seem to be calling the shots and setting the norms which might label deviant certain behavior. The deviant label, queer theorists thought, was being used to regulate—even outlaw—behavior out of line with what those in power thought normative.

Queer theory seems to have emerged partially out of feminism, copying and qualifying the earlier movement. Second-wave feminism (that current in the 1960s, 1970s, and early 1980s) was intent on challenging the assumption that behaviors—for example, interpersonal communication—that were truly masculinist were the norm. Thus, this version of feminism established feminist as equal to masculinist. They were viable alternatives, not a norm and an other. This project was well intended and, at its time, worthwhile, but it encountered a number of objections—from women. One was that it essentialized the female gender, not recognizing how socially constructed gender is; another was that it preserved a dichotomy, even though its own theory noted how the insistence on dichotomies was characteristic of the masculinist discourse second-wave feminists wanted to oppose.

Those who were objecting, strongly influenced by the work of Judith Butler, argued that there are many versions of female. Furthermore, when it comes to sexual orientation, there are positions other than heterosexual and homosexual. Sexuality cannot be reduced to two choices, just as gender cannot be reduced to two possibilities. Second-wave feminists elevated other to equal. Those who criticized the second wave were interested in gender definitions outside the two now-equal possibilities, gender definitions some might label deviant. Those interested primarily in both enlarging the sexual orientation choices and eliminating any and all evaluations of choices were the core queer theory critics.

Essentializing and setting up dichotomies is not limited to gender or sexual orientation. When it comes to race or social class or religion, dominant discourse falls into the same traps. We essentialize blacks or Muslims; we divide the economic picture into rich versus poor. Essentializing and creating dichotomies are understandable cognitive tendencies because they are neat and offer stability in society where reality may be messy. (They are also very much a part of the dominant rational discourse Foucault tried to undermine.) Queer theory consciously rejects this stability because it is false, because it is not true to the way life is.

Like the ideological approaches already outlined, queer theory pursues two directions. First, it critiques texts that offer false stability. It "queers" them. Second, it valorizes texts that assume a social situation that lacks essentializing and easy dichotomies. Ideological criticism, then, in general, pursues two courses—critique and valorization.

Method

How does one pursue these courses?

Critique requires that one closely read, looking for evidence of bias in favor of those who possess power and privilege in a society. On the level of content, one might ask if only the matters that are of interest to those power-up find their way into texts. Related, one might ask, if matters of interest to those power-down do find their way into texts, how are they treated? Are they trivialized? Are they pushed off to the side? Another way to critique is to consider perspectives. Those with power and privilege have a different perspective on issues than those without. On the issue of social services that the government might provide, those with power, who do not need such services, may have a financial perspective, asking how much services cost and how tax rates might be affected. Those without power might be much more focused on the stories—the plights—of those who need the services.

A third way to critique might be to consider matters of language. Is a certain kind of language being privileged—maybe even insisted on? Good grammar is learned in schools, but so are conventions of discourse that extend to matters larger than subject-verb agreement. Are these conventions being insisted on? Or is discourse that, either by accident or by choice, fails to observe the conventions being frowned upon or, worse, rejected?[6]

Valorizing requires some knowledge of what power-down groups want to bring into discourse and how they want to express themselves. In other words, a critic who wants to valorize must find his or her way into the power-down culture. This task can pose a problem, for the sympathetic critic is quite frequently a member of the elite and, as such, has internalized the norms of power/privilege and does not know, except as an outside observer, the norms of the group he or she wishes to valorize.

Those who have arguably been oppressed by an ideology may instinctively know how they wish to come across in a discourse that they may appropriate. Those looking on from outside have to ask about or read about the oppressed and then hope that they grasp what the power-down groups are attempting to do. Mistakes—mistakes backed up by a good measure of sincerity—are often made. These quite frequently occur on the level of language. Many power-down groups have rejected the prevailing language (its small and its large aspects) because they see language as far from neutral. Language in their view embodies existing power and privilege. So, these groups sometimes use their own language. They may also create, outside the dominant practices, discursive practices that are new and can, therefore, be defined by them. (Sometimes, the use of such practices both provides a neutral medium and parodies the media of the privileged.)

The important dimensions in ideological criticism, then, may be good intentions and persistence. A so-so attempt will at least reveal the intended critiquing or valorizing edges. With self-criticism—and perhaps an awareness of the insights of those who know the subject position of the oppressed—the ideological critic can persist at it and get better at it. So, persisting and improving is certainly part of the commitment to act.

Application: *Hamilton*

The application coming up soon in this chapter will feature the Broadway musical *Hamilton*. Before I turn to it, I will say a bit about two other musicals, *Gypsy* (1959) and *Rent* (1996). Let me mention *Rent* quickly in the context of queer theory, for it is the kind of text that queer theory would valorize, for the musical rejects the easy straight versus gay dichotomy that many adhered to before seeing *Rent*. Just before *Rent*, a downturn for the LGBTQ community was former Miss America and orange juice advocate Anita Bryant's "Save Our Children" campaign. It not only essentialized gays and pushed a simplistic straight versus gay dichotomy, but made moral judgments about those labeled deviant. The Save Our Children texts would be precisely what queer theorists would want to "queer." They would do so for what we might term political reasons (i.e., to defeat Bryant's intolerance in favor of *Rent's* "seasons of love") but also to free those essentialized, forced into a dichotomy, and labeled deviant from these traps. Queer theory, then, destabilizes, not just to destabilize, but because a world without the complexities it acquires through queering denies freedom of choice.

Broadway is not the place where most would expect to find what Foucault labels counter-discursive, especially if one's focus is on the Broadway musical. It is thought, by many, to be a "lite" genre, and at one point in its history it was. But in recent decades, there have been several musicals that not only raise serious issues, but challenge the prevailing ideology. The 1959 musical *Gypsy* and the 1996 musical *Rent* are very different, but both represent challenges.

Gypsy, on the surface, is the story of stripper Gypsy Rose Lee, but focusing on Gypsy (stage name for Louise) ignores, first, that the story is more that of Louise's mother Rose, who is trying desperately to live vicariously through her daughters June (who flees at the end of Act One) and Louise and, second, that all of them, mother and daughters, are the victims of the changing theatre business. The variety act that they once staged is no longer viable. Because the audience changed, the urban theatres' fare changed to somewhat off-color comics and strippers. So, with June gone, the only viable course is for the less-talented Louise to shed her clothes. In other words, the capitalist (i.e., theatre owner) was compelling the proletariat (i.e., Louise and others) to do work they found undesirable or face ruin. The scenario is one the Marxist critic would want to expose: The critic would want to highlight how, in the musical, the workers are being exploited.

Rent is more obviously political. It was originally staged at a time when AIDS was not only becoming epidemic, but being presented by some in politics and some in the media as a disease affecting only gay males or illegal drug users. In *Rent*, however, the characters do not fit the stereotype: They are young, and they are not necessarily gay. *Rent*, therefore, calls into question the prevailing ideology on AIDS, replacing a negative view of AIDS-sufferers with a very human one. The musical seemed to change the view many held on the subject; it was successful as a challenge. The ideological critic would highlight how the musical enacted this success.

A still more recent musical, Lin-Manuel Miranda's *Hamilton,* is a more complex attempt to counter the dominant discourse. This Broadway smash continues in the sociopolitical tradition we see in musicals as different as *Gypsy* and *Rent*. It also continues in another tradition, that of bringing to the stage racial, ethnic minorities. Miranda's preceding musical, *In the Heights* (2008), was part of that tradition. Set in the Washington Heights section of Manhattan, it featured a host of characters from different Caribbean nations. It was counter-discursive insofar as the stories of such people rarely made it to the Broadway stage. But Miranda was only beginning the ideological work that the rhetorical critic should respond to by illuminating and valorizing.

In *Hamilton*, Miranda tells the story of Alexander Hamilton. It stresses how he was an other. He was an other, in the musical, in three ways. He was bi-racial, he was a bastard, and he was an immigrant. These traits are stressed in the musical's opening number, "Alexander Hamilton." He then was most certainly not part of the revolutionary era establishment. Although George Washington recognized Hamilton's worth both during the war and during Washington's administration, neither John Adams, on one political side, nor Thomas Jefferson and James Madison, on the other, thought highly of him. Adams, at least in the play, termed Hamilton a "Creole bastard"; Jefferson and Madison treated him with contempt. The musical offers the audience a flawed hero: Both his hubris and his lust lead to his ruin, long before Aaron Burr's bullet takes his life. This flawed hero, however, is presented by the musical as a hero on behalf of both the nation he served and those excluded groups he represents.

Excluded groups were numerous in 1775 and the decades beyond. Immigrants were not welcomed, even though, as the Marquis de Lafayette and Alexander Hamilton sing, "we get things done" right before the Battle of Yorktown.[7] Women were not embraced within the electorate, and, of course, slaves were not. Angelica Schuyler (eventually Hamilton's sister-in-law) voices the women's objection to their exclusion, and the play repeatedly notes that one of the three Hamilton friends we meet early in the tavern, John Lauryns, was making defeating slavery his special cause. The revolutionary war was fought for freedom, but the play makes it very clear that some groups were not included in that mandate for freedom.

Miranda reinforces this point by how he cast the musical. Those playing the many, very white founding fathers—and associated women—were people of color. Hamilton, initially played by Miranda, had a Caribbean heritage; Burr, Washington, Lafayette/ Jefferson (same actor), etc., were enacted by performers of color—by design. Miranda makes his point about who was marginalized in America by showing the audience the racial and ethnic diversity it denied back then and, perhaps, still denies, on Broadway and in society at large.

Miranda also used music to reinforce his point about exclusion. In *In the Heights*, Miranda departed from the Broadway norm and used a mix featuring rap and Latin. Not all Broadway music has, down through the years, been what many term "show tunes": There have been a fair number of departures from that norm. Nonetheless, Miranda's was striking. Just as characters and stories, such as those in *In the Heights*, had not been featured on Broadway, the music in that Tony Award-winning show had not been featured on Broadway. Miranda does much the same thing in *Hamilton*, but with a twist. He draws attention to the music by having historical characters such as Hamilton, Burr, and the Schuyler sisters singing to it. Miranda is making his point about the marginalization of certain groups in America doubly—by having performers of color in very, very white roles and then by having these performers doing rap or hip-hop. Miranda brings those often excluded both on the stage and in the nation before the Broadway audience, and he brings the musical styles of the excluded before that audience.

Finally, Miranda makes an important point about history. Miranda began working on what would become *Hamilton* after reading Chernow's biography of Alexander Hamilton. As Miranda saw things, Hamilton's story had been, to an extent, lost in the shadow of the likes of Washington, Jefferson, etc. Why? Did it have anything to do with Hamilton's lack of an elite pedigree? Miranda then decided to complete the work Chernow had done through writing his biography by bringing Hamilton's story to the musical theatre stage.[8] History had not told Hamilton's story well. Miranda would correct that oversight.

In the musical, Miranda generalizes about history, for he realized that many stories have been lost, and he realized that it was frequently the stories of the marginalized that were either lost or distorted as they were relayed by those power-up. As Miranda's George Washington tells Hamilton, who tells one's story is important. The goal is not just getting into the history. Thus, in the play, Eliza Schuyler Hamilton, after taking herself out of the narrative because of her husband's infidelity, puts herself back in once grief—at their son's death—brought the couple back together. Furthermore, after Alexander's death, she takes the lead in trying to keep her late husband's story alive and understood correctly. Despite her noble effort and her long, noble life, she does not succeed—perhaps because she was a woman and outside the dominant discourse. But in Chernow's book and in Miranda's musical, Hamilton has found two who will tell his story.

What happened to Hamilton (i.e., his story finally being recognized)—Miranda suggests—should happen to others. Many stories have been lost or distorted. Those of Native Americans were mentioned earlier—lost until historian Dee Brown put them on paper in *Bury My Heart at Wounded Knee*. Those of African slaves have also been found and offered. But there are many others. And, implicit in Miranda's musical is that the process of losing or distorting is, more often than not, not neutral. Those who are out of history—or barely in it—are often victims of the powers that determine what history consists of. If included, the stories of those on the margins are often victims of distortions authored by the powers that control the process.

One early reaction to *Hamilton* was amazement that the story of the first U.S. Secretary of the Treasury could be both a musical and a hit. That reaction misses the point that *Hamilton* makes about history, for the musical, although certainly about a particular man, is also about all of those excluded both from histories and from the fullness of the American vision fought for back in revolutionary times.

Strengths and Limitations

The ideological approaches outlined in this chapter can be politically powerful. They talk to power—revealing how discourse is often used to control and suppress. In doing so, they reveal power dynamics that many overlook on the assumption that the prevailing discourse is the normal discourse. The approaches also serve the cause of those who have been oppressed by valorizing their discourse, sometimes after discovering it. This valorization speaks to power by stressing the voices that have been marginalized or lost, revealing what they have to say and how they say it.

This very political approach is not what everyone pursuing academic criticism wishes to do. In doing it, one puts one's self on the line on behalf of specific causes. Not all want to put themselves on the line, and not all are comfortable with the politics undergirding these ideological approaches. These approaches, then, are exciting and rewarding for some, but are not the tasks that all critics are interested in. Those who decline this approach note that power dynamics are not all that is relevant in a text. While this may be true, ideological critics would assert that power dynamics, especially since they are not always apparent, are so important that they dwarf other dimensions of a text.

As noted earlier in this chapter when discussing method, ideological criticism is not easy to do, not because of political exposure, but because those who choose to critique and valorize may be doing so from outside the oppressed group they are trying to help. What these critics do can be interpreted as condescending, and what these critics do can be based on an inadequate understanding of the situation the oppressed face and what the group's preferred discourse might be. Being a good ideological critic, then, may require a great deal of work—listening, reading, research—so that one's critiquing and valorizing accomplishes what the critic wants these activities to accomplish.

Exemplars

Condit, Celeste Michelle. "Hegemony in a Mass-Mediated Society: Concordance about Reproductive Technologies." *Critical Studies in Mass Communication* 11, no. 3 (1994): 205–30.

Hanke, Robert. "Hegemony Masculinity in *Thirtysomething*." *Critical Studies in Mass Communication* 7, no. 3 (1990): 231–48.

Roy, Abhik. "The Construction and Scapegoating of Muslims as the 'Other' in Hindu Nationalist Rhetoric." *Southern Communication Journal* 69, no. 4 (2004): 320–32.

Wander, Philip C. "The Rhetoric of American Foreign Policy." *Quarterly Journal of Speech* 70, no. 4 (1984): 339–61.

Suggested Applications

Speech Applications

- Critique George H. W. Bush's address to the Republican National Convention in 1988. What ideologies are apparent in it? What ideological approaches might be used to question it?

- California Senator Kamala Harris delivered her "maiden" address to the U.S. Senate on February 8, 2018. How might an ideological critic approach it?

Non-Speech Applications

- Monument Avenue in Richmond, Virginia, is a grand boulevard, along which there are numerous monuments to heroes of the Confederacy. How would an ideological critic approach this street as a text?

- View an early episode or two of the television program *Law and Order*. What might an ideological critic say about this very popular series?

Notes

1. McKerrow, Raymie E. "Critical Rhetoric: Theory and Praxis." *Communication Monographs* 56, no. 2 (1989): 91–111.

2. Thiong'o, Ngugi wa. *Decolonizing the Mind: The Politics of Language in African Literature.* London: Heinermann, 1986; and Achebe, Chinua. "The African Writer and the English Language." In *Colonial Discourse and Post-Colonial Theory*, 428–34. New York, NY: Harvester Wheatsheaf, 1993.

3. Ashcroft, Bill, Gareth Griffiths, and Helen Tiffin. *The Empire Writes Back: Theory and Practice in Post-Colonial Literature.* London: Routledge, 2002. 4–6.

4. Morris, Richard, and Philip Wander. "Native American Rhetoric: Dancing in the Shadows of the Ghost Dance." *Quarterly Journal of Speech* 76, no. 2 (1990): 164–91.

5. McKerrow, Raymie. "Critical Rhetoric: Theory and Praxis." *Communication Monographs* 56, no. 2 (1989): 91–111.

6. Orbe, Mark. "'Remember, It's Always Whites' Ball': Descriptions of African-American Male Communication." *Communication Quarterly* 42, no. 3 (1994): 287–300.

7. Hamilton. By Lin-Manuel Miranda. New York, NY. http://www.themusicallyrics.com/h/35/hamilton-the-musical. (Lyrics quoted sparingly because of the difficulty securing permission)

8. For information on the play's genesis and creation, see McCarter, Jeremy, and Lin-Manuel Miranda. *Hamilton: The Revolution.* New York, NY: Grand Central Publishing, 2016.

Figure credit

Fig. 11: Source: https://commons.wikimedia.org/wiki/File:Lin-Manuel_Miranda.jpg.

Ellen Johnson Sirleaf, the first woman president of the African nation of Liberia.

CHAPTER 12

Feminist Criticism

This chapter could be read as an extension of the previous one. There, a range of ideological-based approaches to the criticism of texts were explored. Some had very specific ideologies in mind; others were broader. Marxist criticism focuses on the plight of the working class; post-colonial criticism focuses on the plight of those who were—and still are being—colonized. Queer theory focuses more broadly on those groups or behaviors labeled deviant by the prevailing power; critical rhetoric focuses even more broadly on any and all who may be oppressed by the dominant discourse. All these approaches had two important dimensions: critique and valorization. They examined critically texts that might be argued to be oppressive, and they examined favorably texts that gave the oppressed a voice. Feminist criticism will also feature critique and valorization. Because it has a long history, it will also feature some twists and turns that have, gradually, both complicated and enriched the critical approach.

From Feminism to Feminisms

Feminist criticism is but one of the projects undertaken by feminism, so it makes sense to begin by tracing feminism's course. Those who trace its history speak in terms of waves, pointing to a first wave, a second wave, and—beyond that—a number of internal critiques that have taken feminism several different directions, some of which constitute what is referred to as a third wave.

This brief history, because of its brevity, necessarily oversimplifies many complex matters. My hope is that it traces the contours of the movement accurately and thereby positions today's feminist critics accurately.

The first wave is rooted back in the nineteenth century. Its primary concern was suffrage. It achieved its success in 1920 with the ratification of the Nineteenth Amendment to the U.S. Constitution. We associate the Seneca Falls Convention and the declaration it issued in 1848 as part of this wave, perhaps its rhetorical beginning. So, it will take seventy-plus years for the first wave to meet its goal!

The second wave emerges after a gap, primarily in the later twentieth century. What evoked it was the existence of discrimination in many areas of life. Gender roles had settled in since the nineteenth century, and many of these roles placed women in an inferior position—perceived as inferior and treated in an inferior manner. This second wave will address issues in education, employment, sexual behavior, reproduction, and marriage. It will borrow energy from the American Civil Rights Movement, and it will play off what has been termed the "sexual revolution." The second wave, then, had many concerns, but almost all these concerns were those that affected women from developed nations, especially women from higher social classes. That it had this focus was a reflection of who was leading and a part of it, not any formal design to discriminate. That the second wave tilted in this direction should not detract from its significance. The wave led to significant advances in a number of important areas of life. However, it did neglect the concerns of many women, particularly women of color.

The second wave also promoted a feminine perspective to counter the masculine one that was blindly assumed by many to be the norm or the standard. For example, when it came to rhetorical style (i.e., the way in which a rhetor would present his or her discourse), second wave theorists and researchers would present—and advocate—a feminine style to counter the masculine one. In interpersonal communication, these theorists and researchers would point to "a different voice," different from the presumed normal/standard one used by males. This work was valuable, but it stumbled into two problems. First, it inadvertently essentialized all those gendered female, implying that they all proceeded in the same manner with regards to communication and other activities. Second, it inadvertently accepted a female-male, feminine-masculine dichotomy. That dichotomy was not only an over-simplification of life, but it inadvertently reflected the A versus B mode of thinking that dominated the masculinist thinking and that undergirded the oppressive us versus them, we versus others dichotomies found in society.

So, second wave feminism, despite its significant accomplishments, had problems. As a result, it prompted a set of third waves. Some, outside the privileged group that focused on matters of education and employment within the Western world, insisted on a feminism that recognized the issues facing women globally. Internationally, this insistence gave rise to a third-world feminism. Others, strongly arguing that gender was not a given but rather socially constructed, insisted on a feminism that did not insist on a single vision of the feminine. Many lesbians found this perspective attractive, for they did not enact feminism as their heterosexual sisters did. Bisexual and transgendered women also found this perspective attractive. Sexual identity was not, however, the only variable that might differentiate one socially constructed feminism from another. African American women, for example, following bell hooks's powerful critique of the women's movement, conceived of feminism in terms different from the white, American, usually middle- or upper-class women who dominated the second wave.

Many in these groups, especially those not heterosexual, would embrace queer theory, described in the previous chapter. Many in these groups would take their thinking a step further and speak of intersectionality. By this term, they meant that a person might not be just gendered female (however that gender might be socially constructed). Rather, this person might be gendered female, be of color, and hail from a disadvantaged social class. This person's identity is determined not by one dimension of being, but rather by how different dimensions intersect. A crucial implication of this insistence on intersectionality is the recognition of the many differences that might exist within feminism as a movement. A black lesbian feminist in America will be radically different from a white heterosexual feminist in western Europe. Given these differences, it is important that feminism recognizes common ground as well as respects differences and the different perspectives they may evoke.

There may well be still another group—those who are post-feminist. They argue that feminism has achieved both its first wave and its second wave goals. Given this victory, there are a number of possible paths to take. One can celebrate the power one has gained. One can re-embrace certain stereotypical feminine traits that the second wave, for rhetorical reasons, suppressed on the assumption that they have been reinscribed in such a way that they are no longer viewed negatively. One can simply move on, assuming that the anger thought to be characteristic of some feminists is no longer necessary. Those who want to move on are sometimes upset by the both the insistence by some enduring feminists on totally destroying the patriarchy and by replacing it with pro-feminist structures. The movement, then, in the eyes of some has ignored its victories and continues to pursue a radical—a too radical—course. In universities today, many men and women react negatively to the term feminist. This negative reaction, one which has held back some women in political life, reflects the fact that many students today are considering those who endure as feminists as necessarily radical feminists. Truth be told, there are many students today who would quickly affirm many of the principles of feminism but reject the label. The label, with its very complicated meaning, has become something of a barrier in some arenas. As we move from history to criticism, it is crucial to note that, just as there are many ways to be a feminist (with or without the label), there are many ways to be a feminist critic.

And Criticism?

During the second wave, feminist criticism began, and it took the same two courses we saw for the ideological approaches outlined in chapter 11: namely, critique and valorization. Texts that were arguably masculinist were critiqued as such, with the reductive and prejudiced ways they presented the feminine noted—strongly noted. So, if a politician's speech to a national audience seemed to presuppose he (we'll assume "he") was only addressing a male audience, that observation would be made. Or, if a genre of television programs—let's say situation comedies—only presented women in subordinate roles, that observation would be made.

The valorization project was more complex. When it comes to speeches—we're in the 1960s and 1970s and the primary object for rhetorical criticism was still speeches—there *seemed* to be little by women to examine. If one believed the many anthologies of famous speeches in print at the time, there was not much of merit by women to look at. In literature, the same issue existed, and several women, most notably Sondra Gilbert and Susan Gubar, set out to correct the imbalance. Gilbert and Gubar would eventually edit an anthology published by Norton of just women's writing. A parallel effort was made in speech by Karlyn Kohrs Campbell (and her many graduate students) at the University of Minnesota. The 1989 two-volume study and anthology, *Man Cannot Speak for Her*, was the result. And other anthologies began finding and including more women's voices.

It was easy to find media products—television programs, motion pictures, and poplar music—that deserved feminist critique. However, media products featuring women were slow to develop, but, as they did, feminist media critics valorized them. So, the television police drama *Cagney and Lacey*, the film *Thelma and Louise*, and the many musical artists associated with "Lilith Fair" were duly valorized.

But, in valorizing, critics had a problem. What did they point to? Theorists, up to that point, were overwhelmingly male. What they were implying was that good communication might well be good *male communication*. Roman rhetorician Cicero talks about a vigorous style. Was that a vigorous *male* style? Kenneth Burke talks about scapegoating. Is that a gendered strategy? These questions led some female theorists to posit the existence of a feminine style, describe it, and use it as a basis for assessing discourse by women. For example, here is an attempt by Jane Blankenship and Deborah Robson to define a feminine style in politics:

> Based on the data base analysis and the interpretive works reviewed, we conclude that there is, indeed, a feminine style of political discourse, and that the commonalities we have identified are manifested in five fundamental characteristics of that style. These characteristics are not near; they overlap, intersect, and intertwine in a number of powerful ways. The five characteristics we have identified are [as follows]:

1. Basing political judgments on concrete, lived experience.
2. Valuing inclusivity and the relational nature of being.
3. Conceptualizing the power of public office as a capacity to "get things done" and to empower others.
4. Approaching policy formation holistically.
5. Moving women's issues to the forefront of the public arena.[1]

Initially, efforts such as this one by Blankenship and Robson were applauded, but then they were subject to criticism, for they both implicitly essentialized the feminine gender and probably converted certain preferences exhibited by many white, well-educated women in the Western world into the norm for all gendered feminine, regardless of background. (That Blankenship and Robson limited their definition for a particular sphere (politics) limited the criticism somewhat.)

So, moving beyond the second wave, feminist critics attempting to valorize the texts by those gendered female have had to exhibit considerable subtlety. They have had to intuit what the rhetor wished to do based on how she defined her gendered self and then use that definition as the basis for criticism. The shadow of essentializing has haunted the enterprise, but most feminist critics have been willing to grant, for academic purposes, certain categories. So, categories such as black feminist rhetoric or third-world feminist rhetoric or lesbian feminist rhetoric were used with the understanding that, within those broad categories, there might well be several socially constructed subcategories. Feminist criticism, then, was walking a tightrope, with a fall into essentializing always a possibility.

One last point is worth making here: Those who are gendered female are often working in arenas such as government or commerce that are either arguably male defined or, by the second decade of the twenty-first century, arguably no longer as strikingly gendered. Women in the former situation may choose to speak in the manner common in that arena, and they have every right to do so. Women in the latter may choose to speak in the uni-gendered mode that may be emerging. And that is fine too. Most feminist critics would presume that those gendered female have many choices, just as those gendered male do. Both deserve the freedom to move among the possibilities as they choose the approach and the style of their discourse. Feminist critics would valorize all that rhetors who are gendered female do, but they would probably find those texts with more of a gendered fingerprint more interesting to analyze and discuss. In other words, in politics, a female who chooses to speak in what some might consider a male manner or in what some might consider a gender-neutral manner would not be criticized, but a female who chooses to speak in a manner thought to be, in some ways, more aligned with some variation on the female gender, might find herself applauded. (If you know your current US Senate, it's the difference between the rhetoric of the two California Senators, Dianne Feinstein, who—although not a lawyer—presents her arguments in a lawyer-like manner, and Kamala Harris, who mixes narrative and pathos as she argues.)

Method

In the previous chapter, two paths were outlined for the ideological critic—critique and valorization. The same is true here for this particular case of ideological criticism.

Critiquing masculinist texts can proceed on the levels of content, perspective, and style.

Is the content that is important to those gendered female excluded from a text? If included, is it trivialized or pushed off to the side? On many occasions since 1991, the women in the US Senate have complained that matters important to women do not find their way into committee discussion, floor debates, and approved legislation. In 1993, for example, the seven women then in the Senate asked for a block of time to voice their opposition to a four-star retirement for an admiral. Why? Because he had been in charge when a convention of naval aviators (Tailhook '91) that featured drunkenness, pornography, and sexual assault occurred and had responded inadequately. They knew they would lose, so why did they spend hours speaking? They did so because they wanted to announce that matters of sexual discrimination, sexual harassment, and sexual assault anywhere in government would now be raised in the Senate because there were now, after the 1992 elections, seven women in the body.[2] Well, the women in the Senate—now a larger number—still feel that their issues do not make it forward as they should or are treated as not very important if they do. New York Senator Kirsten Gillibrand, for example, is, in 2013—twenty years after the women in the Senate made Tailhook '91 an issue—still trying to get Congress to address sexual predation in the armed services.

Is the perspective of those gendered female represented in texts under examination? In politics, does debate tend to ignore how women (and their children) may be affected by either problems or proposed solutions? In work environments, are the views of those gendered female heard on matters such as healthcare, leave, flextime, home-work balance, on-site daycare—matters that affect women more or differently than they affect men. If the female perspective is present, is it validated or pushed aside?

Is the style of texts being considered unrelentingly masculine? Is the reasoning, based on the facts and statistics those gendered male are said to privilege, based on strong assertions over more nuanced statements?

In all these cases, one has to be cautious about essentializing gender. One also has to be aware, when discussing issues and perspectives, that those of upper middle-class white females in the United States do not turn into *the* issues and perspectives of a gender. These cautions, however, should not prevent those critiquing from identifying and exposing texts that are oppressive of the female gender. What those critiquing need to be alert to is how a text might be oppressive of not all but some of that group's subsets. For example, a text oppressive of African American females ought to be critiqued as fully and as vigorously as any other.

Valorizing the discourse of those gendered female requires a similar breadth of knowledge and perspective. The aspiring critic needs to, first, come up with a good sense of what female discourse should be. Good means not just accurate; in addition, it means appropriate for the sociocultural circumstances. How a working-class woman of Caribbean origin but living in London might choose to express herself would differ from an American-educated African woman from an elite group in her native land. There are many female styles. The critic must be aware of the multiplicity. And, if viewing a style from the outside, he or she must do a considerable amount of work to acquire something approximating—but never achieving—an insider's sense of things.

The critic needs a sense of what discourse should be like. Then, the critic needs to assess the extent to which a text matches this sense, saluting the text if it does. The goal goes beyond just saluting the particular text: The larger goal is to create, through a current of criticism, an environment in which a variety of authentic styles based on genders are empowered.

Application: Broadway Musical/Film *Grease*

Grease debuted on Broadway in 1971 and ran until 1980; then, it became a feature film in 1978; then, it returned to Broadway for a revival in 2007. It's a teenage musical set in an urban community (perhaps Chicago where some seem to speak with a Jersey accent) back in the 1950s, its central story being a romance between bad boy Danny Zuko and the new good girl Sandy Dumbrowski at the high school. There are other plots, but the romance between Danny and Sandy drives the musical. It sounds like both simple fare and, probably, innocuous fare. A feminist critic, however, might find much in the show to criticize, for the girls are depicted in a manner that is both limiting and sexist.

Sandy is an outsider to the high school—unfairly kicked out of the nearby Catholic school in the original version. She has higher aspirations than most of the students at her new school, certainly higher than the girls who are focused on snagging a man while, maybe, having a back-up career as something such as a beautician or a counter girl at Woolworth's. They, of course, sing their way through various ups and downs, not questioning if there might be a higher road they might take—even though Teen Angel urges one, who has failed as a beautician, to get back to academics in the song "Beauty School Dropout." Sandy is aware of that higher road, but, to fit in at the school, she must more or less abandon it. Conforming not only compels Sandy to lower her sights, but it compels her to change her personality. She is initially depicted as being much like wholesome teen star Sandra Dee, who is "lousy with virginity" and "won't go to bed till I'm legally wed." Like Sandra Dee, Sandy does not smoke, drink, or "rat [her] hair."[3] This persona, however, not only does not allow her to fit in with the other high school girls, but becomes a barrier in her romance with Danny. He does not want someone who's wholesome; rather, in the terms used today, he wants someone who's "hot." She resists and resists, but eventually exchanges her white dress for tight-fitting black leather to sing the duet "You're the One that I Want" near the show's end (in the movie and stage revival). In conforming, Sandy not only ceases to be true to herself, but adopts a highly sexist persona to please Danny.

Grease, then, is about conforming, but, more than that, it is about conforming to a limiting, sexist definition of a young American girl. This definition not only does not include many matters a young woman might value, but the way it is pushed compels female listening to accept the definition as accurate and any more positive alternative as a silly idea. But the sexism in the play goes deeper. One of the show's big hits was the song "Summer Nights," sung, in alternation, between the teenage girls and the teenage boys, with Sandy and Danny sometimes singing solo. The song provides backstory, telling of a summer romance between Sandy and Danny that supposedly had ended because they, at that point, came from different schools. The lyrics are revealing. When referring to a summer romance, the girls want to know "Was it love at first sight?" while the boys want to know "Did she put up a fight?" The girls are focusing on love; the boys, sex. It is not entirely clear in the song what the female summer lover yielded, with or without a fight. Was it as innocent as a kiss? Was it as serious and consequential as sex? (And, of course, Danny, not knowing Sandy will unexpectedly appear at his school, is probably sexualizing and exaggerating the story by telling the boys that "she got friendly in the sand" and "she was good, if you know what I mean"). Whether Danny is telling the truth or not, think of what the boys are asking. They are not only focused on sexual conquest, but are asking to what extent was the intimacy forced (i.e., to what extent was it rape). When one realizes this, it imparts to the popular song a disturbing quality.

This last song would especially disturb a feminist critic, but what might be even more disturbing is how the show obscures its demeaning, disturbing qualities by being, on the surface, entertainment that one is not expected to analyze too deeply. A rhetorical critic, in general, is intrigued by texts that seem to do one thing while doing another. These texts are exhibiting tensions that might, if the audience is attentive, create dissonance. The problem with *Grease* is that the tensions probably were never felt by most, who treated the show as simply a nostalgic depiction of urban teenage life in the 1950s. A feminist critic would want to increase the tensions by presenting the plot and the song lyrics in a critical light informed by issues such as gender-based discrimination and sexual abuse. A feminist critic would want the dissonance between the "lite" show and its disturbing messages to be pronounced—so that the viewer would realize that the show is far from innocuous, insofar as it may lead people in the audience to accept the musical's gendered messages as the way it was—and maybe is. That the message is arguably pitched at young teenage girls makes the situation quite disturbing. Even worse is the Disney *Beauty and the Beast,* which in Kathryn M. Olson's reading, tries to slip (largely unnoticed) a disturbing message about gender and violence past even younger girls.[4]

As a counterpoint to *Grease,* consider another Broadway musical, *Hairspray.* It started as a low-budget film directed by John Waters in 1998; then, to Broadway in 2002; then, back to the silver screen in 2007. It is set back in time—early 1960s—in Baltimore. The central story is weight-challenged Tracy Turnblad's desire to dance on a popular afternoon teen-dance show. In these three texts, it was the "Corny Cornish Show." In reality, it was the "Buddy Deane Show" on WJZ, Channel 13: Yes, the plot is based in fact. Tracy rather comically represents an oppressed group, but, as she struggles to get on the show, she discovers another oppressed group, African Americans, who are not allowed on the show except, about once a month, when there is "colored day." Over-weight rights and civil rights then merge, and, by the end of show, we learn that "You Just Can't Stop the Beat" of progress. *Hairspray* serves as a counterpoint to *Grease* insofar as the former shows you don't have to accept the norms of an earlier time when doing a "retro" work, and you don't need to avoid serious issues when doing a show with teen appeal.

The examination of *Grease* is an example of how a feminist critic might critique discourse to reveal its sexism. The following illustrates how a feminist critic might valorize a woman's words.

Application: Ellen Johnson Sirleaf's Inaugural

Sirleaf, president of Liberia from 2006 to 2018, was the first female head of state elected in Africa. She was a native of Liberia, but spent much of her life outside of Africa. For a long period of time, she resided in the United States, where she received much of her higher education in economics. When she returned to Liberia, the nation was in the midst of a bloody civil war. She got caught up in it, suffering imprisonment and nearly execution, but survived and became the person to which the nation turned to both heal the wounds of the civil war and revitalize a wrecked economy. For her work on behalf of peace in Liberia, she won the Nobel Prize in 2011.

In 2006, Sirleaf delivered her inaugural address. Critics who know the genre, as defined based on American examples, quickly note two characteristics that separate Sirleaf's speech from the norm: its long duration and its treatment of policy matters with a degree of specificity more characteristic of the American State of the Union address. Despite these differences (probably attributable to a different political culture), the speech proceeds much as any incoming president's might. In other words, it seems, through the bulk of the speech, to have very little in it to distinguish it as the rhetoric of a female president.

Let us first praise Almighty God, the Arbiter of all affairs of humankind whose omnipotent Hand guides and steers our nation. Before I begin this address, which signifies the high noon of this historic occasion, I ask that we bow our heads for a moment of silent prayer in memory of the thousands of our compatriots who have died as a result of years of conflict.

Thank you! I also ask your indulgence as I reflect on the memory of my two rural illiterate grandmothers and my mother and father who taught me to be what I am today, and the families who took them in and gave them the opportunity for a better life.

*****

This ritual is symbolically and politically significant and substantive. It reflects the enduring character of a democratic tradition of the peaceful and orderly transfer of political power and authority. It also affirms the culmination of a commitment to our nation's collective search for a purposeful and responsive national leadership.

We applaud the resilience of our people who, weighed down and dehumanized by poverty and rendered immobile by the shackles of fourteen years of war, courageously went to the polls, not once but twice, to vote and to elect Vice President Joseph Boaki and me to serve them.

*****

The tendencies of intolerance of each other's opinion rooted in parochial and selfish considerations—and greed—have driven us into our descent into recent tragedies and paralysis as a nation and people. These negative national tendencies have, in the past, bred ethnic suspicion and hatred, led to injustice, social and political exclusion. They have also weakened our capacity to peacefully co-exist as a people with diverse socio-cultural, economic, and political backgrounds and differences. Consequently, we have witnessed needless generalized conflicts that have profoundly affected the Liberian family, the foundation of our society.

And in the process of resolving the numerous contradictions that have underpinned this struggle, a high price has been paid by many Liberians of diverse backgrounds and social status. I know of this struggle because I have been a part of it. Without bitterness, anger, or vindictiveness, I recall the inhumanity of confinement, the terror of attempted rape, and the ostracism of exile. I also recall the goodness and the kindness of the many who defied orders and instruction to save my life, and give food to the hungry and to give water to the thirsty. I recall their humanity—and thank them.

And so, my Fellow Liberians, let us acknowledge and honor the sacrifices and contributions of all as we put the past behind us. Let us rejoice that our recent democratic exercise has been a redemptive act of faith and an expression of renewed confidence in ourselves. Let us be proud that we were able to ultimately rise above our intense political and other differences in a renewed determination as a people to foster dialogue instead of violence, promote unity rather than disharmony, and engender hope rather than disillusionment and despair.

Ellen Johnson Sirleaf, Selection from Inaugural Address. Copyright © 2006 by Ellen Johnson Sirleaf.

*****

And now I would like to talk to the women, the women of Liberia, the women of Africa—and the women of the world. Until a few decades ago, Liberian women endured the injustice of being treated as second-class citizens. During the years of our civil war, they bore the brunt of inhumanity and terror. They were conscripted into war, gang raped at will, forced into domestic slavery. Yet, it is the women, notably those who established themselves as the Mano River Women's Network for Peace who labored and advocated for peace throughout our region.

It is therefore not surprising that during the period of our elections, Liberian women were galvanized—and demonstrated unmatched passion, enthusiasm, and support for my candidacy. They stood with me; they defended me; they prayed for me. The same can be said for the women throughout Africa. I want to here and now, gratefully acknowledge the powerful voice of women of all walks of life whose votes significantly contributed to my victory.

My Administration shall thus endeavor to give Liberian women prominence in all affairs of our country. My Administration shall empower Liberian women in all areas of national life. We will support and increase the writ of laws that restore their dignities and deal drastically with crimes that dehumanize them. We will enforce without fear or favor the law against rape recently passed by the National Transitional Legislature. We shall encourage families to educate all children, particularly the girl child. We shall also try to provide economic programs that enable Liberian women to assume their proper place in our economic revitalization process.[5]

Feminist critics would be quick to note that, when women enter male-defined realms such as business or politics, they have a rhetorical choice to make. They can use the rhetoric that has been common in these fields, ignoring how it may be patriarchal or masculinist; they can break radically from the traditional rhetoric; or they can forge a rhetoric that reflects both male and female. In politics, many have done the third—so much so and with such success that what one might term an androgynous political rhetoric has emerged that many men and women both now use.

Sirleaf seems to be taking this third course. In thanking the many who have helped Liberia through its crises, she thanks both the men and the women. In speaking of various policy matters, she blends facts and figures with more personal stories, most strikingly the story of the children who kept telling Sirleaf they voted for her. The facts and figures are, arguably, male rhetoric; the story, female, although, in both cases, the critic must note that she is using stereotypes with a full awareness that they are just that. That Sirleaf is taking a third course is most striking when, toward the end of the speech, she directly addresses the situation of women in Liberia. Many remember John F. Kennedy's 1961 inaugural and how he specifically addressed various groups such as our global foes and our neighbors in Latin America. Specifically addressing different audience groups is quite common in the genre. However, specifically addressing different genders is not.

Sirleaf bluntly talks about what the female experience has been in her nation—a second-class citizenship characterized by oppression and discrimination, one that grew worse during the civil war period with women the frequent victims of rape and gang rape. Feminist critics would be drawn to the paragraphs in the inaugural in which Sirleaf addresses the plight of her nation's women. They would praise her for speaking about that situation so directly, and they would praise her calls for specific government action to end all abuse. As these critics would see it, Sirleaf departed from the inaugural norm just enough to signal that her presidency meant that ill treatment of women in Liberia would no longer be tolerated—and that women would play an unprecedented major role in a Sirleaf administration. If one wanted to, one could take the definition of a feminine style in politics offered by Blankenship and Robson, note that it may not be a perfect fit for Liberia, and then proceed one through five through their list. The result would be a degree of conformity that extended beyond the section of the inaugural in which Sirleaf specifically addresses women's experiences in her nation, for the Blakenship and Robson definition considered how political matters were talked about (e.g., inclusivity, getting things done, holistic perspective), not just how women's particular political issues were addressed.

Sirleaf is, by training, an economist. She is not inclined to high-flying, empty rhetoric; rather, she has a tendency to focus on the immediate and the quantifiably real. So, her comments on the situation of women in her country lack flamboyance, but for every measure of flamboyance it lacks, it gains a measure of firmness. Her tone, when delivering the paragraphs focused on women, made it clear that their situation was one the nation under her leadership would address, not just discuss. That tone, in general, characterizes Sirleaf's entire address.

Strengths and Limitations

As with the ideological approaches outlined in the previous chapter, the feminist approach is highly and unapologetically political. The approach may be very radical or less so; its tone may vary as well. But even when the political implications are kept a bit at bay, feminist criticism is engaged in how texts deal with gender, often dealing poorly with the many ways the feminine is socially constructed. Exposing sexism and valorizing the upfront presentation of the feminine, no matter how defined, are tasks well worth pursuing. But not all are comfortable being quite so political.

Being so also can lead to certain dimensions of a text being overlooked. *Grease* deals with inter-ethnic conflict; Sirleaf's speech defines, for Liberia, a very specific foreign policy that involves neighboring nations, the United States, and international entities such as the World Bank. A feminist critic might not note these—or might note them in passing. But almost all lenses a critic might adopt focus her or him on certain dimensions of a text to the exclusion of others. That is the very nature of a lens. All critics who adopt a particular lens need to remind themselves of what they might not be noting—so as not to distort the text while discussing it. The narrower the lens, the more this caution may be necessary.

The feminist critic also must be aware of how complex the question of the female gender is. It is very easy to fall into the traps of essentializing or speaking primarily of privileged white, Western females as if they represent all females. There are many gendered possibilities; there are also many ways in which the gendered possibilities intersect. The critic needs to keep these complexities in mind. Doing so can be difficult, making good feminist criticism challenging.

Exemplars

Campbell, Karlyn Kohnrs. "The Rhetoric of Women's Liberation: An Oxymoron." *Quarterly Journal of Speech* 59 no. 1 (1973): 74–86.

Coupland, Justine, and Angie Williams. "Conflicting Discourses, Shifting Ideologies: Pharmaceutical, 'Alternative,' and Feminist Emancipatory Texts on the Menopause." *Discourse & Society* 13, no. 4 (2002): 419–45.

Dow, Bonnie J. "Hegemony, Feminist Criticism, and *The Mary Tyler Moore Show*." *Critical Studies in Mass Communication* 7, no. 3 (1990): 261–74.

Henke, Jill Birnie, Diane Zimmerman Umble, and Nancy J. Smith. "Construction of the Female Self: Feminist Readings of the Disney Heroine." *Women's Studies in Communication* 19, no. 2 (1996): 229–49.

Sellnow, Deanna D. "Music as Persuasion: Refuting Hegemonic Masculinity in 'He Thinks He'll Keep Her.'" *Women's Studies in Communication* 22, no. 1 (1999): 66–84.

Suggested Applications

Speech Applications

- Most of the speeches referred to in this textbook are by male rhetors. This, of course, reflects how males have dominated public discourse. Pick one that struck you as especially sexist and critique it as a feminist critic would.

- Consider the "Seneca Falls Declaration" as both a critique of male discourse and a feminist statement. (Yes, it's from way back in the nineteenth century but nonetheless deserves critical examination.)

Non-Speech Applications

- Consider the Vietnam and Korean Veterans' memorials in Washington, DC from a feminist perspective. (The former, you will discover, had a statue added to it to address feminist critique, but not the latter.)

- The hero of the *Hunger Games* trilogy is a young woman. Discuss what characterizes her heroism. Should a feminist critic be content with how she is depicted?

Notes

1. Blankenship, Jane, and Deborah Rodman. *Communication Quarterly* 43, no. 4 (1995): 353–66.

2. For fuller discussion, see Sheckels, Theodore F. "The Rhetorical Use of Double-Voiced Discourse and Feminine Style: The U.S. Senate Debate Over the Impact of Tailhook '91 on Admiral Frank B. Kelso II's Retirement Rank." *Southern Communication Journal* 65, no. 1 (2009): 56–68.

3. Songs from *Grease*. Directed by Randal Kleiser. Performed by John Travolta and Olivia Newton-John. United States: Paramount Pictures, 1978. http://www.metrolyrics.com/grease/lyrics.html.

4. Olson, Kathryn M. "An Epideictic Dimension of Symbolic Violence in Disney's *Beauty and the Beast:* Intergenerational Lessons in Romanticizing and Tolerating Intimate Partner Violence." *Quarterly Journal of Speech* 99, no. 4 (2013): 448–80.

5. Sirleaf, Ellen Johnson. "Inaugural Address." Address, Presidential Inauguration, Monrovia, Liberia. https://allafrica.com/stories/200601170106.html.

Figure credit

Fig. 12: Source: https://commons.wikimedia.org/wiki/File:Ellen_Johnson-Sirleaf3.jpg.

Michael Douglas, playing the role of President Andrew Shepard, delivering his memorable news conference "remarks" toward the end of the film *The American President*.

CHAPTER 13

Constitutive Rhetoric

Earlier in the textbook, I turned to a historically important work in literary criticism, M. H. Abrams's *The Mirror and the Lamp* (1953). Before addressing the book's major topic, literary criticism during the Romantic period in early nineteenth-century Britain, Abrams offered a useful framework for discussing criticism in general. He used a triangle to illustrate four different approaches. In the middle was objective, which focused on the literary text; at the points were affective (focused on the audience), mimetic (focused on the world beyond the text), and subjective (focused on the author). As Abrams saw things, literary criticism up to 1800 had been objective with affective and mimetic touches, whereas, with the Romantics, it became subjective. That was, in his judgment, part of the reason Romanticism was termed "revolutionary."

What Abrams says of literary criticism prior to 1800 might be said of rhetorical criticism, as it has been sketched thus far in this textbook. The focus has been primarily objective—concerned with the speech or the written document or the media product or the memory site. Some approaches have also dealt with the mimetic. Most ideological approaches, for example, have focused on how texts too often mirror a version of reality that is oppressive to various groups. Other approaches have also dealt with the affective. The Chicago School keeps returning to the final emotional, intellectual effect on the audience in crafting an understanding of how a text works; a Burkean approach focused on terministic screens or a fantasy theme approach focused on socially constructed visions both attend to how a text has an impact on its audience because of how that audience has formed its worldview.

This affective dimension of rhetorical criticism, however, assumes that the goal of texts is persuasion—that the rhetor has a position that he or she wants the audience to embrace. This chapter deals with a kind of criticism that is very affective (in Abrams's terms) but assumes that persuasion is less the goal than creating identity. Put another way, rather than offering an argument for assent, the rhetor, fully aware of it or not, offers insights that help the audience in constructing or constituting its identity.

Those who look at texts with an eye to seeing these identity-forming effects are engaging in what we term "constitutive rhetoric." A number of insightful approaches merge in this effort, most notably those of James Boyd White, Louis Althusser, and Maurice Charland. They bear fruit, especially in the constitutive rhetoric of minority groups, who lacked a strong identity in societies dominated by others. But, before we turn to these approaches and how they have borne fruit, let's look first at some approaches in rhetoric that anticipate what some refer to as a "constitutive turn" in the discipline.

Perelman and Black

European rhetoric Chaim Perelman (writing with Lucie Olbrechts-Tyteca) published *The New Rhetoric* in 1958; it was first translated into English in 1969. The lengthy book tried to be exhaustive, positioning itself to be as thorough as Aristotle's work, which it purported to be a replacement for. The book raises many, many issues. (In discussing classical rhetoric, I referred to how *The New Rhetoric* offers an updated take on the classical *topoi* or *topica*.) One issue it raises is how a rhetor might not so much appeal to the audience right in front of him or her but, through rhetoric, create that audience as an ideal audience, inviting the real one to become the ideal one. This ideal audience would put its prejudices aside and assess a message based on universal standards of good reasoning and, perhaps, universal values. According to Perelman and Olbrechts-Tyteca, constitutuing such an audience is often a rhetor's goal.

A similar idea was advanced by American rhetorician Edwin Black in 1970 in an important journal article.[1] Black noted that speakers (and writers) almost always adopt a persona. For example, one might argue that President Donald Trump alternates among "average Joe," "street-fighting New York businessman," and "president" when he speaks or tweets. These are, arguably, three different carefully constructed masks or personae. According to Black, all rhetors put on such masks, although in many cases the process is not as obvious as in the case of Trump. Black, however, goes a step further and suggests that rhetors not only put a mask or persona on themselves, but put one on the audience. This he terms the "second persona." Basically, subtly or not so subtly, the rhetor tells the audience who the audience is. So, a white supremacist may, through his or her rhetoric, constitute his or her audience as equally white supremacist. Or, a speaker such as Ellen Johnson Sirleaf (discussed in chapter 12) may, through her rhetoric, tell the Liberian people that they are all now beyond the factions that led to civil war and are all now interested in the rebuilding of the nation in a peaceful climate. She, of course, hopes her audience accepts the way in which she has constituted them.

Perelman and Olbrechts-Tyteca and Black treat this rhetorical constitution of one's audience as just one dimension of what the rhetor was doing. It was more central to rhetoric in the theories of others.

James Boyd White

Neither the team of Perelman and Olbrechts-Tyteca nor Black use the term "constitutive rhetoric." That was one of the contributions made by James Boyd White in *Heracles' Bow* (1985). White also extended the discussion of the relationship between rhetor and audience by paying attention to precisely how a rhetor might constitute this audience. There were, according to White, two main routes: overt persuasion and deceitful manipulation. As the terms suggest, one was thought to be positive; the other, dangerous. Using either route, the rhetor's tools are (a) what White (influenced by Freud) calls "condensation symbols" (i.e., references to cultural ideas and values triggered by words and phrases), (b) literature, and (c) narratives. The distinction between the latter two is that literature is the published body of noteworthy creative work within a culture and narratives are less formal "stories" that pepper oratory, conversation, and written works of a non-literary character. All these resources are, according to White, used to constitute an identity that a group is then, overtly or not, encouraged to embrace.

Louis Althusser

Althusser is a French philosopher with a complex body of thought and a complex life. We are only touching on a corner of both, here.

Althusser was a Marxist, strongly influenced by the work of Antonio Gramschi (discussed in chapter 11). To Gramschi's thoughts, he added Michel Foucault's (also discussed in chapter 11). Both Gramschi and Foucault felt that we were trapped in structures that were constructed by a dominant ideology. Althusser agreed, but he also felt that dissident groups created counter-structures that might be just as entrapping. Thus, he critiqued not just hegemony (Gramschi) and discourse (Foucault), but the ideology promoted by Stalin and the Chinese Cultural Revolution, both of which were presented as challenges to the dominant ideology. As Althusser saw things, people were layered ideological subjects. There was indeed a long-held dominant one, but there were also others that people were hailed or interpellated into by rhetoric.

Consider the case of the early Christians. They existed within one or more ideologies: They were already ideological subjects, whether that ideology be rooted in Roman paganism, the Judaism of the Old Testament, or other belief structures common in the Middle East. The initial disciples of Christ hailed them as brothers in Christ. By attending to this hailing, they began the process of acquiring an ideology and associated identities that were different from the ones they had had. The new ideology/identity, however, did not totally replace the original one. Rather, it layered onto it, even though there might well be contradictions between the two. Note also that neither the original nor the replacement is rooted in empirical reality. Althusser was anti-empirical and therefore held that ideology and identity are human constructions that people absorb from existing human constructions. In other words, one becomes a Marxist not because one sees the conditions suffered by workers (empirical reality), but because one is influenced by how others have presented matters rhetorically.

In explaining this embracing of ideology and identity, Althusser is strongly influenced by psychology, especially that of neo-Freudian Jacques Lacan. This is neither the time nor place to try to explain Lacan, but one concept in Lacan is worth noting. Lacan traces the human psyche through a mirror stage, during which we acquire dimensions of identity. Althusser sees the rhetorical manifestations of ideology and identity, be they speeches, documents, media products, or events, as offering something like a mirror that those "hailed" will begin to see themselves in as they become "interpellated." This mirror does not function as the one in your bathroom: It does not show the person before it; rather, it shows what that person will become as he or she becomes constituted.

Charland on the Quebecois

White and Althusser provide rich but complex explanations for the fundamental premise of constitutive rhetoric: that texts of various sorts can constitute an audience, providing that audience with an identity. Probably the classic example of the process in the communication studies discipline's literature in Maurice Charland's article published in the *Quarterly Journal of Speech*.[2] Charland's focus is in the province of Quebec in Canada. As most know, it has a French-speaking majority whose roots are deep in the province. Now, there are undoubtedly many ways in which this group might think of itself, not all of which would produce unity among them. Their history in Canada covered centuries, and, among other divisions, there were sharp social class ones as well as later-emerging ones, separating those living in traditional rural areas from emerging urban ones.

Charland argues, in his essay, that rhetorical processes essentially created the group identity of *peuple Quebecois*. This *peuple Quebecois* would play a major role in the separatist movement that roiled Quebec and Canada decades ago. Charland's startling point is that the group—and the associated political identity—that many observers must have thought had very deep roots was actually much more recent and rhetorically constituted. The major role was not tied to an identity they had long held that rhetoric revived; rather, the role was tied to the rhetoric in texts authored close in time to the separatist campaign.

Several excerpts from Charland's essay reveal the progression of his thinking. In speaking about the *peuple Quebecois*, he says:

> That subject and the collectivized "peuple Quebecois" are, in Althusser's language, "interpellated" as political subjects through a process of identification in rhetorical narratives that "always already" presume the constitution of subjects.

Rhetoric constitutes an identity, and this rhetoric presumes that the identity already exists. But that identity does not already exist:

> From such a perspective, we cannot accept the "giveness" of "audience," "person," or "subject," but must consider their very textuality, their very constitution in rhetoric as a structured articulation of signs. We must, in other words, consider the textual nature of social being.

The identification is textual: "the *peuple Quebecois*, and 'peoples' in general, exist only through an ideological discourse that constitutes them."[3] A consequence of this is that the *peuple Quebecois*, "precisely because they are the subjects within a text, within a narrative rhetoric, must follow the logic of the narrative."[4] Charland agrees that "[w]hat is significant in constitutive rhetoric is that it positions the reader towards political, social, and economic action in the material world and it is in this positioning that its ideological character becomes significant,"[5] so that what is textual (i.e., what is rhetorical) determines some very real consequences."[6]

Before offering his case study, Charland reviews the theory undergirding constitutive rhetoric. That review is well worth reading. If one does, one will note how Charland finds common ground between what White and Althusser say and what Kenneth Burke says concerning identification or consubstantiality. Interestingly, the core idea of constitutive rhetoric may well have been present in theory that was being read and discussed long before anyone turned to White, Althusser, and the many other European philosophers and psychologists they cite.

Dissident Groups, Other Groups

In an earlier chapter, I noted how society has moved away from essentializing definitions of groups, such as those gendered female. For a range of groups, theorists and researchers alike have come to assume that identity as a gender, as a sexual orientation, as a race, as an ethnicity, as a social class, etc., is socially constructed. Constitutive rhetoric plays a major role in how these groups socially construct themselves, and these groups are not monolithic: There is not a single way to be constituted as male or African American, for example. Intersectionality—the fact that a person may be part of more than one socially constructed group—makes matters still more complicated. But, in all these cases, rhetoric plays a role in constituting the group identity or identities.

Despite the complexities, it is still useful to discern how the process of rhetorically constituting a group works. White points to condensation symbols, literature, and narratives as three elements to look for. That list is probably not exhaustive. White also suggests that sometimes the process may be difficult to discern, maybe deceitfully so as we are constituted as a group with traits we might, if we interrogated them, object to. For example, those who identify as white may be constituted into a privileged group, the terms of which they might resist if they knew them. Discerning the process, I would suggest, is important for majority groups but especially important for minority groups, dissenting groups, and marginalized or discriminated-against groups. In these cases, there may well be rival rhetorics constituting them in very different terms. They may be rhetorically chosen without even knowing that they had choices.

Let's go back in time to the early 1960s, when African Americans were victims of systemic discrimination in the United States. The Civil Rights Movement was not unified; rather, there were many groups fighting, but with different emphases and different tactics for the same general goal. There was the National Association for the Advancement of Colored People (NAACP), the Congress for Racial Equality (CORE), the Southern Christian Leadership Conference (SCLC), the Student Non-Violent Coordinating Committee (SNCC), the Nation of Islam (which Malcolm X was initially connected with), and the nameless group organized loosely under his leadership after he left the Nation of Islam. Each of these groups offered its members an identity—overtly through rhetorical processes they could point to and less overtly through rhetorical processes that were beneath the surface and therefore much less visible. Compare, for example, Dr. Martin Luther King, Jr.'s famous August 1963 speech delivered on the steps of the Lincoln Memorial to any of several addresses Malcolm X delivered to urban crowds. These two Civil Rights Movement leaders constituted their race in strikingly different terms. King dreamt of a time when black and white could share a table; Malcolm X envisioned empowered, largely separate black communities. As condensation symbols, King's shared table was far different from the choice between the ballot and bullet

Malcolm X offered, and the stories they told were different. And their followers, when it came to literature, probably read different texts. In the 1960s and 1970s, African American writing found its way into curricula, but there was, in mainstream schools, black writing that was okay to read and black writing that was far too radical for students, black or white, to encounter. This writing constituted the African American group in rather different ways.

So, Martin and Malcolm rhetorically constituted African Americans quite differently. But in both cases, they constituted African Americans in terms that were different from what many white leaders in the American South would use—or even what white leaders such as Presidents Kennedy and Johnson would use. So, pick either black leader and you have vital constitutive rhetorics because they are set against a mainstream rhetoric that was still often demeaning toward, or at least suspicious of, African Americans.

Consider an international example. A sizeable chunk of northeastern Spain is considered Catalonia or Catalunya. At present, there is a large separatist movement in this area. Catalonia's language and culture was suppressed under the dictatorial rule of Francisco Franco. Since his fall from power, the Spanish government in Madrid has very slowly allowed Catalonia to regain its separate identity, but the Spanish government is strongly opposed to secession. But what makes one Catalan? What characterizes this identity and how, rhetorically, was it constituted? History plays a major role—the suppression by Franco, being on the losing side in the Spanish Civil War, and—further back in time—being on the losing side in the early eighteenth-century War of the Spanish Succession, which placed a Bourbon claimant on the throne, not a Hapsburg one. These events and others—and, very importantly—how they are told, play a role, but so do such things as songs and festivals—even soccer. One really cannot fully understand what is currently transpiring in this corner of Spain without knowing how the Catalan identity has been socially and rhetorically constituted.[7] That a Catalan secession movement has recently acquired energy suggests strongly that the way texts of various sorts, especially that of festival days, are telling the story is constituting the Catalan identity that is fueling revolution.

There is an implication of this rhetorical approach that should be considered. Althusser, you will recall, argued that identity is *not* based in a reality that might be studied empirically. Ideology is a human construct, and we swim in a sea of conflicting ideologies. Some might think biology plays a major role in determining matters such as gender and race and ethnicity. This approach, in its purest form, insists on the contrary. Gender identity is not defined by one's sexual organs; race identity is not defined by one's skin color; ethnic identity is not defined by hair color, nose size, or forehead breadth. Identity is constituted through rhetorical discourse. Catalans are not such because of their genes, but rather because of a body of texts that tell their stories.

Method

Perhaps the crucial first steps are (a) identifying a group that is of interest and (b) gathering the texts that may be constituting this group. The latter can be historical, political research if the group is like the *peuple Quebecois* or the Catalans. But, if the group is an ethnic group or a social group, then the critic must determine what texts the group has or is consuming. The texts could be political manifestos but could just as easily be a body of popular music. A rap music culture may have constituted a black male identity; Fox News may be constituting a shared political identity that distrusts the government and distrusts most media news.

Once a body of texts are assembled, then the next step is to extract from them the identity they seem to be presenting. Especially important to note in the texts would be condensation symbols because they offer, in a dense package, a host of sociocultural beliefs. These symbols could be verbal or could be visual. During the latter days of the Civil Rights Movement, Black Power (announced by SNCC) was such a symbol, as was the iconic black panther, borrowed by groups in Oakland, California, and Chicago, Illinois, from a Lowndes County, Alabama, where the icon was first used as part of a voting rights campaign. What may constitute a group goes beyond the sources White pointed to, so be alert to songs, holiday rituals, and heroes as possibly having a rhetorical role.

The critic's task is to put the material together into a coherent identity and then to see if, in the discourse of the group, the identity seems to be functioning. That discourse could be written, but, at least initially, the identity is more likely to be conveyed through conversation. Finding that identity is functioning is a test of what the critic has theorized. It is indeed rewarding to find one's theory seemingly supported. The really interesting rhetorical dimension, however, is how rhetorical texts constitute an identity. The process is especially interesting if the identity is, as in the case of the *peuple Quebecois*, purely textual. But, even when there is some basis for identity that texts reinforce, it is fascinating to see how texts bring identity out of just a few weak hints.

Application: *The American President* and *The West Wing*

This approach is, more often than not, applied to matters such as gender and race or ethnic identity (Quebecois, African American, Catalan), but it can have less profound applications. In high schools, for example, there is a distinct marching band identity. How has it been constituted rhetorically? Although the identity undoubtedly varies from school to school, it is remarkably the same. What rhetorical discourse is operating across the boundaries separating schools, even schools in different parts of the country? The same might be asked of lacrosse playing or cheering on both the high school and college levels; the same might be asked of fraternity or sorority membership.

Perhaps just a tad less profound are groups of fans, who acquire an identity based on who or what they are a fan of. These fans can talk about the movies they are a fan of (the *Star Wars* films), the celebrities they are a fan of (the Kardashians), or the sports team they are a fan of (the Dallas Cowboys) for hours. These conversations involve the sharing of stories. There is a lot of, "Do you remember the episode (or the game) when" going on. But to constitute an identity, there must be more than just shared stories. There must be shared attitudes and values.

An example would be fans of the multiple award-winning television series *The West Wing*, which ran on NBC from 1999 to 2006. It arguably grew out of the movie *The American President* (1995). That film, written by Aaron Sorkin, focused on the kind of president progressive Americans wished they had. Near its ending was a rousing speech by fictitious President Andrew Shepherd, in which he committed himself to doing his job on issues progressives care about, not pursuing the watered-down agenda that was necessary to get reelected. For the spin-off television series, however, Sorkin wanted to focus less on the president and more on the staff. So, he planned an ensemble drama in which President Josiah Bartlet would play a minimal role. It was not long before the dynamics of both television drama and the show itself required that Bartlet be center-stage. That was at the end of season one, in an episode aptly titled "Let Bartlet Be Bartlet." After that, the president was the central performer, with his staff members playing roles of different durations, depending on the week's script. The show proceeded through six more seasons, attracting many devoted fans, even though, in latter seasons, the scripts were uneven. Both the Shepherd speech from *The American President* and an excerpt from the "Let Bartlet Be Bartlet" episodes are reproduced in this chapter.

John Podhoretz's writing in *The Weekly Standard* termed the show "pornography for liberals." This catchy phrase suggests that, despite some conservative touches in early seasons, the Bartlett administration pursued policy directions political progressives applauded.[8] As the nation transitioned from Bill Clinton to George W. Bush, the show highlighted not so much what the Democrats did, but what the Democrats should have done. In real elections, many fans expressed the wish that there might be a candidate like Jed Bartlet to vote for. Bumper stickers calling for his election appeared, as did signs saying "Jed Bartlet is My President."

However, it was not just policy matters that created the show's appeal. There were attitudes and values. President Bartlet and his aides took their jobs very seriously: They were in the White House, not to enrich themselves or serve narrow special interests, but to do what was best for the American people. They were there to serve. They projected a high level of education—Bartlet being a PhD who had won a Nobel Prize in economics, suggesting that they were bringing a high level of aptitude to the task of serving. They were partisan at times; after all, the show was intended to be a realistic portrayal of how the White House worked, but they did not let partisan politics get in the way of doing what was right.

The show was not only realistic, but dramatic, so there were scandals. There were matters in some of the aides' pasts that surfaced, and Bartlett himself ended up censured by the Congress for not disclosing that he suffered from multiple sclerosis when running for president. Despite these scandals—and countless personal dramas—the characters pushed on for principles. There were times in the seven seasons when principles had to yield to political reality, but the characters always projected the attitude that, although they had compromised to do what was possible, they would return to the principles on a later occasion and try to do more.

Excerpt from The American President

For the last couple of months, Senator Rumson has suggested that being President of this country was, to a certain extent, about character. And although I've not been willing to engage in his attacks on me, I have been here three years and three days, and I can tell you without hesitation: Being President of this country is entirely about character.

For the record, yes, I am a card-carrying member of the ACLU, but the more important question is "Why aren't you, Bob?" Now this is an organization whose sole purpose is to defend the Bill of Rights, so it naturally begs the question, why would a senator, his party's most powerful spokesman and a candidate for President, choose to reject upholding the constitution? Now if you can answer that question, folks, then you're smarter than I am, because I didn't understand it until a few hours ago.

America isn't easy. America is advanced citizenship. You've gotta want it bad, 'cause it's gonna put up a fight. It's gonna say, "You want free speech? Let's see you acknowledge a man whose words make your blood boil, who's standing center stage and advocating at the top of his lungs that which you would spend a lifetime opposing at the top of yours." You want to claim this land as the land of the free? Then the symbol of your country cannot just be a flag. The symbol also has to be one of its citizens exercising his right to burn that flag in protest. Now show me that, defend that, celebrate that in your classrooms.

Then you can stand up and sing about the land of the free.

I've known Bob Rumson for years. And I've been operating under the assumption that the reason Bob devotes so much time and energy to shouting at the rain was that he simply didn't get it. Well, I was wrong. Bob's problem isn't that he doesn't get it. Bob's problem is that he can't sell it!

We have serious problems to solve, and we need serious people to solve them. And whatever your particular problem is, I promise you Bob Rumson is not the least bit interested in solving it. He is interested in two things, and two things only: making you afraid of it, and telling you who's to blame for it. That, ladies and gentlemen, is how you win elections. You gather a group of middle age, middle class, middle income

Aaron Sorkin, Selection from *The American President*. Copyright © 1995 by Warner Bros. Entertainment Inc.

voters who remember with longing an easier time, and you talk to them about family, and American values and character, and you wave an old photo of the President's girlfriend and you scream about patriotism. You tell them she's to blame for their lot in life. And you go on television and you call her a whore.

Sydney Ellen Wade has done nothing to you, Bob. She has done nothing but put herself through school, represent the interests of public school teachers, and lobby for the safety of our natural resources. You want a character debate, Bob? You better stick with me, 'cause Sydney Ellen Wade is way out of your league.

I've loved two women in my life. I lost one to cancer. And I lost the other 'cause I was so busy keeping my job, I forgot to do my job. Well, that ends right now.

Tomorrow morning the White House is sending a bill to Congress for its consideration. It's White House Resolution 455, an energy bill requiring a twenty percent reduction in the emission of fossil fuels over the next ten years. It is by far the most aggressive stride ever taken in the fight to reverse the effects of global warming. The other piece of legislation is the crime bill. As of today, it no longer exists. I'm throwing it out. I'm throwing it out and writing a law that makes sense. You cannot address crime prevention without getting rid of assault weapons and hand guns. I consider them a threat to national security, and I will go door to door if I have to, but I'm gonna convince Americans that I'm right, and I'm gonna get the guns.

We've got serious problems, and we need serious people. And if you want to talk about character, Bob, you'd better come at me with more than a burning flag and a membership card. If you want to talk about character and American values, fine. Just tell me where and when, and I'll show up. This is time for serious people, Bob, and your fifteen minutes are up.

My name is Andrew Shepherd, and I AM the President.[9]

Excerpt from The West Wing, *"Let Bartlet Be Bartlet"*

BARTLET:	I really did wake up energized this morning.
LEO:	I know.
BARTLET:	I never go to bed that way.
LEO:	I know.
BARTLET:	Just once, in this job, I'd like to end a day feeling as good as I did when the day started.
LEO:	The memo?
BARTLET:	Yeah.
LEO:	Yes.
BARTLET:	We've heard it all before. Leo, you drive me to politically safe ground. It's not true.
LEO:	I know it's not true.
BARTLET:	Good.
LEO:	You drive me there.
BARTLETT:	What the hell did you say?
LEO:	And you know it too.
BARTLET:	Leo?

Aaron Sorkin, Peter Parnell and Patrick Caddell, Selections from "Let Bartlet Be Bartlet," *The West Wing.* Copyright © 2000 by Warner Bros. Entertainment Inc.

LEO:	We're stuck in neutral because that's where you tell me to stay.
BARTLET:	You're wrong.
LEO:	No. I'm not, sir.
BARTLET:	You want to do this now?
LEO:	Sir?
BARTLET:	You came to my house, Leo.
LEO:	Mr. President?
BARTLET:	You came to my house, and you said, "Jeb, let's run for President." I said, "Why?" And you said, "so that you can open your mouth and say what you think!" Where'd that part go, Leo?
LEO:	You tell me, Mr. President. I don't see a shortage of cameras or microphones around here. What the hell were you waiting for?
BARTLET:	Look. …
LEO:	Everything you do. …
BARTLET:	This morning. …
LEO:	Everything you do says: "For God's sake, Leo. I don't want to be a one-term president."
BARTLET:	Did I not say put our guys on the FEC?
LEO:	No sir. You did not do that.
BARTLET:	Leo!
LEO:	You said—No! You said, let's dangle our feet in the water of whatever the hell it is we dangle our feet in, and we want to make it look like we're trying without pissing too many people off!
BARTLET:	You're writing a fascinating version of history, my friend.
LEO:	Oh, take a look at Mandy's memo, Mr. President, and you'll read a fascinating version of it.
BARTLET:	You brought me in on teachers. You brought me in on capital gains. You brought me in on China. And you brought me in on guns.
LEO:	Brought you in from where? You've never been out there on guns. You've never been out there on teachers. You dangle your feet, and I'm the hall monitor around here. It's my job to make sure nobody runs too fast or goes off target. I tell Josh to go to the Hill on campaign finance, he knows nothing's gonna come of it.
BARTLET:	That's crap.
LEO:	Sam can't get real on Don't Ask, Don't Tell because you're not gonna be there, and every guy sitting across the room from him knows that.
BARTLET:	Leo, if I ever tell you to get aggressive about campaign finance or gays in the military you would tell me, "Don't run too fast or go too far."
LEO:	If you ever told me to get aggressive about anything, I'd say I serve at the pleasure of the president. But we'll never know, sir. Because I don't think you're ever gonna say it.
BARTLET:	I have said it, and nothing's ever happened.

LEO:	You want to see me orchestrate this right now? You want to see me mobilize these people? These people who would walk into fire if you told them to. These people who showed up to lead. These people who showed up to fight.

****

BARTLET:	I don't want to feel like this anymore.
LEO:	You don't have to.
BARTLET:	I don't want to go to sleep like this.
LEO:	You don't have to.
BARTLET:	I want to speak.
LEO:	Say it out loud. Say it to me.
BARTLET:	This is more important than reelection. I want to speak now.
LEO:	Say it again.
BARTLET:	This is more important than reelection. I want to speak now.
LEO:	Now we're in business.
BARTLET:	What's happening?
LEO:	We got our asses kicked in the first quarter, and it's time we moved up the mat.
BARTLET:	Yes!
LEO:	Say it.
BARTLET:	This is more important than reelection. I want to speak now.
LEO:	I'm gonna talk to the staff. I'm gonna take them off the leash.
BARTLET:	You have a strategy for all this?
LEO:	I have the beginning of one.
BARTLET:	What is it?
LEO:	I'm gonna try that out for a little while (showing Bartlet what he wrote down: "Let Bartlet Be Bartlet")

Leo goes to rest of staff.

LEO:	Listen up. Our ground game isn't working. If we want to walk into walls, I want us running into them full speed.
JOSH:	What are you saying?
LEO:	Well, you can start by telling the Hill the President has named his nominee for the FEC. And we're gonna lose some of these battles, and we might even lose the White House, but we're not gonna be threatened by issues. We're gonna put them front and center. We're gonna raise the level of political debate in this country, and let that be our legacy. That sound all right to you, Josh?
JOSH:	I serve at the pleasure of the President of the United States.
LEO:	Yeah.
C.J.:	I serve at the pleasure of the President.
SAM:	I serve at the pleasure of President Bartlet.
LEO:	Toby?
TOBY:	I serve at the pleasure of the President.
LEO:	Good. Then let's get in the game.[10]

Those who were fans of the show became constituted by its rhetoric into a political community. They wanted a president like Jed Bartlet could be; they wanted a White House comprised of highly talented men and women like Leo, Josh, Sam, C. J., and Toby; they wanted certain attitudes and values to govern. These fans were certainly inclined in these directions before *The West Wing* took to the air, but the program consolidated all and constituted the fans into a group that not only could recite plots and lines, but talk with passion about what the Bartlet White House stood for and how the real one ought to imitate the fictitious one. Yes, they could talk in detail about specific episodes, but their fandom went beyond sharing plots. Their fandom embraced policy positions and political identities, giving them a political identity. That identity was constituted through both the episodes themselves and countless conversations among fans about the episodes.

Strengths and Limitations

Constitutive rhetoric—and criticism associated with it—represents, in some eyes, a radical redirection in our scholarship. It attends to audience in a way that other approaches do not—or do so only implicitly. Rhetors have long been told to analyze their audiences, for it is difficult to persuade auditors or readers or viewers if you do not know who they are and, especially, what attitudes they hold and how personally important—or salient—these attitudes are. Criticism has, perhaps, paid less attention to this audience dynamic than the characteristics of the text itself. But, to the extent critics have—the Chicago School talking about the final effect on the audience, Burke talking about playing to audience's terministic screens, Bormann talking about persuading an audience by sharing that audience's fantasy themes—their focus has been on persuasion. Constitutive rhetoric is more concerned with the audience's identity formation. This shift is permitting rhetorical critics to ask a question they largely have not asked. And it is an important question, for one's identity—or complex of identities—is an important part of who people are.

As with many other lenses, this one does focus on one issue to the exclusion of others. It also assumes that rhetorical texts play *the* role in constituting identity. Not all will accept the assumption that empirical reality plays no role in the process. One issue worth raising with this assumption in mind is, "What do you make of the material conditions under which one develops an identity?" Might not growing up in an upper middle-class community affect identity? Might not growing up impoverished or in a third-world slum? Many who embrace constitutive rhetoric would argue that these material conditions *are* rhetorical. They are, in the broadest sense of the word, "texts." White pointed to condensation symbols, literature, and narratives as crucial in rhetorically constituting identity. Contemporary constitutive rhetoricians rather clearly have a much longer list of the constructs that tell us who we are, if the material conditions of our lives are conceived of rhetorically (not empirically) and are among the kinds of things a theorist such as White would point to as constitutive. Broadened in this manner, constitutive rhetoric has incredible explanatory power. Nonetheless, it attends to certain aspects of a text while excluding others, and it attends to one important rhetorical function while excluding the more traditional persuasive one.

Exemplars

Akioye, Akin A. "The Rhetorical Construction of Radical Africanism at the United Nations: Metaphoric Cluster as Strategy." *Discourse & Society* 5, no. 1 (January 1995): 7–31.

Flores, Lisa A., & Dreama G. Moon. "Rethinking Race, Revealing Dilemmas: Imagining a New Racial Subject in *Race Traitor*." *Western Journal of Communication* 66, no. 2 (2002): 181–207.

Orbe, Mark P. (1998). "Constructions of Reality of MTV's *The Real World*: An Analysis of the Restrictive Coding of Black Masculinity." *Southern Communication Journal* 64, no. 1 (1998): 32–47.

Stein, Sarah R. "The '1984' Macintosh Ad: Cinematic Icons and Constitutive Rhetoric in the Launch of a New Machine." *Quarterly Journal of Speech* 88, no. 2 (May 2002): 169–92.

Suggested Applications

Speech Applications

- In 1969, President Richard Nixon declared that he was speaking on behalf of a "silent majority." How did he constitute this group through this speech?

- In the 1930s, President Franklin D. Roosevelt was opposed from his political left by populist Huey Long. Consider one of Long's most famous speeches, "Share the Wealth." How did he try to constitute a group that he hoped would be a political counter to FDR?

Non-Speech Applications

- The Washington, DC African American History and Culture Museum was mentioned in a previous chapter. Here, consider how the place, mainly what it includes, is an attempt to constitute an African American identity.

- Bill Cosby is now not the revered figure he once was, but his fate should not obscure the fact that the long-running *Cosby Show* was influential. How did it attempt to constitute an African American identity?

Notes

1. Black, Edwin. "The Second Persona." *Quarterly Journal of Speech* 56, no. 2 (1970): 109–19.

2. Charland, Maurice. "Constitutive Rhetoric: the Case of the People Quebecois." *Quarterly Journal of Speech* 73, no. 3 (1987): 133–50.

3. Ibid., p. 134.

4. Ibid., p. 137.

5. Ibid., p. 139.

6. Ibid., p. 141.

7. Minder, Raphael. *The Struggle for Catalonia: Rebel Politics in Spain.* London: Hurst and Company, 2017.

8. Parry-Giles, Trevor, and Shawn J. Parry-Giles. *The Prime Time Presidency: The West Wing and U.S. Nationalism.* Chicago, IL: University of Illinois Press, 2006. Parry-Giles, Trevor, and Shawn J. Parry-Giles. *The Prime Time Presidency: The West Wing and U.S. Nationalism.* Chicago, IL: University of Illinois Press, 2006.

9. Excerpt from *The American President.* Directed by Rob Reiner. Performed by Michael Douglas, Annette Bening, and Martin Sheen. United States: Columbia Pictures, 1995. http://www.Americanrhetoric.com/MovieSpeeches/Moviesspeechtheamericanpresident.

10. *The West Wing.* NBC. September 22, 1999-May 14, 2006. http://www/westwingtranscripts.com/search.php?flag=getTranscript&id=19.

Figure credit

Fig. 13: Robert Reiner/Warner Bros, The American President. Copyright © 1995 by Warner Bros. Entertainment Inc.

Writing a Critical Essay

When you write a critical essay during a college course in rhetorical criticism, you are, of course, writing in a limited academic context defined by that course, but I want to begin this discussion by putting you in a much larger context, that of the communication discipline you are now working in.

Back in 1914, when the discipline arguably began, it was firmly in the humanities with touches of the arts. Gradually, the discipline became more and more a social science one. At some colleges and universities today, it has become an entirely social science endeavor, but, if you are taking a course like rhetorical criticism, you are probably enrolled in a program that mixes social science, humanities, and—maybe—arts perspectives. But, among these, the social science one may dominate since its domination is now the case in the discipline nationally.

All this history and discussion of academic categories is relevant because scholars do not write the same way in humanities and social science disciplines. Put simply, writing in the humanities is typically fluid, with an essay having clear goals but not a set pattern, whereas writing in the social science tends to follow a set pattern. One effect of the increasing domination of the social science perspectives in the communication discipline has been a gradual intrusion of this set pattern throughout all areas of the field. So, now, essays in rhetorical criticism sometimes read as if they are pieces of social science writing.

So, let's start with social science writing.

An essay there will typically progress through six parts.

There will be a brief introduction that sets the stage for the research project that the author(s) are reporting about. Then, there will be an extensive literature review. In this second section, the author(s) survey the relevant research on the topic under discussion. Ideally, the review points to one or more questions that need to be answered. These are often listed as research questions, labeled *R1*, *R2*, etc. Sometimes, the author(s) will also, at this point, offer, for each question, the answers he, she, or they think will emerge. These may be labeled and listed *H1*, *H2*, etc., the *H* standing for hypothesis.

The third section of the essay is where the author(s) review the theory undergirding the research and the methods to be followed in that research. The fourth section offers the reader the data that the research generated. If the research is quantitative, the data will look like data; if the research is qualitative, the data may be the comments offered by research subjects. The fifth section is where the author(s) discuss the data, noting what they reveal. The research questions are explicitly answered; often, the hypotheses are explicitly confirmed or disconfirmed. Finally, there is a conclusion where, typically, the author(s) point out the limitations they operated under and suggest what further research is necessary.

These six sections—introduction, literature review, theory and methods, data, discussion, and conclusion—are labeled. One reason they are is that social science essays are commonly not read beginning to end. If the reader chooses to go beyond the abstract, which precedes the essay and offers a preview or a summary, the reader may go directly to the discussion. If the reader is intrigued by the findings, then the reader might look at the data. If the reader is really intrigued, he or she may look at the theory and method section—to see what the researchers did—and the literature review—to see what previous work the researchers built on. The essay, then, is read in a non-linear way, and parts of it may not be read at all.

The humanities essay is very different. It will be read, linearly, beginning to end, and it will likely be read in its entirety. Thus, formulaic section headings are not necessary. Furthermore, it is not necessary that a certain task (i.e., surveying the literature) be performed in a single spot. Many decades ago, the humanities essay was very fluid. The writer approached it as if it were an art work, not a set of boxes in which one reported one's research. However, the gradual intrusion of the social science perspective into the entire communication discipline has now created a context in which the critical essay probably cannot be as free-wheeling as it once was.

So, what I would like to suggest—for classroom use and beyond—is a modification of the social science procedure.

An essay, then, should have an introduction. In this part, the author (usually, in rhetorical criticism, a single person) announces the subject of his or her analysis and offers any background information on the subject that the reader needs to understand the analysis that will follow. The author may, in this introduction, present his or her thesis, or the author may present the question or questions he or she will eventually answer. Either way, the author should suggest to the reader why the subject is worth exploring. The good introduction, thus, creates a reader who wants to proceed onward.

The next two parts are somewhat interchangeable. One presents the theory informing the exploration and how that theory has been operationalized by the critic. The other talks about any previous critical work on the subject that either sets up the new analysis or offers insights that help move the analysis along. Often, if the previous work is strongly connected to a point in the analysis that will follow, the discussion of that work is deferred to that point. So, there may not be a literature review per se. The literature on the topic is, of course, known and discussed; the difference is that, in a humanities essay, the review may not be offered in its entirety in a single section labeled "Literature Review."

In a rhetorical criticism classroom, you are probably moving quickly from type of criticism to type of criticism. Thus, you are probably not being asked—for essays in the course—to investigate what others have said. So, the classroom essay more typically moves from the introduction directly to a discussion of the relevant theory (or theories) and how the critic proceeded.

The next section is the crucial one. It combines data and discussion and presents the author's analysis. It is quite common for this section to be organized by theme or topic. If the analysis revealed three matters, then the essay will typically go 1-2-3, explaining each and offering sufficient textual support from the text to gain the reader's assent. The same if the analysis focused on three topics: 1-2-3 with explanation and support for each.

Once upon a time, critical essays had no headings and subheadings. In fact, they were frowned upon—thought to be a crutch weak writers relied on instead of writing good transitions and good topic sentences. Now, under the influence of the social sciences, critical essays in the humanities tradition do feature headings and subheadings, but they are not the formulaic ones of social science writing; rather, they derive from the essay's content.

So, let's say you have chosen to investigate the rhetoric of the #MeToo movement. You want to mix two very different theories in your approach. You want to discern, in the texts associated with the movement, the balance between logos and pathos, and you are interested in how the discourse fits into the classical categories of deliberative (suitable for legislating) and epideictic (more ceremonial, offering praise and blame). You're thinking that there may well be an interesting blurring of the two modes. And you also, in line with ideological criticism, want to discern to what extent the movement uses parody to undermine sexist discourse and presents the stories of victims in order to validate and valorize their position.

Here are the headings and subheadings you might use:

Introduction
Theory
　　Classical Rhetoric
　　Ideological Criticism
Logos vs. Pathos
Deliberative vs. Epideictic
Use of Parody
Validating/Valorizing Victims' Stories
Conclusion

The conclusion here would probably not talk about limitations and future research. Rather, it would strongly summarize the essay and answer the question "So what?" Conclusions in the humanities tradition are very important opportunities to point to what is important in one's analysis.

If your assignment requires you to look at existing criticism on your chosen text, you could treat that criticism in one of three ways. First, you could add a section after "Introduction," called "Existing Criticism" or, if you want, "Literature Review." Second, you could bring that criticism in where relevant as you present your analysis. Third, if the amount of criticism is limited, as it would probably be in this case because of the topic's recency, you could simply add a paragraph to the introduction.

Most classroom assignments in a rhetorical criticism class are probably not going to require you to survey what is already in print. The goal in such a class is typically to have to try out several approaches, so you are usually asked to encounter a text on your own.

One last example.

Let's say you've chosen to examine the 2017 film *The Post* using feminist criticism. The film, on one level, is the story of how *The Washington Post* transitions from a local paper whose leaders were rather cozy with government leaders to a national paper that eventually brings down a president. The two central characters are the newspaper's editor, Ben Bradlee, and the newspaper's owner, Katharine Meyer Graham. The newspaper was the darling of Graham's father. At his death, he gave control to his son-in-law, Katharine's husband Phil. After his suicide, she becomes the owner. Brought up to play a major role in Washington, DC high society, she found herself in the newspaper business.

Using feminist criticism, you want to discuss how the film depicts the sexist environment Katharine Graham finds herself, how she gradually acquires the confidence to run the newspaper, and how the film depicts her toward its end.

You might structure such an essay along the following lines:

Introduction—introduce topic, summarize film, present theses or questions
Feminist Criticism
    Critique of Sexism
    Valorization of Women's Lives
The Post
    Surrounded by Men
    Not Allowed to Speak
    Increasing Confidence
    Decisions to Publish *Pentagon Papers* Material
    Scene Leaving U.S. Supreme Court
Conclusion—noting that film is about First Amendment *and* about Catharine Graham's triumph over sexism

Again, you can discern the social science pattern, but it has been adapted to fit the humanities discipline better. Except for the phrases that follow "Introduction" and "Conclusion," you could use what is listed as your headings and subheadings. You could even change "Introduction" to "More than the First Amendment" and "Conclusion" to "Triumphing Over Sexism." The headings in a social science essay tend to always be "Data," "Discussion," etc. In accordance with the humanities tradition rhetorical criticism is part of, headings and subheadings (if used) can be much more substantive.

The discussion thus far has focused on structure (what classical theory would term *dispositio*). Using a clear structure is very important, but what makes a critical essay compelling is not as much its structure as how evidence from the text in question supports the arguments that are offered about the text. So, in the chunk of the essay that merges and replaces "Data" and "Discussion," it is crucial to show, explicitly, what in the text informs your analysis. If you're arguing that the #MeToo movement overwhelmingly features epideictic rhetoric, offer examples; if you're arguing that *The Post* depicts men constantly interrupting or talking over Mrs. Graham, point to examples. The true strength of a critical essay is in how persuasive it is, and its persuasiveness depends on the evidence you cite.

Glossary

Active unidirectional double-voiced discourse: According to Mikhail Bakhtin, a type of writing or speaking that admits into the text, without the writer's/speaker's awareness other voices, voices pursuing basically the same point

Active varidirectional double-voiced discourse: According to Mikhail Bakhtin, a type of writing or speaking that admits into the text, without the writer's/speaker's awareness other voices, voices pursuing a different point

Anaphora: A rhetorical scheme in which several phrases or clauses in sequence begin with the same word or words

Antimetabole: A rhetorical scheme in which the word(s) at the end of a phrase or clause are used at the beginning of the next phrase or clause

Asyndeton: A rhetorical scheme in which conjunctions are omitted between all items in a sequence

Carnivalesque: According to Mikhail Bakhtin, a type of writing or speaking in which authority figures (government, church, academe) are treated irreverently, satirically. Frequently but not necessarily uses references to bodily (eating, drinking, procreating, excreting) excesses

Classical allusion: A reference to a character or event in ancient Greek or Roman literature or mythology

Climax: A rhetorical scheme in which a sequence of phrases or clauses is built, with the last item in the sequence departing from the established pattern for emphasis

Constitutive rhetoric: An emphasis on how rhetorical texts can create, virtually out of nothing, an identity for their audience

Consubstantiality: According to Kenneth Burke, the goal of oneness or unity that the rhetor pushes the guilt-ridden audience toward in order to relieve that guilt (much like identification, although Burkean critics do draw distinctions)

Diagesis: The chronological pattern of a narrative as written or spoken, as opposed to the chronological pattern as the narrative, as if in real time

Discourse: According to Michel Foucault, the dominant norms within an era reinforced by many human institutions, including its texts (see *episteme*)

Disposition: According to classical rhetoricians, the second canon or division of rhetoric focused on how texts are organized

Elocutio or **eloquence:** According to classical rhetoricians, the third canon or division of rhetoric focused on the how texts use the resources of language in creating their style

Episteme: According to Michel Foucault, the dominant norms within an era reinforced by many human institutions, including its texts (see *discourse*)

Epistrophe: A rhetorical scheme in which a sequence of phrases or clauses end with the same word or words

Ethos: According to classical rhetoricians, a type of proof offered by a rhetor based on his or her perceived competence, character, and good will (many contemporary rhetoricians replace good will with dynamism)

Exigence: The set of circumstances that creates the need that a particular text will address

Fantasy themes: According to Ernest Bormann, views of social reality, past, present, and future created by a rhetorical community through a process of generating ideas and chaining others on

Final effect: According to Chicago School critics, the emotional and intellectual effect of a text, an effect that other elements in the text contribute to

Hegemony: According to theorists Antonio Gramschi, Stuart Hall, and others, the power that the prevailing power structure has over those within in, especially those in power-down positions within it

Hyperbole: A rhetorical trope in which a matter is deliberately exaggerated for effect

Identification: According to Kenneth Burke, the goal of unity or oneness the rhetor pushes the guilt-ridden audience toward in order to relieve that guilt (much like consubstantiality, although Burkean critics do draw distinctions)

Ideograph: According to rhetorician Michael Calvin McGee, a term that is loaded with sociocultural meanings that brings those readings into a text

Inventio or **invention:** According to classical rhetoricians, the first canon of rhetoric focused on finding the proofs, especially the logical ones, for a text's arguments

Litotes: A rhetorical trope in which a matter is ironically understated for effect

Logos: According to classical rhetoricians, a type of proof offered by a rhetor consisting of substantive arguments, such as striking comparisons, citing examples, or noting consequences, the different possibilities often listed as commonplaces or common topics

Memoria or **memory:** According to classical rhetoricians, the fifth canon of rhetoric focused on how to memorize one's speech, which, in the present day, can be focused more on how one uses one's script or one's notes

Metonomy: A rhetorical trope in which a quality or characteristic of an item is used to stand for the item

Metropolitan center: According to post-colonial theorists, the center of the once-empire that, earlier in time, directed affairs in the colonies and, today, may still determine the sociocultural norms of the former colonies

Monomyth: According to mythological critics, the single all-encompassing myth that informs all human texts

Narrative coherence: According to Walter Fisher, a necessary quality of a persuasive narrative requiring all the pieces to be present and function together clearly

Narrative fidelity: According to Walter Fisher, a necessary quality of a persuasive narrative requiring the plot, the characters, and the implicit values to "ring true" for the audience

Passive unidirectional double-voiced discourse: According to Mikhail Bakhtin, a type of writing or speaking that admits into the text, with the rhetor's awareness and control, voices pursuing the same point as the rhetor

Passive varidirectional double-voiced discourse: According to Mikhail Bakhtin, a type of writing or speaking that admits to the text, with the rhetor's awareness and control, voices pursuing a different point than the rhetor

Pathos: According to classical rhetoricians, a type of proof that appeals to a variety of human emotions

Pentad: According to Kenneth Burke, the five crucial elements of drama, those being act, agent, scene, agency, and purpose

Peroration: According to classical rhetoricians, the culminating part of the oration in which the rhetor makes his or her strongest, grandest case

Persona: The character, among the many a rhetor possesses, that he or she chooses to take on as voice in a text

Pluralism: According to Chicago School critics, the belief that, in explaining how a rhetor brings about a final effect, a critic can and should range through the focal points commonly associated with multiple critical approaches, should they seem relevant

Polyphony: According to Mikhail Bakhtin, the language of a text is comprised of the many voices that inform human language that are admitted into that text

Polysyndeton: A rhetorical scheme in which conjunctions occur between all items in a list

Polyvalence: The presence of many meaning in a text produced by its openness

Primacy: Occurring first in a list and thereby acquiring emphasis, second only to recency

Pronuncitatio: According to classical rhetoricians, the fourth canon of rhetoric that focuses on the delivery of a message

Prosopopoeia: A rhetorical trope in which the imagined words of a person or group are presented

Rational world paradigm: According to Walter Fisher, the assumption that learned reasoning processes are necessary in assessing human reasoning

Ratios: According to Kenneth Burke, the relationships between all the terms in the pentad, used to determine which term and which pairings are dominant in a human drama

Recency: Occurring last in a list and thereby acquiring emphasis over all other items in list

Rhetoric: Traditionally, the art of discovering and then putting to use the best available means of persuasion

Schemes: Artful ways of arranging phrases and clauses into sentences or sequences of sentences

Second persona: According to rhetorician Edwin Black, the audience that the rhetor attempts to create through his or her text

Stylization: Using words, phrases, and even syntax in a manner that seems to echo a previous speaker or writer

Synecdoche: A rhetorical trope in which a part stands for the whole

Terministic screens: According to Kenneth Burke, the words and phrases that a person or a group assembles to represent his, her, or its social reality that, once created, admits discourse containing the terms while excluding discourse using alien terms

Topoi or **topica:** In classical rhetoric and afterwards, list of places where a rhetor might go to find arguments, with places being not literal places but common types of argument

Tropes: Figurative, non-literal uses of language such as metaphor

Univocal discourse: According to Mikhail Bakhtin, the language of a text if stripped of all echoed voices and entailments brought in from previous uses, often found in the discourse of law, government, science, and technology

Index

CPSIA information can be obtained
at www.ICGtesting.com
Printed in the USA
LVHW010017031221
705112LV00005B/22

9 781516 523801